CONTEMPORARY SOCIETY: TRIBAL STUDIES

VOLUME FOUR
SOCIAL REALITIES

CONTEMPORARY SOCIETY: TRIBAL STUDIES

Edited by

DEEPAK KUMAR BEHERA

AND

GEORG PFEFFER

VOLUME ONE	—	STRUCTURE AND PROCESS
VOLUME TWO	—	DEVELOPMENT ISSUES, TRANSITION AND CHANGE
VOLUME THREE	—	SOCIAL CONCERN
VOLUME FOUR	—	SOCIAL REALITIES

THE EDITORS

Deepak Kumar Behera is Reader in the Department of Anthropology, Sambalpur University, Sambalpur, Orissa (India).

Georg Pfeffer is Professor and Head of the Department of Ethnology, Freie University of Berlin (Germany).

CONTEMPORARY SOCIETY: TRIBAL STUDIES

VOLUME FOUR

SOCIAL REALITIES

Edited by
DEEPAK KUMAR BEHERA
Department of Anthropology
Sambalpur University
Sambalpur - 768 019
Orissa
India

GEORG PFEFFER
Freie Universität Berlin
Institut für Ethnologie
Drosselweg 1 - 3
D-14195 Berlin
Germany

CONCEPT PUBLISHING COMPANY, NEW DELHI - 110 059

Associate Editors
Sudhansu Shekhar Guru and
Arun Kumar Basa

ISBN 81-7022-640-6 (Series)
ISBN 81-7022-738-0 (Vol. IV)

First Published 1999

Published and Printed by
Ashok Kumar Mittal
Concept Publishing Company
A/15-16, Commercial Block, Mohan Garden
New Delhi - 110 059 (India)

Phones: 5648039, 5649024
Fax: 0091-(0)11-5648053

ACKNOWLEDGEMENTS

We are grateful to all the contributors to the volume. Their academic generosity has enabled us to complete this work sucessfully. We offer our special thanks to Mr. Ashok Kumar Mohapatra, Dr. Sudhansu Shekar Guru and Mr. Arun Kumar Basa for their untiring help and co-operation at various stages of the project. Without their support the volume would not have seen the light of the day. We also express our deep sense of gratitude to all others who helped us directly or indirectly for the successful completion of the volume. Last but not least, we are thankful to Concept Publishing Company for showing interest to take up the publication project *Contemporary Society: Tribal Studies.*

DEEPAK KUMAR BEHERA
GEORG PFEFFER

CONTENTS

SECTION III

COMMUNITY LIFE

INTRODUCTION

DEEPAK KUMAR BEHERA AND GEORG PFEFFER

Documentation of various facets of tribal social reality is very much essential before they are totally eclipsed by the rapid process of globalization of the world economy. While examining the current literature on tribal societies we notice a curious absence of scientific studies based on intensive fieldwork among a large and important section of the world population. The series *Contemporary Society: Tribal Studies* tries to fill in this gap and thereby attempts to remove our ignorance on many aspects of tribal social reality. The ongoing series has already brought out three earlier volumes, namely, (I) *Structure and Process,* (II) *Development Issues, Transition and Change,* and (III) *Social Concern.* The first volume, consisting of twenty-five chapters, is devoted to the study of structural and ethnic relations, gender, ecology, and ideology in contemporary tribal societies. The chapters in the second volume, thirty-three in number, deal with development issues, transition and change in various sectors of tribal life. The third volume consisting of twenty-two chapters, works out empirical parameters of knowledge-production and examines their inherent social concern. It critically examinet various issues that have affected tribal society and culture.

Titled *Social Realities* this volume, under the series *Contemporary Society: Tribal Studies*, draws a number of social scientists together into a commonly scholarly quest for the understanding of different aspects of tribal society. It documents the said aspects through the contribution of many eminent social scientists of India and abroad. The papers in this volume have been presented under three sections, viz. (1) Kinship and Domestic Groups, (2) Ethnicity, Uprising and Revivalism, and (3) Community Life.

The objects of knowledge do not exist *per se*. Nor is the volume of knowledge self-evident. What is required in the analysis of knowledge is a consensus of the people in a community in defining and using it in terms of common cultural perceptions and goals. Accordingly, it becomes essentials for the social scientist to formulate the necessary perceptive on knowledge and the methodology of its analysis in correspondence with the said communal consensus relating to knowledge. This volume ventures into the analysis of the objects of knowledge—in our case, those like the social realities of the tribals in India and abroad. It is belived that the documentation of this objects of knowledge will enrich our understanding on tribal social realities.

The first section includes three articles, all on kinship and domestic groups. In the first article under this section Georg Pfeffer offers a comprehensive account of the kinship vocabulary of two southern Munda languages, i.e. Gutob and Remo. Each presents closed unified system of symmetric affinal prescription. Pfeffer is critical of the traditional diagrams or "terminological types" used for analysis, since they do not allow a differentiation of "direct" and "indirect" affines. Further, he compares the pattern of vocabulary with the patterns of marriage rules and practices, rituals, descent constructs and techniques of production. He shows that the vocabulary directly differentiates ego's junior and senior affinal relationships.

M. Suryanarayan analyzes the kinship terminology of the Saoras, a Mundari speaking Scheduled Tribe of Andhra Pradesh. From his analysis he concludes that the kinship terminology of the Saoras shows to a considerable extent correspondence with its cultural practices. The author feels that the Guinea-Dakota continuum helps explain the changes that have taken place in the kinship terminology of the Saoras of the sample areas.

A.R.N. Srivastava explores the interrelationships among demography, economy and organization of domestic groups of the Korwa, a small semi-agricultural tribe of Palamau, South Bihar (India). A review of literature on family and domestic life of non-technological societies points out the growing interest of anthropologists in studying the crucial role of demography in controlling the developmental cycles in domestic groups. Srivastava offers a model that explains various forms of developmental cycles of domestic groups and their relative probabilities (frequencies) over time. He also indicates that these are the outcome of a few fundamental demographic and economic variables.

The second section on ethnicity, uprising and revivalism contains as many as nine articles. In the first article Peter T. Suzuki offers a definition of ethnic group and raises some theoretical issues associated with it by taking the case of the Winnebago tribe of Nebraska. The tribe itself has undergone rapid changes during the past few years, much of which can be attributed to a favourable economic condition. Suzuki opines that the Winnebago tribe is currently taking a rebirth together with a stronger sense of ethnicity and tribalhood. The type of ethnicity being experienced is an indirectly managed ethnicity, which is in contrast to the directly managed ethnicity as in present-day Yugoslavia under President Milosevic.

Soheila Shahshahani studies an area close to Tehran that is extremely rich in its ethnic component. She shows that the three prevalent ideologies of the state, religion and communism have all tried to attenuate the importance and functionality of ethnicity there. The area is losing colour and importance very fast. It is no longer possible to find there an all-encompassing human environment in which one takes birth, chooses one's spouse, speaks its language, eats its food and wears its clothes and fights to keep its identity through self-affirmation in disputes. Yet ethnicity is still a buffer to protect individuals. It gives them a network of social relations. It is also the ground for self-realization and shared imagination, although it is not an aim in itself. In order to find the ethnic identity of Varameen, Shashani looks into its history, its mode of subsistence, everyday culture and the imaginations of its people.

Manis Kumar Raha discusses the problem of ethnic identity in the context of tribal India. The members of some tribal groups have been able to maintain their traditional ethnic identity in the changing social milieu. Some other tribal groups have changed their ethnic identities for one reason or another. There are also tribal groups, who after shifting their identity temporarily, have again switched over to their traditional identities to meet the demands of the changing socio-political situation. The author substantiates his argument by citing numerous examples in tribal India context.

R.M. Sarkar critically examines the nature of tribal ethnicity in Santal Parganas. He unfolds the traditional history behind the tribal ethnicity in Santal Parganas. Tribal ethnicity of this region is in fact the reflection of the situations of the Santals through time and space. The author shows as to how the Santal uprising against the British helped those tribals to strengthen their ethnic identity.

Rajat Kanti Das argues that in the contemporary situation the notion of cultural uniqueness has assumed a new dimension with an increasing number of tribals are trying to use it for political purposes. He stresses the need to develop organizational strategies at the socio-political level. This would be a timely deterrent to the political parties that aim at subverting the identity of tribals instead of promoting and reinforcing them. He cites, for instance, the political objective of the Jharkhand movement which has ultimately led to the strengthening party-organization. In the political conflict the Jharkhandis have been drawing strength from their traditional socio-political organizations.

Krishna Reddy, Rathnaiah and Narasimha Raju have made an attempt to analyze the historical process of integration of the tribals during the pre-independence period. They have also studied the assimilation of the tribals with regional movements and their search for identity. It is well known that tribals participated in the freedom movement at various stages in different forms in the country. The tribal movements in Andhra Pradesh are entirely different from those elsewhere, given the divergent socio-economic and political conditions in the tribal areas in the country. Krishna Reddy, Rathnaiah and Narasimha Raju deplore that in spite of the great sacrifice made by the tribals during the Gandhian phase of freedom movement, most of their socio-economic and other problems remain unsolved, even after 50 years of Independence. The land they lost has not yet been resorted, and their rights on forest have not yet fully protected. Without proper appraisal of their significant role in the struggle for independence, the history of India's freedom movement would remain incomplete.

Debendranath Jena deals with the Adivasi-Harijan conflict in Phulbani which took place in recent past. He examines its deep-rooted socio-cultural causes and consequences. Although the conflict is regarded by most of the people as politically motivated, Jena's findings explains the economic deprivation of Kandhas and the socio-cultural persecution of Panas as the major causes of the genesis of communal antagonism. The existing political factors only acted as a catalyst of the antagonism.

Tripathy and Nayak depict the role of Birsa Munda as an apostle of social justice. They discuss the factors that led this charismatic leader to start the movement for social justice. The germination of the movement occurred due to the conversion of Mundas from adivasi religion to Christianity. Birsa appeared on the scene to oppose the interference of *diku* (outsiders). His reforms and reorganization in the subsequent period made the movement more meaningful. His humanistic teaching drew innumerable followers towards him.

Mukherjee and Mollick present the case of Gond revivalism and reintegration in Madhya Pradesh. This movement has occurred because of the dissatisfaction of the Gond with the current social and economic conditions. The movement is launched against the prevailing irrational practices and social evils prevailing in order to achieve a social reconstruction. For the preservation of their religious and cultural identity they have formed different social and political organizations.

The last section deals with various aspects of community life among the tribal people. In the first article under this section R.E.S. Tanner examines the traditional social system of the Sukumas of north-western Tanzania, which was based on personal achievement and geographical mobility. The Sukumas had neither obligatory rites of passage, except funerals, nor any age grades. Their religious system was based on a belief in spirits. Few converted to institutionalized religions. There was no institutionalized political system either. Tanner feels that their characteristics seem to parallel some western social practices, and this may account for the absence of tension among the Sukumas arising from modernization.

R.E.S. Tanner's second article is also related to the same population. There he analyzes various reasons of the reluctance of the Sukuma to convert either to Christianity or Islam. He highlights the fact that only 12 per cent of the five million Sukuma are Christians or Moslems despite more than a century of their exposure to these ideas. Their traditional religion is without institutions and has easily adapted to changing conditions. Quasi-traditional healers and diviners are widely available and cope adequately with their personal problems for which both Christianity and Islam do not have appropriate and readily available rituals.

The Sukuma evaluate their religious practices pragmatically rather than ideologically.

The paper by Babu, Kusuma and Naidu presents an ethnographic profile of the Jatapu, an agricultural tribe inhabiting the Eastern Ghats of the north coastal Andhra Pradesh. The Jatapu is a patriarchal endogamous group with several exogamous patrilineages that are totemic by nature. They have their own religion that centres on supernaturalism. However, the influence of Hinduism is noticeable in their beliefs and practices. The paper also narrates the current political, social and economic aspects of the tribe.

Amal Kumar Das discusses Totos, one of the least known tribal communities of India. There is a misconception that the Totos are a vanishing tribe. But the demographic situation does not speak so. They live in a single village in Totopara in Jalpaiguri district of West-Bengal under a sub-Himalayan terrain. They belong to the Mongoloid racial stock and are grouped under "Bhutia" scheduled-tribe of West-Bengal. They are one of the three identified "primitive tribes" of West-Bengal, the other two being the Lodha and the Birhor. Besides the Totos, twenty-four other communities are living at present in Totopara. Previously, the Totos were accustomed to shifting cultivation but they have become settled agriculturists for about five decades. They are an endogamous group having thirteen clans. This inter-breeding of a small population within thirteen of its clans might have biological consequences affecting the gene pool. Due to the planned developmental programmes some changes have now taken place in their life and outlook. A neo-elite group has emerged and it is eager to serve the community. They are no more a closed society and are inclined to march ahead with others.

In their paper Mandal and Sanyal deal with the socio-economic life of Saharia, a primitive tribe of Madhya Pradesh. A major bulk of the tract inhabited by Saharia tribe is covered by forest and the Vindhaya mountains. The traditional villages of the Saharias in the forest area are usually small. Now-a-days the Saharias are living in multi-ethnic villages in the plains and are not apparently much different from the other people around them. Except for bits and pieces of information recorded in census of India by the British administrators, no detailed anthropological account of this tribe has yet been prepared. The Saharias who have settled down in such multi-ethnic villages have greater socio-economic relations with the people of other ethnic groups than their counterparts in the forest. Such contact has brought about some socio-economic changes among the Saharias living in the plains.

In the next article Mohammad Taghi Sheykhi discusses the changing socio-economic life of some nomadic tribes of Iran. These people play a vital role in the animal-food production of their country. Their cultural homogeneity has for centuries forced them to maintain a moving or unsettled way of life, although in recent years various socio-economic factors have started to shrink them demographically. With the introduction of some welfare measures for their children they have now started to choose a settled way of life.

In the tribal areas where traditional values continue to be important, the position of the aged is expected to be better than it is in the urban areas. However, the tribal areas known for their traditional customs and practices are now witnessing rapid changes under the impact of various modernizing forces. P. Venkata Rao feels that these changes have a bearing on the living conditions of the aged. His case study of the Chenchus shows that the position of the aged in tribal village is not very comfortable, contrary to the general expectation.

The paper by Sinha and Das is based upon an intensive fieldwork carried out among the Kamar tribe residing in three villages of Gariaband tahsil of Raipur district of Madhya Pradesh. The study seeks to provide a comprehensive account of the political organization and customary laws of the Kamar, one of the seven primitive tribal groups of Madhya Pradesh.

The number of papers in this volume is not large enough to provide our readers with comprehensive understanding of various issues of social concern and social reality in our contemporary tribal societies. Nonetheless the empirical depth and analytical rigour of the papers, it is hoped, will be a modest help in this regard. We wish to receive feedback from scholars of tribal studies on the strength and weakness of this volume. As we get on with the preparation of the forthcoming volumes under the *Contemporary Society: Tribal Studies* series, a word of appreciation will encourage as much in the way as constructive criticism would enlighten us.

SECTION I

KINSHIP AND DOMESTIC GROUP

ONE

GADABA AND THE BONDO KINSHIP VOCABULARIES *VERSUS* MARRIAGE, DESCENT AND PRODUCTION

GEORG PFEFFER

Introduction

Studies of Indian kinship vocabularies, including those of tribal languages, have been treated in a descriptive or historical frame of reference, until Louis Dumont introduced his structural analysis of the "Dravidian Kinship Terminology" (1953) and initiated a prolonged debate on Indian data as well as method of analysis, culminating in Dumonts final discussion of "Affinity as a Value" (1983). The major contribution to this research is Trautmann's work on "Dravidian Kinship" (1981).

In the course of these debates, several authors discussed the differences of the south Indian "Dravidian" structure when compared to the Indo-European vocabulary of north India, but the peculiar middle Indian tribal classification of kin terms remained aside, before I introduced some variations 15 years ago (Pfeffer 1982 and 1983). More recently Robert Parkin (1992) added an elaborate comparative study of a number of middle Indian tribes, naming it "the Munda", because all of them speak languages belonging to the Munda family. His title is deceptive, because the uninformed reader might confuse the people called "the Munda" by Parkin with the Scheduled Tribe called "the Munda" by every other publication, but "the Mundari" by Parkin. Confusion is also created by the subtitle promising "an account of their social organization." In reality Parkin, having never visited India, is comparing bits and pieces of a wide variety of publications on tribal ethnography, intending to analyze the kinship vocabulary of the numerous tribes combined under this title. In fact he is offering a mixed bag, choosing a limited selection of terms—found suitable in several languages—and gracefully ignoring the rest.

The present paper will avoid such short-lived manoeuvres and prefer to offer two separate attempts of accumulating the complete vocabulary of kinship from two languages of the Munda family. This material is the result of primary ethnographic research. Hopefully it will be revised by further fieldwork in future. Beyond the mere ethnographic aspect, my paper also attempts to conceive the terminological structure of the whole and the logic it is based upon.

The analysis will be concerned with the languages of the Gadaba[1] and the Bondo[2], who speak Gutob and Remo respectively. Both ethnic units are part of the middle Indian tribal complex and in many ways related to some 40 major tribal communities settling in the vast hilly regions between Ganges and Godavari and comprising a population of about a hundred million people.[3] Very little primary anthropological research has been carried out in this region and the best recent studies—excellent in many other respects—suffer from serious defects[4] when discussing what is know as "kinship terminologies". This rather confusing state of affairs may justify a return to the more general question. Why should we study "systems of kin classification" or "relationship terminologies"?

Kinship and "Kinship"

The essential arguments of the case appear to have been raised long ago by the timeless contributions of Morgan (1871) and Kroeber (1909). The latter stressed a given or universal grip of kin-types and those principles of classification which, in some form or the other, were applied by each particular culture in order to come to terms with such universal relations. In an omnipresent domain of kinship Californian and Plains' Indians as well as modern Europeans of various nations classed the kin-types in a number of different ways, designating these classes by a limited vocabulary. Once this process of classification as such was clarified, Kroeber saw no reason to pay much attention to terminological analyses.

Morgan's pioneer research seems to have led the way towards a differentiation of kinship and "kinship", the universal domain and the particular status of the kinship vocabulary in certain societies. Thus the Amerindian social order as such was largely expressed in the language of kinship. This type of constitutional expression was rather different from the bureaucratic Constitution of the state. Thus the pattern of the "kinship" vocabulary did not simply classify a separate domain of that name but was subjected to and representing the basic ideas of the unified social order in such holistic societies. When this pre-state type of society gave way to civilizations on some continents, "kinship" terms elsewhere remained important sources for the study of the human evolutionary process.

Kroeber saw the same methods of classification at work in all systems of kinship. Arguing indirectly against Morgan, all terminologies were "classificatory" for him. Morgan, however, saw holistic patterns in some "kinship" vocabulary and a lack of such patterns in others called "descriptive", because ego's description of certain kin-types was their only systematic feature. Patterns of "classificatory systems", on the contrary, coincided with the other social patterns.

To the present day this basic controversy has not been settled. Some scholars, mostly those coming from the field of linguistics, were happy to discover further-comparable-principles of classification in the universal domain Kroeber had conceived, but others, while admitting many errors in the details of Morgan's studies, followed him in differentiating vocabularies of a limited domain in civil societies[5], such as the Polish or the Portuguese, from the terminologies of holistic societies such as the tribal orders of America or Oceania.

The latter course will be persued in the present article. The same constitutional importance has been discussed by modern authors such as Maurice Godelier (1986a:142-3), who has repeatedly seen the "relations of production" of tribal societies articulated by the "kinship" order. Where human energy is the prime "force of production", the social relations concerned with reproduction are the relevant property relations. Thus "kinship" is the central issue of the "mode of production" in technologically simple societies. The mental conceptions of the world and the material provisions for physical survival are jointly articulated within the framework of "kinship".

While agreeing with Godelier on this basic premise, I am unable to discover anything like evidence in his monograph on the tribal Baruya (1986b). His theoretical argument is lacking a clear link-up with his ethnography. Moreover, his description of the marriage rules is avoiding elementary information on the diachronic perspective,[6] and with regard to the kinship vocabulary, we are only informed of the terminological equation of grand parents and grand children and of the "Iroquois type" of cousin terms *(ibid.* 19). The relevance of these data with regard to the general frame of reference remains obscure. Why are they mentioned at all? In case any kind of data will suffice to bolster the hypothesis, we can do without them. If, however, kinship relations "on the ground" are supposed to represent "relations of production" in particular tribal societies, specific evidence must be supplied in confirmation of the thesis. The present article will therefore also probe into the relation between the pattern of the kinship vocabulary and other socio-economic patterns in order to offer at least glimpses of a structure applied to "kinship" as well as to production.

The Basis of Terminological Analyses

Terminological Types

Terminological "type" such as "Iroquois", "bifurcate merging" or "Hawaiian" were brought into fashion by Lowie (1920) and Spier (1925) in the nineteen-twenties, and the reason for their lasting popularity may be found in their simplistic conception. Anybody can identify similarities and differences of "cousin terms" in G0 or "collateral terms" in G+1[7] and, applying the proper jargon, lend professional respectability to such a finding. Even more impressive phrases like "bifurcate collateral type in G+1 and Hawaiian type in G0 or similar combinations in cases, when collaterals are differentiated only in the parental generation and not in ego's. More than two decades ago Rodney Needham[8] (1974: 50-61) delivered what then appeared to be the death-blow to the "terminological type", but in spite of his detailed criticism, they live on and are likely to survive in the jargon for many more decades. I shall avoid their use because of basic defects shortly recalled here: First, they refer only to a very small portion of the kinship vocabularly. Secondly, they refer to certain kin-types seen as important consaguinal positions in "Western" society but not necessarily so in others. Finally, without the slightest justification, the exotic names imply an air of ethnographic substance. Following Needham, the present paper will therefore avoid such familiar jargon.

Completeness

The point of this short criticism is to recall the basic principle of all terminological analyses which usually remains unmentioned, because it is either violated or self-understood. Only the complete account of all the kinship categories of a given tribe or linguistic unit can lead to comparable[9] results regarding patterns of classification. On the other hand, the selection of "suitable" terminological extracts for analysis and the simultaneous and tacid disregard for "unsuitable" portions of the kinship vocabulary of a given linguistic unit disqualifies the whole exercise.

The point is rather important for the study of middle Indian kinship vocabularies, since most authors were not aware of it when supplying various lists of kin terms in their ethnographics. As far as I can see, only Bouez (1985), Deeney (no date), McDougal (1963), and von Fürer-Haimendorf (1979) respect the criterion of completeness. Other authors (e.g. Bhattacharya, 1968: xvii) are professional enough to offer a few references concerning the ethnographic scope and the difficulties encountered during fieldwork. Some even mention the linguistic bias of their research and the fact that "there are therefore some important omissions in the terminology"[10] (Bhattacharya, 1970:

445).

Perhaps an anecdote will offer the best impression of ethnographic conditions in middle India: In February 1981, the late Dr. L.P. Vidyarthi, a former President of the World Association of Anthropological and Ethnological Sciences, kindly invited me to his department, introduced me to his staff and guided me to several tribal villages in the neighbourhood of Ranchi/Bihar, where we were able to conduct elaborate discussions with members of the Munda and Oraon tribes. In the course of these debates it soon became clear that my host did not take the slightest interest in kinship studies, his fields being religion, politics and economic development. His crucial—and controversial—ethnographic contribution to the kinship vocabulary of the *Maler* (Vidyarthi, 1963:218) was meaningless to him. He did not recall when and how the data were collected, since such efforts for him must have been an insignificant part of his main endeavour.

The difficulties mentioned above all lead to a central issue of middle Indian ethnography in general and accounts of the kinship vocabulary in particular. All members of Scheduled Tribes grow up with a command of at least two if not three different languages, and almost all ethnographers are in no position to learn the respective tribal idiom[11], since all government agencies are trying their best to reduce the relevance of these "minor" tongues.[12] The Gadaba case may serve as example. Since their settlements lie on the border of Orissa and Andhra Pradesh, most tribal speak their own Gutob language (of the Munda linguistic family) and have a full command of the local dialects of Oriya (an Indo-European language) and Telugu (a Dravidian language). Similarly, all Bondo are at least bilingual and continue to mix Oriya and Telugu kinship terms into their daily conversations. The criterion of completeness would therefore question the ethnographers right to select some kinship terms used regularly by these people and discard others.

The only way out of this dilemma appears to be a somewhat artificial isolation of those terms belonging etymologically to the (Munda) Gutob and Remo languages and ignoring the rest. Some individual terms such as *budhi* (yZ, HyBW) and *somdi* (SWM, SWF, DHM, DHF), however, are clearly of Indo-European origin and used in many north Indian languages. At the same time they lack a Munda substitute. Others, such as *bayi* (FF, MMB, eB) are of doubtful origin.

Thus it should be clear that the kinship vocabulary presented for discussion offers only terms from Munda languages in addition to those from other linguistic families not substituted by Gadaba or Bondo speakers in any other form. Assuming a complete account in this respect, my report is breaking the usual taboo on references to tribal multilingualism, so that a lack of completeness in the general sense of the spoken language must be admitted. Since the tribal speakers have no problems in shifting from one language to the other within the same conversation (or even sentence), I realize that my exclusion of most Indo-European and Dravidian terms does not reflect the day-to-day linguistic practice of the people described.

Scope

Another crucial issue is the scope of the terms under study. All of the tribes I have visited[13] live in local acephalous communities united by bonds of consanguinity and affinity, and within these *Gemeinschaften* of upto about fifty small villages, a member refers to any other by a kinship term irrespective of a genealogical distance. The work of McDougal (1963) and others also shows that kin terms are not "extended" from "focal types" to others. In fact collectives as such are named with terms reserved for individuals in "Western" classifications. Beyond the boundaries of such a community outsiders are named as such, even if they belong to the same Schedule Tribe or linguistic unit. Within the class of strangers, Gadaba and Bondo do, of course, differentiate tribals from clients[14] and locals from immigrant traders and administrators[15] applying other terminological instruments. Thus all Bondo, living off the beaten track in almost inaccessible hills, must be seen as such a homogeneous *Gemeinschaft* while there are several different local groups within the Gadaba tribe, and these communities have, in the course of history, developed differences regarding rituals, kinship rules and social categories. Such a differentiation will come into play, when I compare the uniform vocabulary of kinship within fluctuations among marriage rules and property relations.

Ethnography

Given these ethnographic problems the manner of data-collection must also be mentioned. Since 1981, I have frequently lived in a number of Gadaba villages of various subregions often only accessible by long hikes. My hosts were rather communicative and I had no difficulties whatsoever in observing and discussing social relations. Both men and women regularly engaged with me in the "play" of demands and counter-demands as the regular and manageable feature of daily conversation. Only during bouts of drunkenness at major festivals communication occasionally became disagreeable. As a result of these long-term contacts, I am fairly confident about the reliability of the data presented here.

The Bondo connection was of a different kind: In January 1981 I was able to conduct my first interview with two Bondo men who had just completed the usual five-year term in jail after a murder case. In order to be readmitted into their village community they bought the provisions for a big feast at the local market place. There I talked to them in the company of their—always communicative—Dombo clients. After the long absence from home, the two men were sober[16], talkative and in a way nostalgic about their language and community. During each one of my later excursions I managed to repeat such conversations with a few sober individuals away from Bondo settlements. But usually contacts at market place failed completely. Three times I spent a day of hiking into the forested Bondo Hills in several attempts to gain acceptance in the different villages near the track. I was employing the very competent help of a local guide who was wellknown and respected by the villagers. The following conversation at the village centre, the megalithic platform, would usually develop after my initial salutations:

Villager: Are you bringing clothes[17] or medicine?
I.: Neither, I have just come to chat with you.
V.: I see no point in chatting.
I: What a big village? Are all of you of the *hantal* clan?
V.: No, but even those of my clan are scoundrels. *Mangal Sisa* (or some other name) in that lane over there shot an arrow into my eye (chest, arm, leg etc.). If he shows his face, I'll kill him.
I. When did it happen?
V.: This is none of your business. Give me money and leave!
I: How about some *bidi* (local cigarettes)?
V.: Pass them on and get lost.
I.: Will we meet at the weekly market in X?
V.: No. get out immediately.

Other conversations of the same result were less extended. I dare to introduce these features of ethnography, because several authors (Elwin, 1950, Fernandez, 1969; and Bhattacharya, 1968 and 1970) have conducted primary research on the kinship vocabulary of the Bondo, and disagreements have developed over minute details of their data. Given the ethnographic conditions described above, I would not blame any of these scholars.

Elwin's excursions in the early nineteen-forties were accompanied by police escorts, since the Bondo were not really known for their friendliness, and their homicide-rate is among the world's highest. Fernandez, an American, only had very short contacts in the nineteen-sixties, while Bhattacharya could conduct some of his interviews in jail. The few communicative Bondo men mentioned several Europeans, presumably Ethnographers, who had vainly tried to live in a Bondo village. Given such conditions, the basis of my own data must be very slender.

The Vocabulary[18]

The Gutob Denotata (see Table 1.1 and 1.2)

G+2	
bayi	FF,MMB
ia	FM, MFZ
umbang	MF, FMB
miming	MM, FFZ
igloy	FF, MM, FM, MF
G+1	
afong	F, FB, MZH
uang	FZ, HM, WM, MBW
iong	M, MZ, FBW
mamung	MB, WF, HF, FZH
GO:	
bobroyn	WB,B w.s.
bulon	WZ, Z w.s.
buyan	HB, B m.s.
tonan	HZ, Z m.s.
bayi	eB, FBSe, MZSe, HeZH, WeZH
ia	eBW
bobo	yB, FBSy, MZSy, HyZH, WyZH
kiliboi	yBW, HyZ
miming	eZ, FBDe, MZDe, HeBW, WeBW
umbang	eZH
budhi	yZ, FBDy, MZDy, HyBW, WyBW
erel	yZH, HyB, WyB
irilboi	HeZ, WeZ
giking	HeB, WeB
giring	WyZ
kimboy	W, woman
remol	H, man
imbing	BW w.s.
maranger	MBD, MBS, FZS, FZD
somdi	SWF, DHM, DHF, SWM
G-1:	
odu'on	S, BS m.s., ZS w.s.
ono'on	D, ZD w.s, BD m.s.

kimingay	SW
ariyo	DH
mason	BS w.s., BD w.s., ZD m.s., ZS m.s.

G-2:

igloy	DD, SS, SD, DS

Analysis

The relational pattern of the vocabulary as a whole is discussed in its more important aspects now and will be finally represented by Tables 1.1 and 1.2. Initially the whole must be differentiated from the subset, i.e. the pattern within the central generational level. The structure of such a subset is determined by the opposition of relative age. In a way the subset offers the logical oppositions of the whole as a microcosm, because the whole is equally determined by the opposed categories of alliance and seniority, but the elements of the latter are generational levels rather than respective age. My analysis will discuss the whole only. N.J. Allen's analytical tools, the three forms of "classical" terminological equations (Allen 1989: 176-7), have proved to be most useful terms for the presentation of the structure found in the vocabulary.

Classificatory equations: Same-sex siblings of different kin-type are equated throughout, but in G0 this classificatory principle is encountered by the principle of relative seniority which differentiates eZ and yZ, WeB and WyB as well as similar categories of that level. In G+1, I may add, the relative seniority is expressed by a prefix, e.g. *modafang* (FeB) or *ninafang* (FyB).

Prescriptive equations: The terminology is systematically equating affines and consanguines at the two upper generational levels. Thus the "Dravidian" equations of *uang* (FZ, MBW, WF, HF) and *mamung* (MB, FZH, HF, WF), for example, prescribe symmetric affinal exchange within G+1. In ego's generation the very same symmetry is also maintained by equations such as *miming* (eZ, WeBW), *budhi* (yZ, WyBW, HyBW) and *erel* (yZH, WyB) or *bayi* (eB, WeZH, HeZH) and *bobo* (yB, WyZH, HyZH).

At the same time, the differentiation—or lack of equation—of such affinal categories as *ia* (eBW) in relation to *irilboi* (WeZ) or *ubang* (eZH) in relation to *giking* (WeB) is crucial. While within G0 the junior affinal categories (ZH and WB) are equated, the senior ones differentiate two separate classes of affines.

A contradiction of the relational pattern comes into light, when we study the reciprocal relations of *uang* (HM, WM, FZ, MBW) and *mamung*

TABLE 1.1: Gutob Kinship Vocabulary (Male Bias)

	Consanguines		--	Affines		Affines		=	Quasi-Consanguines	
	male	female		female	male	male	female		female	male
G+ 2	*bayi*/FF *(igloy)*	*miming*/FFZ *(igloy)*		*ia*/FM *(igloy)*	*umbang*/FMB *(igloy)*	*umbang*/MF *(igloy)*	*ia*/MFZ *(igloy)*		*miming*/MM *(igloy)*	*bayi*/MMB *(igloy)*
G+ 1	*afang*/F	*uang*/FZ		*iong*/M	*mamung*/MB	*mamung*/WF	*iong*/WFZ		*uang*/WM	*afang*/WMB
e G0 y	*bayi*/eB WeZH *buyan*/B *bobo*/yB	*miming*/eZ WeBW *tonan*/Z *budhi*/WyBW		*ia*/BW *irilboy*/WeZ *kimboy*/W *giring*/WyZ *kiliboy*/yBW	*umbang*/eZH *erel*/yZH/WyB	*somdi*/DHF *maranger* MBS/FZS	*maranger* FZD/MBD		*somdi*/SWM	
G-1	*odu'on*/S,BS	*ono'on*/D,BD		*kimingay*/SW	*ariyo*/DH	*mason*/ZS	*mason*/ZD			
G-2	*igloy*/SS	*igloy*/SD		*igloy*/SSW	*igloy*/SDH	*igloy*/DS	*igloy*/DD		*igloy*/DSW	*igloy*/DDH

TABLE 1.2: Gutob Kinship Vocabulary (Female Bias)

	Consanguines		=	Affines		Affines		=	Quasi-Consanguines	
	female	male		male	female	female	male		male	female
G+2	*miming*/mm *(igloy)*	*bayi*/MMB *(igloy)*		*umbang*/MF *(igloy)*	*ia*/MFZ *(igloy)*	*ia*/FM *(igloy)*	*umbang*/FMB *(igloy)*		*bayi*/FF *(igloy)*	*miming*/FFZ *(igloy)*
G+1 +1	*iong*/M	*mamung*/MB		*afang*/F	*uang*/FZ	*iong*/HFZ	*mamung*/HF		*afang*/HMB	*uang*/HM
e G0 y	*miming*/eZ HeBW *bulon*/Z *budhi* yZ	*bayi*/eB HeZH *bobroyn*/B *bobo*/yB		*umbang*/eZH *giking*/HeB *remol*/H *erel*/yZH/HyB	*ia*/eBW *irilboy*/HeZ *imbing*/BW *kiliboy*/yBW	*maranger* FZD/MBD *somdi*/DHM	*maranger* MBS/FZS		*somdi*/SWF	
G-1	*ono'on*/D,ZD	*odu'on*/S,ZS		*ariyo*/DH	kimingay/SW	mason/BD	mason/BS			
G-2	*igloy*/DD	*igloy*/DS		*igloy*/DDH	*igloy*/DSW	*igloy*/SD	*igloy*/SS		*igloy*/SDH	*igloy*/SSW

(WF, HF, FZH, MB), since their reciprocals differentiate into *kimingay* (SW) and *ariyo* (DH), on the one hand, and *mason* (BS w.s., BD w.s., ZD m.s., ZS m.s.) on the other. Furthermore in ego's generation BW, ZH, WB and HZ are never equated with MB's or FZ's children, i.e. *maranger* in the present case. Thus the "Dravidian" order is ruled out inspite of the equations FZ=HM or MB=WF.

The terminology as a whole offers two lines at the two upper generational levels and more than two lines in G0 and G-1. If *somdi* (SWF, DHM etc.) is taken into account, a fourth line would be represented, but such a demonstration is not really necessary, since any system of symmetric affinal prescription offering a third line implies the same symmetric relation, i.e. a fourth line, for all lines involved. This point must be stressed, since all tribal vocabularies of kinship in middle India use the Indo-European term *somdi* to denote the same kin-types. I have yet to find a language of the Munda or Dravidian linguistic family[19] with an "indigenous" term for *somdi* and therefore conclude, that it is not essential for the representation of the holistic pattern, even though it is known everywhere to the bilingual-speakers and mentioned in proper place in the course of an ethnographic enquiry. In regular informal discourse, the term *somdi,* however, stands for all affines irrespective of sex or generational level.

Alternate generation equations: The terms *bobo* (yB, WyZH) and *budhi* (yZ, WyBW) may be of Indo-European origin. In most north Indian languages *baba*–pronounced *bobo* in Oriya stands for "old man" and *budhi* for "old woman". Even if we leave aside such an equation–and remain concerned with Munda terms of the only—not just individual categories are equated in alternating generations, but the same affinal links appear simultaneously in G+2 and G0. The grandparental symmetric exchange of *bayi* (FF) and *miming* (MM) on the one side and *ia* (FM) and *umbang* (MF) on the other is repeated in the very same terms in Ego's generation. In addition to this repetition only the categories of G2 offer similar equations.

Additional observations: The discovery[20] of certain special Gutob terms of G0 is also of interest, since they are restricted to either male or female speakers, i.e. *bobroyn* or B, *bulon* or Z and *imbing* or BW (for female speakers only) and *buyan* or B, *tonan* or Z (for males only). They help to solve a general issue in Indian households, the question of terminological adjustment to the spouse system of reference. A man may thus refer to his wife's siblings or affines in the same terms, as she does, and vice versa, but both can also make use of general or–with regard to the speaker—"neutral" terms *miming* (eZ) and *budhi* (yZ), *bayi* (eB) and *bobo* (yB) or *ia* (eBW) and *kiliboy* (yBW) according to the situation.

At the level of G+2 terms are duplicated. The general *igloy* is applied reciprocally indicating the alternate generation equation of the even levels, just as the special terms such as *ia* (FM) are equated in Ego's generation. These special terms, on the other hand, differentiate the lines. The same differentiation in G-2 would be technically impossible, since each one of the four grandparental terms has a male as well as a female reciprocal. The elementary mechanism of preventing a "pure" reconstruction of the past in the future, the change from married predecessors (F and M) to sibling successors (D and S), has to be taken into account. The duplication in G+2 is thus a compromise between the lineal principle and the idea of alternate generations.

Preliminary Conclusions

Kinship categories of the Gadaba (see Table 1.1 and 1.2) represent a closed and unified system of symmetric affinal prescription. This system of affinal exchange as a whole, always differentiating ego's consanguines and affines, can only be represented in a sex-biased manner, i.e. by either M or F as part of a consanguinal pair of siblings in G+1 and by equating ego with same-sex siblings. In this manner the sibling status of ego's son and daughter can be mirrored into the parental generation. The upper generational levels can easily be represented by *bayi* (FF) and *miming* (MM), involved in affinal exchange with *umbang* (MF) and *ia* (FM) of the grandparental generation, and by *afang* (F) and *uang* (FZ) as exchange-partners of *iong* (M) and *mamung* (MB) in G+1.

In G0, however, the exchange is becoming more refined. Initially the process of G+2 is copied in an identical manner. The message is clear. The affinal link of the grandparental generational level is repeated. The alternate generations are equated in opposition to the adjacent generations. The diachronic perspective does register continuity, but not the identical pattern of adjacent generations. The affinal exchange is not repeated immediately, as is the case in the south Indian "Dravidian" systems (see Trautmann, 1981), because the cross-cousins are not equated with the spouses or spouses' siblings in G0. Diachronic affinity is rather expressed by repetitions in alternate generations.

The even and the odd generational levels operate with different direct affines respectively, but since the affinal contacts of the preceeding and succeeding generational levels continue to appear in G0 and G-1, the other terms represent "indirect affines" or a second type of affinal link involved in an exchange with a mostly nondescript but logically necessary fourth line of "quasi-consanguines".[21]

Within ego's generation the children of affines or *maranger* are differentiated from affinal exchange-partners whose children, or mason, are again excluded from exchange with ego's children. Some help from another discipline may be relevant at this moment: The literal meaning of *maranger* is "the senior one". Similarly senior direct affines within G0 are differentiated into two categories—of wife-takers and of wife-givers—whereas junior direct affines, i.e. *erel* (ZH, WB) and *kiliboi* (BW, HZ) represent takers and givers simultaneously. In short, juniors represent prescribed exchange, seniors prescribed distance.

Diagrams

The diagrammatic representation of terminological patterns generally remains problematic and has regularly led to misunderstandings. Thus Radcliffe-Brown (1953) was confused by Dumont's version of the ideal "Dravidian" system in print (Dumont 1953:10), but the latter form of a diagram could hardly cope with empirical diversity. Later Thomas Trautmann (1981: 40) was able to master this task and design an elegant framework suitable for all empirical versions of "Dravidian" terminologies. In the case of the middle Indian systems more visual emphasis should be added to the principle of alternating affinal prescription. The diagram or table should therefore stress a different overall pattern for the systematic presentation of the terms (see Tables).

The Remo Denotata (see Tables 1.3 and 1.4)

G+2:	
tuta	FF, MF
ia	MM, FM
G+1:	
ba	F
iong	M
bus'a	MeZ, FeB, MeZH, FeBW
mbu	MyZ, FyBW
kuku	FyB, MyZH
uang	FZ, MBW
mamung	MB, FZH
inking	HF, WF
kianr	WM, HM
G0	
Mang	eB
ombing	eBW
mé	yB
kimiyun	yBW

ming	eZ
umbang	eZH
kui	yZ
arju	yZH
maranger	MBD, FZS, FZD, MBS
imbing	MBSW, FZSW
somdi	DHF, SWM, SWF, DHF
umfor	H
kunui	W
inking	WeB, HeB
kianr	WeZ, HeZ, WeBW, HeBW
giring	WyB, HyB
iong	WyBW, HyBW
giringboi	WyZ, HyZ
bailo	WyZH, HyZH
G-1	
o'on	S, BS m.s., ZS w.s.
u'un	D, ZD w.s., BD m.s.
kimiyun	SW
arju	DH
mason	BS w.s., ZD m.s., ZS m.s., BD w.s.
bailo	BDH w.s., ZDH w.s.
G-2	
iglei	DS, SS, SD, SDH, SSW, DSW, DDH

Analysis

Although the languages of Gutob and Remo are closely connected and the kinship terms of the Gadaba and the Bondo are mutually understandable, differences of details remain.

Classificatory equations: Same-sex siblings of different kin-type are equated frequently, but the principle of seniority differentiates them in G0 as well as in G+1. Thus the terms for F *(ba)* and M *(iong)* in the parental generation stand for one kin-type only, even though *iong* reappears as WyBW and HyBW in G0, indicating the consanguinal character of these kin-types.

Prescriptive equations: In G+1 affinal exchange is prescribed in the usual manner, but in an extraordinary style. A single category *(bus'a)* ignores the principle of sex-differentiation and thus unites the kin-types of FeB, FeBW, MeZ and MeZH. As the most striking difference with regard to the Gutob pattern, the terms for MB/FZH *(mamung)* and FZ/MBW *(uang)* are not equated with those of WF *(inking)* and WM *(kianr)* respectively. Thus four and not two lines are represented in G+1.

Alternate generation equations: The Remo vocabulary offers no hint of such equations.

Additional observations: Several terms of adjacent generations are equated. Two of them *(iong, bailo)*–equating M and WyBW as well as WyZH and "husband of cross-niece"–stress the consanguinal character of the category, two others *kimiyun* and *arju* or yBW/SW and yZH/DH, must be seen as the terms for "direct junior affines" as such. Compared to the Gutob scheme, the order of Remo terms emphasizes the same principle of seniority within G0 by equating WeZ/HeZ with HM/WM *(kianr)* and WeB/HeB with HF/WF *(inking)*. Thus these affines of ego's generation are equated with their seniors of G+1, a method observed in many Indian terminological orders. In the present case of the Bondo, their unusual marriage rule[23] does not contradict the terminological distance of ego's senior affines within G0, since the equation does not contain a sex bias.

Preliminary Conclusions

While the extreme generational levels of G2 are hardly differentiated at all, the prescriptive nature of the Remo vocabulary (see Tables 1.3 & 1.4) is conveyed by the pattern of affinal exchange in G+1. Prescription is adjusted to the principles of seniority-within G0 and G+1– and alternation. The latter issue is not at all expressed by alternate generation equations, but by differentiating "spouse's parents" from MB and FZ, "spouse's siblings" from cross-cousins, and "children's spouses" from Cross-nephews and cross-nieces. Thus repetition of affinal exchange in adjacent generations is categorically excluded. If the system of kin terms is seen as a unified whole, as it must be, four terminological lines are the minimal requirement for diachronic affinity. The system of the Bondo allows more latitude when compared to the Gadaba order. Whereas the latter prescribes the identical repetition of symmetric exchange in alternating generations by equating grandparental and senior sibling terms, the former prescribes symmetric exchange and allows alternating exchanges as "shortest route" for the preservation of diachronic affinity. Separate terms for "indirect affines" at the three central generational levels exclude immediate repetition of exchange.

TABLE 1.3: Remo Kinship Vocabulary (Male Bias)

		Consanguines		=	Affines		Affines		=	Quasi-Consanguines	
		male	female		female	male	male	female		female	male
G+2		*tuta*/FF	*ia*		*ia*/FM	*tuta*	*tuta*/MF	*ia*		*ia*/MM	*tuta*
G+1	e	*bus'a*/FeB			*bus'a*/MeZ						
G+1		*ba*/F	*uang*/FZ		*iong*/M	*mamung*/MB	*inking*/WF			*kianr*/WM	
G+1	y	*kuku*/FyB			*mbu*/MyZ						
G0	e	*mang*/eB	*ming*/eZ		*ombing*/eBW	*umbang*/eZH					
G0		*kianr*/WeBW			*kianr*/WeZ	*inking*/WeB	*somdi*/DHF			*somdhi*/SWM	
G0					*kunui*/W		*maranger*	*maranger*		*imbing*	
G0		*bailo*/WyZH			*giringboi*/WyZ	*giring*/WyB	MBS/FZS	FZD/MBD		MBSW/FZSW	
G0	y	*mé*/yB	*kui*/yZ		*kimiyun*/yBW	*arju*/yZH					
G-1		*o'on*/S,BS	*u'un*/D,BD		*kimiyun*/SW	*arju*/DH	*mason*/ZS	*mason*/ZD			*bailo*/ZDH
G-2		*iglei*	*iglei*		*iglei*	*iglei*	*iglei*	*iglei*		*iglei*	*iglei*

TABLE 1.4: Remo Kinship Vocabulary (Female Bias)

	Consanguines female	Consanguines male	=	Affines male	Affines female	Affines female	Affines male	=	Quasi-Consanguines male	Quasi-Consanguines female
G+2	*ia*/MM	*tuta*		*tuta*/MF	*ia*	*ia*/FM	*tuta*		*tuta*/FF	*ia*
e	*bus'a*/MeZ			*bus'a*/FeB						
G+1	*iong*/M	*mamung*/MB		*ba*/F	*uang*/FZ	*kianr*/HM			*inking*/HF	
y	*mbu*/MyZ			*kuku*/FyB						
e	*ming*/eZ	*mang*/eB		*umbang*/eZH	*ombing*/eBW					
	kianr/HeBW			*inking*/HeB	*kianr*/HeZ	*somdi*/SWM			*somdi*/DHF	
G0				*umfor*/H		*maranger*	*maranger*			
	iong/HyBW	*bailo*/HyZH		*giring*/HyB	*giringboi*/HyZ	*FZD*/MBD	*MBS*/FZS			
y	*kui*/yZ	*mé*/yB		*arju*/yZH	*kimiyun*/yBW					
G-1	*u'un*/D,ZD	o'on/S,ZS		*arju*/DH	*kimiyun*/WS	*mason*/BD	*mason*/BS		*bailo*/BDH	
G-2	*iglei*	*iglei*		*iglei*	*iglei*	*iglei*	*iglei*		*iglei*	*iglei*

Comparison

Practices and Marriage Rules

The relation between categories, rules and practices of kinship remained a bone of contention among experts until Rodney Needham's (1973) seminal article on prescription. Thereafter, it was understood that the phenomena of these three analytical frames of reference were to be analized separately. It is therefore not permissible to explain features in one of these domains, e.g. a particular form of affinal prescription, by reference to features of another, e.g. statistical frequencies of a certain type of intermarriage. The regularities of each sphere can only be compared as such.

Unfortunately I am in no position to provide any reliable account of the frequencies in marriage links among the Gadaba or Bondo in a manner that is statistically relevant. Marriage rules vary. All informants emphasized the symmetric nature of marriage agreements. Those who are allowed to "take" a virgin must sooner or later "give" one in return. But in some subregions, for example in the neighbourhood of Lamptaput, the marriage rule also provides for an interval of one generation. Those families who have intermarried in the previous generation must not do so in the present one. At the same time, the "reopening" of the grandparental path is considered to be the standard. Since villages are exogamous, alliances are supposed to be maintained with at least two different affinal villages. Such links do not necessarily tie a lineage as a whole to two outside settlements only, since marriages are usually arranged at the sublineage level. Thus the principles of symmetry, seniority and alternation are expressed by the kinship vocabulary as well as by the marriage rules.

Other subregions, e.g. the Onukadili area, offer a slightly different picture. Here the Gadaba follow the simple "Dravidian" pattern of immediate repetition of intermarriage or "restricted exchange", simplistically called "bilateral cross-cousin marriage" by anthropological jargon. The propagation of this rule of repetition in adjacent generations may have been facilitated by the south Indian social environment of the district as a part of the former Madras presidency, but most of the Telugu traders and administrators of the neighbourhood in fact prefer "matrilateral cross-cousin marriages". The Gadaba have never accepted such an asymmetrical preference, but on the issue of immediate repetition they may have been influenced by neighbouring Hindus.

The account of the marriage rules, therefore, offers a picture not dissimilar to the pattern of the vocabulary, where a part, i.e. the two upper generational levels, coincides with the south Indian "Dravidian" system, while G0 and G-1 imply at least four terminological lines of exchange. The more refined alternating order may have been the earlier feature, the version of direct repetition a later historical development. It is possible, though not all necessary, that "cross-cousin marriage" of the simplistic type has led to a removal of separate categories for "parents-in-law" in the Gutob vocabulary.

Whatever information the Bondo informants would provide on this subject appeared to stress the interval of one generation and the prohibition of immediate re-enactment of intermarriage. I was, however, unable to attend any Bondo marriage, whereas a guest of several Gadaba weddings, I could enquire about the regularities of each case. The Bondo rules insist on village exogamy and symmetric exchanges and explicitly disallow a bride from a man's maternal village. At the same time villages are classfied as "brother" *(bhai)* or as affinal *(bondhu)* settlements, and brides must be brought from the latter category only.[24] So a sublineage may entertain alliance partners in several villages simultaneously, two being the minimum. This relational pattern of rules is thus equivalent to the pattern of terminological categories.

While the Gadaba norms and vocabulary both look as if they have at least partly been subjected to historical changes, no such influence is reflected by the Bondo patterns. The contradiction of the Gadaba vocabulary, i.e. the prescriptive equations (FZ=WM and MB=HF) as opposed to the alternate generation equations (MM=eZ and MF=eZH), goes together with at least two contradictory marriage rules—immediate vs. delayed repetition of intermarriage—according to different subregions, while the rather isolated Scheduled Tribe of the Bondo, the "junior sibling" of the Gadaba, offers none of such contradictions.

Rituals

When I entered Bondo villages on two occasions, unaware of the fact that major rituals were being performed, I was disallowed to participate. Informants did, however, mention the same categories of bond-friendship I was familiar with Gadaba rituals. Presumably a similar "ritual language" is articulated, while details are likely to differ.

The most important Gadaba ritual is the secondary funeral called *gotr* which is seen as the "senior" or superior form of a marriage. An ordinary wedding is an affair of the whole village community in the month of *Magh* (January/February). Interrupting the annual wedding festivities, once in every generation at this time, the deceased of the past period are "given" to hereditary exchange partners of other villages. The dead are represented by buffaloes and devoured by the partners who bring menhirs for the lineage platform in exchange. In 1988, for example, I was able to witness how 162 buffaloes were given away in a certain village. The most important structural message of the ritual appears to be the inversion of the marriage pattern. Whereas at ordinary weddings, two types of agnates from other settlements have to sit in opposed rows acting as witnesses of the exchange between affinal villages, at the "senior" form of marriage, as the secondary funeral is conceived, the same affines have to act as witnesses of the exchange of souls between villages mutually defined as agnatic.[25]

The lineage ritual identifies four categories of exchange partners. The two agnatic ones are the so-called "bone-brothers" who take the majority of the buffaloes and others called "bond-friends"[26] or *moitr* who will always mutually give in to any kind of demand. The affines are differentiated into those who are aggressive and dispute the agnatic claim of the buffaloes by emphasizing their close genealogical connection to the deceased FZ or MB, as well as those who come as witnessess and cooperate by providing cows[27] for the feast (see Pfeffer, 1992). Thus in this major potlatch-like ritual the Gadaba world is subdivided into cow-bringers and buffalo-takers, those who dispute and those who fulfil all demands. Altogether four categories appear, two of which qualify for symmetric exchanges and two others are excluded from ritual reciprocity. This pattern of material transfers is coinciding with the pattern of alternate exchanges in the kinship vocabulary.

Descent

All ethnographers of the Bondo confirm the general social framework of two patrilineal exogamous moieties named cobra and tiger. Among the Gadaba subregional differences may again be observed. In the area of Lamptaput four exogamous patrilineal clans (cobra, tiger, monkey and sun) exchange, "sisters" while other such descent categories are added in other subregions. Most of the many different tribal societies settling in the southwest of Koraput town—at a distance of some 50 miles—are in fact structured by either the cobra/tiger moieties or by the above named quartet or by eight exogamous, patrilineal totemic clans comprising fish, cobra, cow, tiger, bear, monkey, vulture and sun. It should also be clear that neither the orders of four clans nor those of eight units offer a particular pattern of intermarriage. Thus Gadaba of the cobra clan may entertain affinal alliances with those of the tiger, monkey or sun category.

Simultaneously all of those tribes[28] maintain a limited set of universally applied non-exogamous patrilineal status categories named after positions of sacred or secular leadership. Each clan *(bonso)* includes representatives of all status categories *(kuda),* and each one of such honorific titles is found in all clans. In the Lamptaput subregion the Gadaba only operate with the status categories *boronaik* (senior secular leader), *munduli* (junior secular leader), *sisa* (senior sacred leader) and *kirsani* (junior sacred leader). These are the most popular titles of other subregions and tribes—including that of the Bondo—as well, but several other names come up in addition, e.g. *charan* or sacred leader. All of these terms are of Indo-European origin, but we have no means to trace their history. It should be clear, however, that the village community offers a given status to each member, implying different secular and sacred obligations. Everywhere the categories are again differentiated according to the principle of seniority. All members of a village are thus related to one another by the ritual obligations that go along with the status categories. Irrespective of the statistical representation of these titles within each village, they represent the dichotomies of two values, i.e. the sacred/ secular and the senior/junior hierarchies.

Comparing these socio-centric structural units with the ego-centric kinship categories we find that the pattern of Bondo moieties and status concepts does not fit in an exact manner, even though the principles of symmetry and seniority may be shared. The Gadaba everywhere permit members of a clan to engage in affinal exchanges with several other clans. They offer alternatives. Most Gadaba operate with four clan categories only. Of the groups representing the four Gadaba status categories in each village, two conduct rituals and two are reponsible for political decision-making. This opposition may be seen in analogy to that of consanguines and affines of the kinship vocabulary, and the same applies to the senior-junior dichotomy.

Production

Hunting and collecting are the only tribal occupations restricted to gender categories. The meagre rest of wild animals in the Eastern Ghats must be hunted by all men at the major spring festival *chait*, when women "close" the villages and cross-dress until the men return with game. Women on the other hand move to the forest all year long to dig out wild tubers with their long metal-tipped sticks. These root-crops are a considerable addition to the daily diet, while the gains of hunting are materially insignificant among the Gadaba. Even Bondo men, permanently armed with bows and arrows, axes and swords, rarely kill animals outsizing a rat.

Perhaps the hunting tradition has been a liability in the field of animal husbandry. The tribals are excellent butchers but show only minor skills in breeding their domestic animals. Cows and buffaloes are given to the clients to tend and pigs, sheep, goats and chicken are not bred systematically but left to run around unattended until offered for some sacrifice.

The other traditional form of production is swidden cultivation. The tribal "lords of the land" used to distribute the fields according to the family needs and the labour-power available. In 1982, however, the government raised a settlement-camp of administrators in the region and "settled"[29] the land once and for all by providing the cultivators—of the time—with *pattas* or certificates of permanent ownership.[30] This raised new difficulties, since quite a few of the Gadaba—but none of the Bondo-villagers were working in the tea plantations of Assam as long-term migrant labourers. By their absence they lost their claims to the village lands. Many of them are involved in litigation nowadays while other have remained permanently in the slums of the Assamese plantation-towns. On the other hand some of those who happened to be present during the settlement-work–or who were recalled by their relatives–have become quite affluent.

If these modern developments are ignored for a moment, the traditional avenues of production of the two tribes must be seen in hunting and gathering, keeping animals for sacrifice and swidden cultivation, two short term and two long-term engagements.

Today manured gardens for vegetables, rain-fed fields for dry-rice or various species of millet, terraced river-beds for wet-rice, and rotating slash-and-burn cultivation on the hilltops may be seen as a similar fourfold division.

Conclusions

Women work in agriculture, men contribute to domestic work without major gender differences. Before the "settlement" labour used to be the most important factor of production and labour to this day has no gender-based value. An outmarrying woman would be a major loss for her agnates. Though cows and other valuables are given as bride-wealth at marriages, they are usually consumed on the spot at the wedding feasts and come nowhere near a compensation for the loss of labour-power incurred by the bride-giving party. Thus the general rule of symmetric exchange, prescribed by the vocabulary, among other things guarantees a mutual adjustment of labour among the parties involved. The principle of alternation[31] duplicates such long-term intensive contacts between affinal allies. As I have shown before (Pfeffer, 1982) most tribal communities of middle India share the value-ideas of symmetry, seniority and diachronic alliance contained in the idea of alternation. These ideas give shape to the "relations of production" since production cannot be isolated from other social and intellectual spheres.

Tribal institutions have, of course, been subjected to historical changes and their patterns would never fit exactly. But the unified order of values remains. Perhaps more extended research would have to be invested into the process of swidden cultivation, nowadays more important among the Bondo than among the Gadaba. The periodically alternating phases of cultivation and fallow of a piece of land must have had a major influence upon the worldview and the periodic alternations it prescribes.

The two Gadaba ideas of marriage also involve alternation: The "junior" marriage unites young affines who may join in sexual intercourse in order to reproduce new humans. The "senior" marriage, i.e. the secondary funeral, unites older agnates who eat one another in order to remove the humans[32] long after their physical death. Both rituals are accepted as interrelated and necessary. They also have a material basis. The great *gotr* ceremony is seen as the main reason for people to work and save the fruits of work. In every generation the villagers blow all their savings on the four days of this ritual.

The terminological equations shaping the structure of the kinship vocabulary are in fact formulas of the general principles that determine the tribal values. Thus "classificatory equation" is a shorthand version for the holistic principle governing these societies "prescriptive equation" is the neatest code for the idea of interdependence which is so prominent among the tribes. An "alternate generation equation" is a parsimonious articulation of the principle of seniority. The adjacent juniors must depend upon other links than their seniors. Juniors are different from seniors and yet unmarriageable. They are non-affinal others. In combination all of these classificatory instruments imply opposition and interdependence of allied sides and levels as well as hierarchy of seniors between and within these levels.

The idea of a holistic interdependence of seniors and juniors is a characteristic value in general. Thus the Gadaba are related to the Bondo as "senior siblings" are to their "juniors", and all over middle India endogamous tribes as well as major sections of these tribes are related to one another by a hierarchy expressed in the language of seniority and agnation (see Pfeffer, 1983:90-101). This language is providing the basic framework of the intra- and intertribal hierarchy. The affinal partners of siblings must be different from the partners of their parents, and members of the-relatively junior-Bondo or Munda tribe must not marry those people reserved for the—relatively senior—Gadaba or Ho tribe.

The concept of alternating prescribed affinal exchange is furthermore relevant to evolutionist reconstructions. Three decades ago Rodney Needham (1967) tried to elaborate an evolutionary sequence of possible affinal combinations beginning with the constraints of a simple behavioural and terminological "two-section system" (Needham, 1967: 46) and followed by successive stages of "symmetric prescriptive terminology plus assymetric alliance" *(ibid)* and then asymmetrical prescriptions and preferences upto the disintegration of these simple principles of interdependence. Inspired by this frame of reference, I tried to show that a "four-section terminology" (Pfeffer, 1983: 109), as discovered among the Juang, offers relatively more latitude and less constraints than a simple moiety order. It also indicates a direction for an evolution that diversifies alliance patterns and finally abolishes all positive marriage rules (*ibid.,* 119/20). This divergent evolutionary "route" could have altogether avoided stages of asymmetry.

Later N.J. Allen's refined approach presented the "tetradic model" (Allen, 1986: 90) underlying realisations such as the Gadaba and the Bondo scheme. In the model of a quadripartite society the simplest kinship terminology differentiates siblings and spouses as well as parents and children. In relation to the model the empirical societies discussed in the present article duplicate the marriageable categories, thereby duplicating the parent/child categories. A single affinal exchange is no longer prescribed, and in the course of the given alternative it becomes clear that the fourth line of "quasi-consanguines" need not be named, may be left open, or can generally be treated in a negligent manner offering a possible door to further evolutionary changes. Thus a reference to the tetradic model clarifies primary possibilities of variation and latitude.

Middle Indian tribal society is simple enough to allow kinship relations to govern others in a manner not too far removed from conditions in a quadripartite society. The complex society of castes and classes in south India, on the other hand, has been quite different for the last thousands of years. In the limited or private sphere of kinship, the "Dravidian" terminology may be seen as a simple system of "Cross-cousin marriage", but this very simplicity is perfectly suitable for a complex order of the political economy, just as a descriptive terminology would be. With the growing outside influence the Gadaba vocabulary and marriage rules are simplified and at least partially adjusted to the "Dravidian" scheme.

Finally, quite apart from the evolutionary issues, I would like to discuss the "sustained development" tribal India is supposed to undergo, since kinship vocabulary and rules are not just academic toys of armchair anthropologists but indirect indicators of massive oppression. For the last decades the central and the provincial budgets have reserved large sums for the development of the Gadaba, the Bondo and other tribes of the region. Most of these funds were diverted into private channels the invisible kind, but year after year the very presence of the administration has increased.[33] Because of this growth more outsiders find opportunities to cut the forest for commercial purposes and encourage the tribals to grow cash crops in order to purchase commodities from plains people. The administration also interferes directly into Bondo marriage practices or Gadaba secondary funerals. Culture change is the declared aim. The tribes are supposed to be brought, "into the cultural mainstream of India", whatever that may mean. Such a growing presence of the plains people and their cultural priorities will further reduce the tribal forms of production, descent and marriage, and—provided a certain delay—will be measurable in the language and the structural changes of the vocabulary of kinship.

Postscript on the Vocabulary of the *Didye* (or Gītare) and the *Parenga* (or *Gorum*)

During an excursion in spring 1998 those neighbours of the Gadaba and the Bondo were visited who are officially known as *Didaye* and *Parenga* but call themselves *Gītare* and *Gorum* in their own languages belonging to the southern Munda family. The *Gītare* denotata were the following: *N'ta* (FF, MF); *n'ja* (MM, FM); *bai* (MM, eZ); *mong* (MB, FZH); *n'we* (FZ, MBW); *n'tang* (FyB, MyZH); *b'ssa* (FeB, MeZH); *m'ba* (F); *iang* (M,MZ, FBW); *te'tang* (HF, WF); *m'in* (WM, HM); *dohneselabai* (W); *kehar* (WeZ.); *Sadu* (WeZH); *nang* (HeB); *m'pe* (HyB, HyBW, HeBW); *m'baing* (HZ); *ba'ari* (HZH); *graing* (MBS, FZS; WyB); *graingboi* (FZD, MBD, WyZ); *bai'ang* (WyZH); *n'kuin* (WeB) *baiang* (B,MBDH); *m'bang* (BW); *tona* (Zm.s., FZSW, WBW); *buling* (Zw.s); *m'be* (Zhm.s.); *rajahoing* (ZHw.s.); *hoing* (S,BSm.s., ZSw.s.; D, ZDw.s., BDm.s.) *kiming* (SW); *m'bing* (DH), *matson* (Zsm.s., ZDm.s., BDw.s., Bsw.s.); *ailae* (DD,DS,SD,SS).

The *Gorum* denotata were the following: *Ona* (FF, FMB, eB); *akang* (FM, eBW); *dada* (MF,MMB); *bibkuila* (MM); *mama* (MB,FZH); *ota* (FZ, MBW); *chatara* (HF, WF); *chatari* (WM, HM); *oba* (F); oya (M); *malo* (FeB, MeZH); *bodai* (MeZ, FeBW); *asuaya* (MyZ, FyBW); *kiki* (FyB, MyZH); *mena* (MBD, MBS, FZS, FZD); *sakha* (yB); *konun* (yBW, SW); *abi* (eZ, WeBW;HeZ); *bhatu* (eZH,HeZH); *oguni* (WyZ); *tonan* (yZ); *juin* (yZH, DH); *kadaman* (W); *mara* (H); *susur* (WeB, HeB); *sala* (WB); *ilil* (WyZ, HyZ); *datu* (WyZH, HyZH); *bhanja* (ZSm.s., BSw.s.); *bhanji* (BDw.s.; ZDm.s.); *angun* (S,Bsm.s., Zsw.s.); *kola* (D,ZDw.s., BDm.s.); *ileng* (DD,SD,DS, SS).

Though this preliminary collection may contain several mistakes, the major result–comparable to the *Remo* and *Gutob* vocabularies—is the fact that the line of ego's direct affines differs from those of ego's parents' or children's direct affines.

NOTES

1. Some 50,000 Gadaba of Orissa (Tripathi, 1971: 326) inhabit the mountain area called Eastern Ghats and several thousand more are living in the neighbouring province of Andhra Pradesh. The name Gadaba is derived from the river Godavari, the southern border of the tribe.
2. Some five to six thousand Bondo *(ibid.)* live in the "Bondo Hills" of the Eastern Ghats as neighbours and "junior siblings" of the Gadaba. They call themselves and their Munda language Remo or "human".
3. Numerous inhabitants of the tribal areas have not been mentioned on the administrative schedules, thus failing to qualify for the Census status of Scheduled Tribe.

4. Thus Piers Vitebsky's brilliant study of Sora Shamanism (1993) clearly shows the author's lack of interest in terminological issues, and Simeran M.S. Gell's fine monograph on the Muria Gond offers "the" kinship terms in a special table (1992: 43) adopting Trautmann's (1981) form of a diagram but failing to mention the—important–separate perspective of a female speaker. The author also does not take into account the multitude of other kinship terms she is mentioning in the text.
5. Societies constituted by the citizens of a state were called "civilizations" by Morgan.
6. We are told (Godelier, 1986b: 20-3) that the Baruya must exchange one woman for another and avoid matrilateral cross-cousin marriage. A man can marry his patrilateral cross-cousin to complete the cycle, if his paternal aunt was "given" without the equivalent return gift. Thus the reader may venture intelligent speculations about the diachronic perspective, but the author does not mention any rule, even though affinity is certainly inherited.
7. G0/G1/G2 should stand for the generational levels of ego, and the levels removed by one or two generations respectively. An additional "plus" or "minus" stands for upper or lower levels respectively.
8. What I wish to propose therefore is quite seriously that this kind of typology, i.e. one in which types are defined by isolated features of named societies arbitrarily selected as paradigm cases, should be entirely abandoned. (Needham, 1974: 53)
9. A basic error may be demonstrated by the usual textbook equation of Inuit and European terminologies under the heading of "Eskimo type." Apart from a few cousin-terms, the patterns of the vocabularies in fact differ markedly.
10. Only the linguist S. Bhattacharya (1970) has so far collected and published data on the kinship vocabulary of the Gadaba. They contain considerable omissions and mistakes and are presented in the course of a linguistic comparison of most Munda languages and not in an anthropological frame of reference.
11. Vitebsky provides the admirable exception to this rule. A handfull of others made attempts. The main difficulties arise due to the fact that foreigners are not permitted by the government to stay longer than three months within a specific tribal area.
12. If schools are opened in the tribal areas, the staff would never dream of teaching in a tribal tongue. Very few printed books are available in tribal languages (none in Gutob or Remo) for a market that usually consists of urban intellectual "rebells" against the dominance of the Hindu and Muslim plains people.
13. In February 1972, I visited the Kond and Sora areas for the first time. Later longish excursions to most tribal areas followed in 1980/1, 1982, 1983, 1987, 1988, 1990, 1994, and 1996.
14. Members of the "Scheduled Tribes" are seen as owner-cultivators of the tribal territory. Crafts (weaving, smithery), commerce and cattle-herding are the traditional tasks of clients who are found among all tribes as culture brokers. Almost all ethnographers of middle India have ignored this important symbiotic relationship and the more prosaic tasks of the clients.
15. The Gadaba and Bondo live in the southern Koraput District where more than 90 per cent of the population (the inhabitants of the rural areas) are tribal. They communicate with immigrants at market places or in the course of administrative action.
16. Palm wine *(salap)* is a major source of daily nutrition for all Bondo and hard liquor *(mahua)* is regularly produced out of the fruits of the *bassia latiflia* and consumed at all times of the day. Thus the Bondo consumption of liquor may approach German standards, but the rest of the diet is meagre.
17. Since the nineteen-seventies the government is running a "Bondo Development Agency" in the Hills which is trying to popularise clothes among the "naked" Bondo women who wear miniskirts only. Since 1992 the District Commissioner of Malkangiri is paying cash

to Bondo women who agree to dress more elaborately and stop shaving their skulls.

18. I cannot accept the dogma that the small number of kin-types mentioned here are supposed to include the "focal kin-types" of a term which would be "extended" to others in a later logical step. For this reason, the kin-types mentioned here refer only to some of the possible positions the terms are actually applied to.
19. In the course of my fieldwork I have collected the vocabulary of kinship among 32 ethnic groups of the tribal areas.
20. The same kind of sex-specific terms of the Bondo are provided by Bhattacharya (e.g. 1968: 70), but I was unable to confirm them under the given ethnographic conditions.
21. In my first work on middle Indian terminologies (Pfeffer, 1982: 65), I adopted this expression from Vatuk's analysis of north Indian terminologies by quoting her work (Vatuk, 1969: 101). I was pleased to learn that other specialists for middle India later followed suit.
22. I am rather impressed by Michelle Z. Rosaldo's diagram of two cross-cutting concentric series of circles (Rosaldo, 1980:12) without any reference to kin-types, because such clear demarcations would have misrepresented Ilongot ideas.
23. According to the explicit norm, most male Bondo marry women who are their seniors by five to six years.
24. All middle Indian tribes recognize this diachronic form of affinity. The terms *bhai/ bondhu* are adopted from north Indian languages.
25. No genealogical links can be discovered between such "brother" villages. As in all middle Indian tribal ideologies agnation is defined by the exclusion of intermarriage.
26. The Gadaba *moitr* status is inherited at the level of the sublineage and should not be confused with individual "bond-friendship" prevalent all over the tribal areas.
27. In contrast to the Hindus who advocate the consumption of milk and discourage the consumption of beef, the middle Indian tribals advocate beef during communal feasts and abstain from milk and milk products.
28. No ethnographic fieldwork has ever been conducted among these tribes. This may be due to the less exotic Indo-European languages they speak, since the fallacy of equating language and culture is a widespread syndrome. The patterns of their kinship vocabularies, however, differ greatly from the north Indian regularities and closely resemble those of the Bondo and the Gadaba.
29. The administrative process of settlement camps may be the most important heritage of the British colonial Government in India.
30. Cultivators were evicted, however, in vast areas where water-reserves and dams for hydroelectric projects had been constructed. Compensation was absolutely insignificant. In fact the population concerned was left to starve.
31. To my knowledge Dumont (1966, 1971) was the first to compare systems of alternating marriage alliances. He called these systems "Aranda". When discussing the Juang alliances of two generation-sets in each village I wrote accordingly: "They therefore maintain a structure which Dumont defined as characteristic for the Aranda system". (Pfeffer, 1982: 53). Other publications have later ridiculed this finding. At the same time they did not hesitate to adopt my results regarding marriage alliance and affinal prescription of the Juang (Pfeffer, 1982: 51-3;67) without reference. In the same unorthodox manner they have incorporated and elaborated numerous other original data and conclusions several years after my book, but I see no reason to mention such "adoptions" in detail.
32. Buffaloes represent the dead. For details see Pfeffer (1992).
33. Recently, for example, the old Koraput district has been subdivided into three new ones.

REFERENCES

Allen, N.J. 1986. "Tetradic Theory: An Approach to Kinship," *JASO*, XVII (2): 87-109.

Allen, N.J. 1989. "The Evolution of Kinship Terminologies," *Lingua*, 77: 173-185.

Bhattacharya, Sudhibhushan. 1968. *A Bonda Dictionary*. Poona: Deccan College.

—. 1970. "Kinship Terms in the Munda Languages," *Anthropos*, 65: 440-465.

Bouez, Serge. 1985. *Réciprocité et hiérarchie. L'Alliance chez les Hos et les Santal dans l'Inde*. Paris: Societe d'Ethnographie.

Deeney, J (ND) *Ho Grammar and Vocabulary*. Chaibasa: Xavier Ho Publications.

Dumont, Louis. 1953. "The Dravidian Kinship Terminology as an Expression of Marriage," *Man*, Art. 54.

—. 1966. "Descent of Intermarriage? A Relational View of the Australian Section System," *South-Western Journal of Anthropology*, 22: 231-250.

—. 1971. *Introduction á déux théories d'anthropologie sociale*. Paris: Mouton.

—. 1983. *Affinity as a Value. Marriage Alliance in South India, with Comparative Essays on Australia*. Chicago: The University of Chicago Press.

Elwin, Verrier. 1950. *Bondo Highlander*, Bombay: Oxford University Press.

Fernandez, Frank, 1969. "A Critique of Verrier Elwin's Anthropology: Hill Bondo Social Organization and Kinship Analysis", in M.C. Pradhan, R.D. Singh, P.K. Mishra and D.B. Sastry (eds.), *Anthropology and Archaeology. Essays in Commemoration of Verrier Elwin, 1902-64*. London, Oxford University Press.

Fürer-Haimendorf, Christoph Von. 1979. *The Gonds of Andhra Pradesh*. New Delhi; Vikas.

Gell, Simeran M.S. 1992. *The Ghotul in Muria Society*. Chur: Harwood.

Godelier, Maurice, 1986. *The Making of Great Men. Male Domination and Power among the New Guinea Baruya*. Cambridge; Cambridge University Press.

—. 1986; *The Mental and the Material*. London; Verso

Kroeber, Alfred. 1909. "Classificatory Systems of Relationship," *Journal of the Royal Anthropological Institute*, 39: 77-84.

Lowie, Robert. 1920. *Primitive Society*. New York: Bouiand Liverright.

McDougal, Charles W. 1963. *The Social Structure of the Hill Juang*. Unpublished Ph.D. Dissertation, University of New Mexico, Ann Arbour UMI.

Morgan, Lewis Henry, 1970. *Systems of Consanguinity and Affinity of the Human Family*. Smithsonian Contributions to Knowledge, No. 218, Washington D.C. Smithsonian Institution.

Needham, Rodney. 1967. "Terminology and Alliance II-Mapuche; Conclusions," *Sociologus*, 17(1): 39-54.

—. 1973. Prescription. *Oceania* 43: 166-181.

—. 1974. *Remarks and Inventions. Skeptical Essays about Kinship*. London: Tavistock.

Parkin, Robert, 1992. *The Munda of Central India: An Account of their Social Organization*. New Delhi. Oxford University Press.

Pfeffer, Georg. 1982: *Status and Affinity in Middle India*. Wiesbaden. Steiner.

—. 1983. Generation and Marriage in Middle India: The Evolutionary Potential of "Restricted Exchange", *Contributions to Indian Sociology*, (N.S.) 17(1): 87-122.

—. 1992. "Der intro-agnatische 'Seelentausch' der Gadaba beim groben Lineageritual," (pp. 59-92) in M. Laubscher (ed.), *Beitrage zur Ethnologie Mittel-und Südindiens*. Munich. Anacon.

Radcliffe-Brown, A.R. 1953. Correspondence. *Man* article. 169.

Rosaldo, Michelle Z. 1980. *Knowledge and Passion. Ilongoi Notions of Self and Social Life*. Cambridge: Cambridge University Press.

Spier, Leslie. 1925. *The Distribution of Kinship Systems in North America*. Seattle: University of Washington Publications in Anthropology, Vol. 1.

Trautmann, Thomas R. 1981. *Dravidian Kinship.* Cambridge; Cambridge University Press.

Tripathi, B. 1971. *A Portrait of Population, Orissa.* Census of India 1971, Cuttack: Govt. Printing.

Vatuk, Sylvia. 1969. "A Structural Analysis of the Hindi Kinship Terminology," *Contributions to Indian Sociology* (N.S.) 3: 95-115.

Vidyarthi, L.P. 1963. *The Maler: A Study in Nature-Man-Spirit Complex of a Hill Tribe in Bihar.* Calcutta: Bookland.

Vitebsky, Piers. 1993. *Dialogues with the Dead. The discussion of mortality among the Sora of eastern India.* Cambridge: Cambridge University Press.

TWO

IMPACT OF DRAVIDIAN MARRIAGE PRACTICES ON A MUNDARI SPEAKING SAORA KINSHIP TERMINOLOGY

M. SURYANARAYANA

Kinship terminology in any culture is a product of language that the people speak. Lowie (1932) says that "language represents reality and in so far it is related to the social phenomena it is likely to mirror them." In the context of the above statement the kinship terminology of the Saoras, a Mundari speaking Scheduled Tribe of Andhra Pradesh, is examined in this paper.

Saoras are one of the important Scheduled Tribes of India inhabiting the Srikakulam and Vijayanagaram districts of Andhra Pradesh, Koraput and Ganjam districts of Orissa. The population of Saoras in Andhra Pradesh is 81.227. The present paper primarily aims to focus on the impact of Dravidian preferential marriage practices on the Saoras and the consequent changes that have resulted in the kinship terminology of the Saoras.

Field work was carried out on the Saoras of Parvathipuram, Palakonda and Seethampeta taluks of Vijayanagaram and Srikakulam districts between 1965-67 and again a re-visit was made in 1976 to observe the changes that have taken place. Three different Saora villages from three different areas (Seethampeta, Badharagiri and Mandasa Blocks) from the taluks mentioned above were selected for intensive study. The areas differ from one another in the extent of their contacts with the non-tribal caste Hindu Dravidian population resulting in significant changes in their kinship terminology (Suryanarayana, 1977).

Guinea-Dakota Continuum in Saora Society

Murdock (1949) has suggested logical sequences of changes through several successive types of social structure. He has evolved eleven types of social organization mainly basing on descent, residence and cousin terminology. He has further shown how logically a change in any one of the above factors, i.e. the type of descent, residence and cousin terminology affect the social organization. The social organization of the Saoras is analyzed following the logical sequences of changes proposed by Murdock.

The kinship terminology of the Saoras of Seethampeta-Bhadaragiri area conforms to the Mundari pattern, while the Saoras of Mandasa who are subjected to more contacts with Dravidian groups have different kinship terms. Between the Saoras of Seethampeta and Bhadaragiri, the Saoras of Bhadaragiri are more in contact with Dravidian groups than the Saoras of Seethampeta who are comparatively isolated. Those Saoras that are relatively in more contact with the Dravidian groups, i.e. the Saoras of Bhadaragiri and Mandasa, have accepted cross-cousin marriage and sister's daughter marriage while the Saoras of Seethampeta have not fully accepted the cross-cousin marriage of the Dravidian groups. Thus the adoption of cross-cousin marriage and sister's daughter marriage has its consequent impact of the kinship terminology of the Saoras.

Murdock (1949) while discussing the multiple historical influences in determining the kinship terminology says "the inductions from comparative studies become appreciably more dependable than influences from historical analysis". As mentioned earlier, the Saoras of the three areas under study are subjected to changes but we find relative differences between them. Hence, an attempt has been made to compare the kinship terminology of the Saoras in these three areas and a logical analysis is presented.

The earlier studies about the Saoras, Ramamurthy (1931), Sitapati (1938-43) did not throw much light on their social structure. Ramamurthy gave a list of relationship terms in his book *A Manual of the Saora Language* which are similar to those kinship terms found in Seethampeta area. The relationship terms mentioned by Ramamurthy are of Hawaiian type (cousin terms). Sitapati (1938-43) mentioned about the rules regulating marriage wherein he states that marriage with the following categories of relatives is forbidden among the Saoras:

(1) with mother's sister
(2) with father's sister
(3) with brother's daughter
(4) with sister's daughter
(5) with first cross-cousin

According to the rules reported by Sitapati, a person should not marry his cross-cousin as well as his sister's daughter. The same is reflected in the kinship terminology of the Saoras of Seethampeta area. Fig. 2.1 represents the kinship terminology of the Saoras of the past, which incidentally becomes

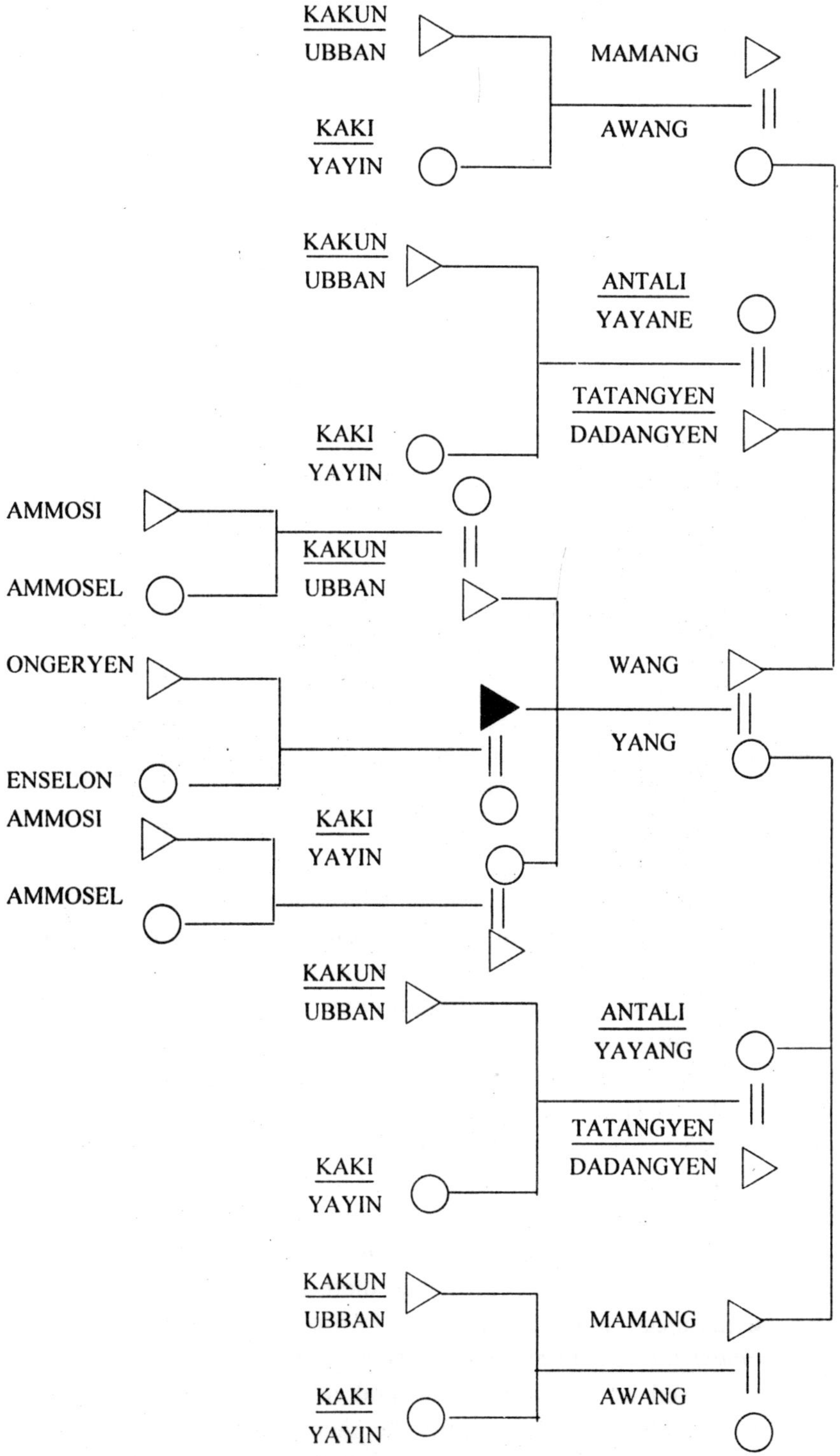

FIG. 2.1: Cousin, Aunt and Niece Terms in Seetampeta Area

true of the Saoras of Seethampeta area. To a certain extent, it also represents about Saoras (Bhadragiri) who have adopted cross-cousin marriage very recently but not yet changed their kinship terminology. In this typical terminology we find all cross and parallel cousins being designated by the name terms as those used for one's own siblings (i.e. *kakun/ubban* for males; *kakin/yayin* for females). The brother's daughter and sister's daughter are called by the same term *ammosel,* while brother's son and sister's son are called by the same term *ammosi.* By this we can infer safely that Saoras of the past did not practice cross-cousin and sister's daughter marriages, and any breach of the rule must have been opposed vehemently by the society. This interpretation is not only consistent with terminology and historical records (Sitapati, 1938-43) but also provides a clue for understanding how subsequent terminological changes took place.

The statistical data showed a constant increase in cross-cousin and sister's daughter marriages from Seethampeta to Bhadragiri and thence to Mandasa area. For want of spcae, the statistical data are not furnished here.

The salient features of the Saoras of Seethampeta area show Hawaiian type of cousin terminology, bifurcate collateral type of aunt terms, linear type of niece terms, patrilineal descent, presence of lineage units, patrilocal and neolocal residence, monogamous and polygamous marriages, clans and demes absent, and bilateral extension of incest taboos. The above characteristics almost fit into the Guinea type of social organization of Murdock (1949) which is characterized by patrilineal descent, patrilocal residence, Hawaiin type or Eskimo type of cousin terminology and exogamous patrilineal kin-groups.

As a result of the adoption of the cross-cousin and also sister's daughter marriages from the Dravidian speaking caste Hindus, it is logical to infer that the kinship terminology also changed accordingly.

Fig. 2.2 shows the kinship terminology of the Saoras of Bhadragiri area who are in transition, i.e. those who accepted cross-cousin marriage recently but did not influence the kinship terminology fully. The major change we find is in the cousin terminology. With the adoption of cross-cousin marriage, a person calls his female cross-cousin as *arrelboi* (if she is younger than ego) and *bonnin* (if she is older than ego), but for the male cross-cousins a single term *boung* is applied whether he is older or younger than ego.

It is interesting to observe that in Bhadragiri area the cousin terms mentioned earlier are used only when there is a marriageable cross-cousin. But, for the niece terms they continue to use the traditional terms *(ammosel* and *ammosi* for female and male respectively). This transitional stage can also be viewed as a result of "cultural lag". As Murdock (1949) writes "kinship terms frequently exemplify the phenomenon of cultural lag." Lowie (1932) also says "one . . . factor that must always be considered in the time

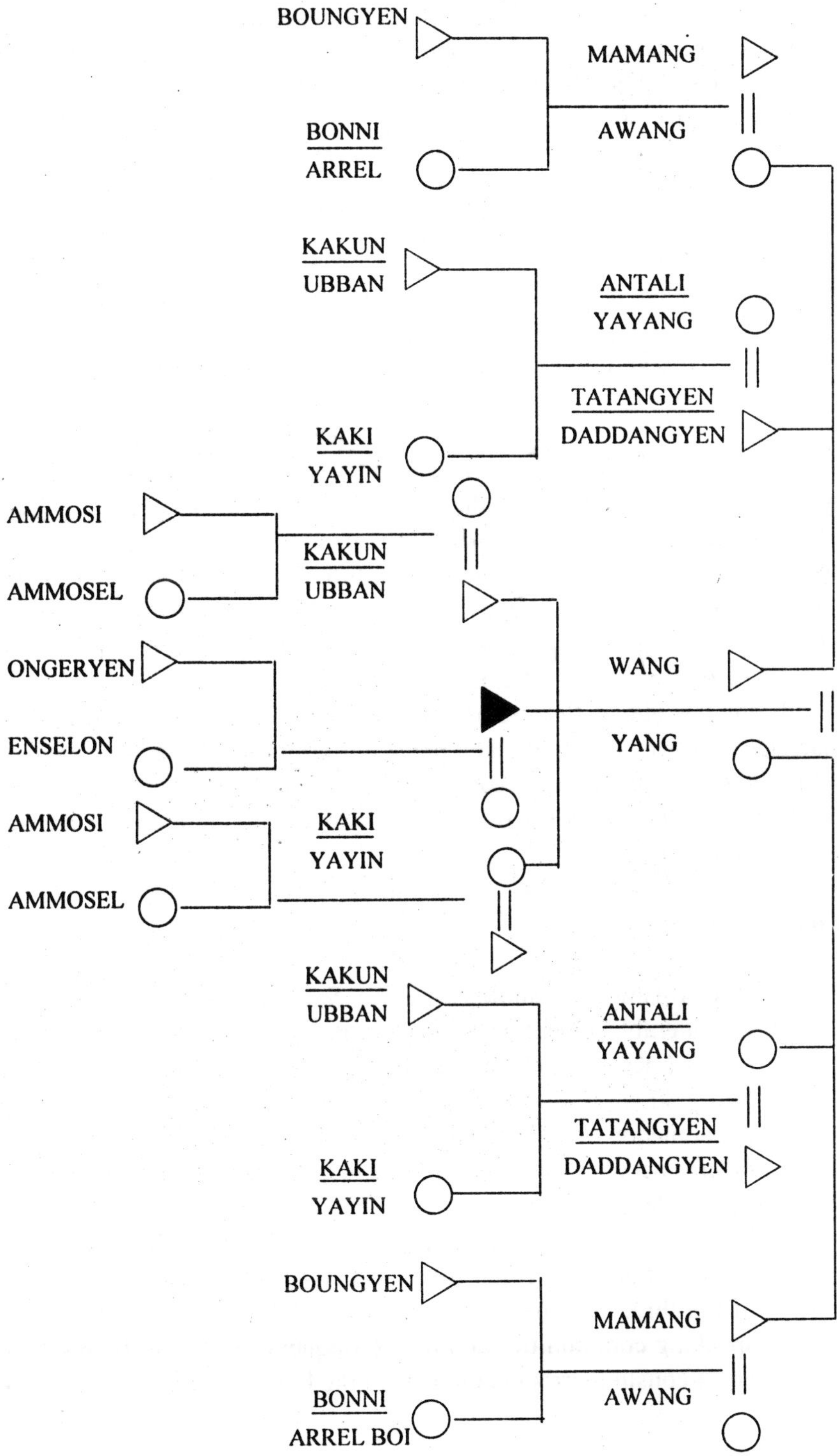

FIG. 2.2: Cousin, Aunt and Niece Terms in Bhadragiri Area

element. A recently acquired custom may not yet have developed appropriate nomenclature, while . . . the nomenclature may survive after the custom has been obsolete". The above mentioned stage represents the transitional stage of development showing the tendency towards the Dakota type of social organization as described by Murdock (1949).

We find in Fig. 2.3 some new kinship terms in place of the old terms. *Paruyiyen* and *madangoryan* are the terms used for the male cross-cousins, *kinarboi* and *madenselon* for female cross-cousins with respect to age. Brother's children and sister's children are also differentiated as follows:

Brother's son: putraoon; Brother's daughter: Jayariyan
Sister's son: Badangiyen; Sister's daughter: Badingiyan.

With the aforementioned changes in the kinship terminology, the Guinea type of social organization of the Saoras of this area has gradually changed towards the Dakota type of social organization, characterized by Iroquois cousin terminology, bifurcate merging or bifurcate collateral type of aunt and niece terms. The major changes in the kinship terminology of the Saoras of Mandasa is from Hwaiian cousin terminology to Iroguois type and from lineal type of niece terms of collateral type.

From the above discussion, we can observe that the changes in the marriage practices have not taken place uniformly in all the three areas. This differential acceptance of cross-cousin and sister's daughter marriage has resulted in the development of Guinea-Dakota continuum among the Saoras of Andhra Pradesh.

Conclusions

1. The kinship terminology of the Saoras shows consistency to a considerable extent with its cultural practices (marriage practices, rules of descent and the associated kinship behaviour).
2. Saora kinship terminology of the transitional type exhibits the phenomenon of "cultural lag" as we find the recently acquired custom of cross-cousin marriage did not help in developing the appropriate nomenclature.
3. The Guinea-Dakota continuum framework helps in explaining the changes that have taken place in kinship terminology of the Saoras of the three regions which are differently exposed to the Dravidian speaking communities and the consequent impact of the preferential cross-cousin marriage practices of the latter over that of the former.

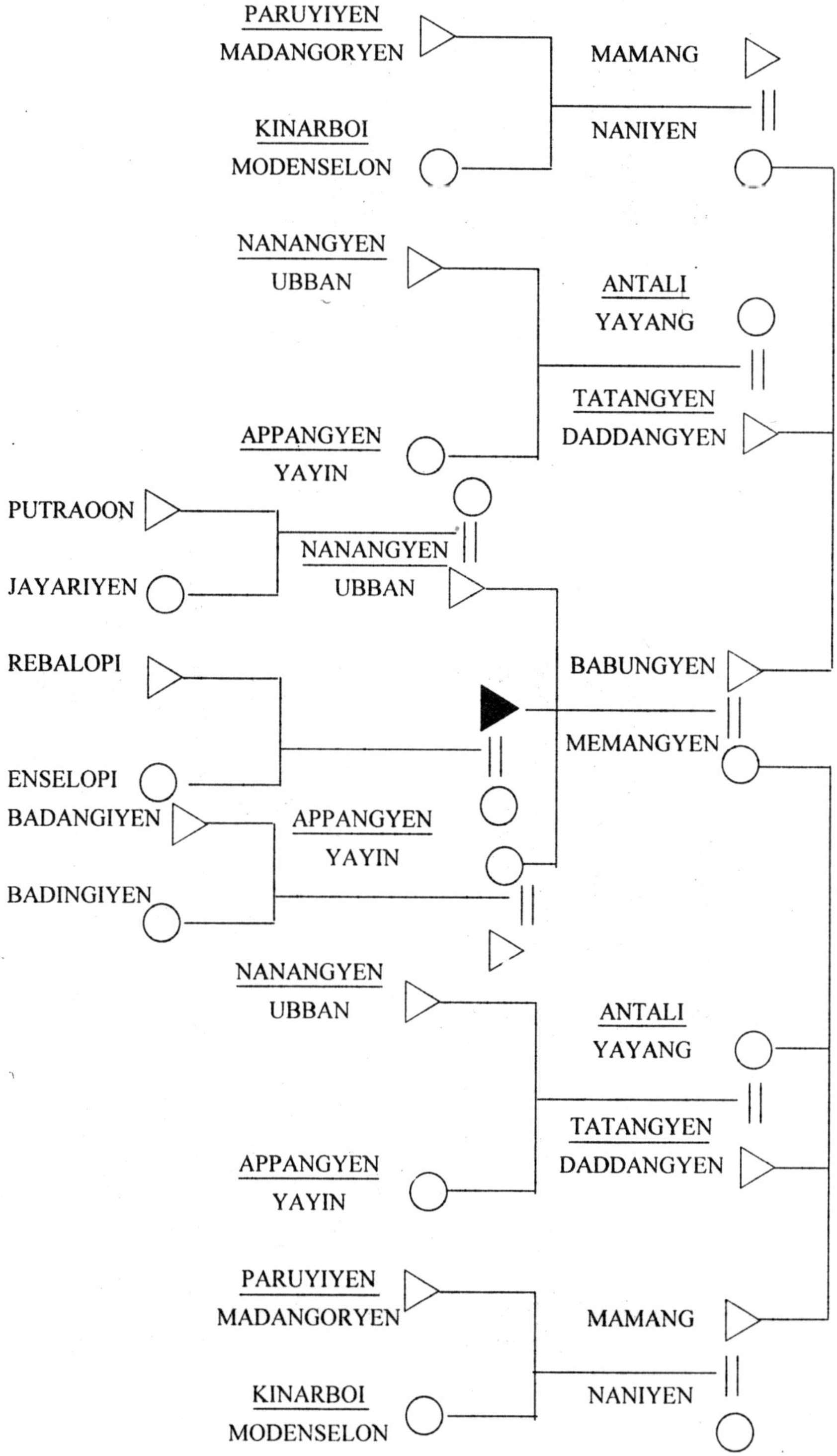

FIG. 2.3: Cousin, Aunt and Niece Terms in Mandasa Area

REFERENCES

Lowie, R.H. 1932. "Kinship", *Encyclopaedia of Social Sciences,* Vol. VII.

Murdock, G.P. 1949. *Social Structure,* New York: Macmillan Company.

Ramamurthy, G.V. 1931. *A Manual of the Saora Language.*

Sitapati, G.V. 1938-43. "Saoras and their Country", *Journal of the Andhra Historical Research Society.*

Suryanarayana, M. 1977. Marriage, Family and Kinship of the Saoras of Andhra Pradesh, Unpublished Ph.D. thesis, Andhra University, Waltair.

THREE

ANTHROPOLOGICAL STUDIES ON FAMILY, HOUSEHOLD AND DOMESTIC GROUP AMONG THE KORWA
Then and Now

A.R.N. SRIVASTAVA

The Theoretical and Methodological Background

The family, household, domestic group, its structure, and its relationship to other aspects of society have been of central interest to social anthropology since the beginning. During the past four decades students of family, for the most part, centered their discussions around three topics:

(i) Analytical distinction between family, household and domestic unit
(ii) Typological approach to family
(iii) Processual approach to family

I would first briefly dwell on the first two dimensions and heavily concentrate on the third dimension relating it to the theme of social anthropology in general terms.

Family and household are frequently treated as synonymous, the terms being used interchangeable. Many definitions of "family" incorporate common residence as an integral part. Pioneer field anthropologists (e.g. Malinowski, Lowie, Murdock, and others) did not make analytical distinction between these terms. They showed the existence of conjugal type family among the societies of all levels. Malinowski, for example, observed and concluded "the individual conjugal family was a unit playing an important part in the social life of the natives (Australian) and well defined by a number of moral, customary and legal norms; it is further determined by the sexual division of labour, the aboriginal mode of living, and especially by the intimate relation between the parents and children" (1913: 303-4).

Field anthropologists of sixties and onward have made distinction between family and household, and have suggested the term "domestic unit" central to the analysis of social structure and social organization of societies of all levels.

Murdock (1949) states that the nuclear family consists of a married man and woman with their offsprings. The nuclear family is a universal human social grouping. Either as the sole prevailing form of the family or as the basic unit from which more complex familial forms are compounded, it exists as a distinct and strongly functional group in every human society. Whatever larger familial forms may exist... the nuclear family is always recognizable and always has its distinctive and vital functions, sexual, economic, reproductive and educational.

Murdock and his followers seem to be right in seeing the nuclear family as a convenient social instrument for handling a series of human problems. Therefore Murdock's comments on the functional efficacy of the nuclear family cannot be denied or contradicted by the existence of a few societies in which nuclear family is absent.

The problem is of another dimension. This is of generalization on comparative ground. Since the aim of social anthropology is to examine and understand the human societies cross-culturally, our purpose should be to develop a set of concepts to describe and compare all human societies. Thinking in this way Murdock's notion on elementary or nuclear family is inadequate or even misleading (for details see Buchler and Selby, 1968).

Diverse Forms of Family

Text-books and articles devoted to the institution of family and marriage are full of statements concerning various types of families. Some consider the number of persons including the number of mates as the basis of classification; other stress the degrees of genealogical relations, the relative importance of kinship versus conjugal ties; and still others consider the activities of members for classification. The issue of typology of family has become somewhat confused owing to different criteria being used. Below are noted the popular views on the classification of family found in standard text-books.

I. Conjugal or nuclear family
II. Consanguineal family
III. Composite conjugal (a) polyandrous, (b) polygynous
IV. Composite unilineal or extended family
 (a) patrineal, (b) matrilineal, (c) joint family (See Fig. 3.1)

I & II

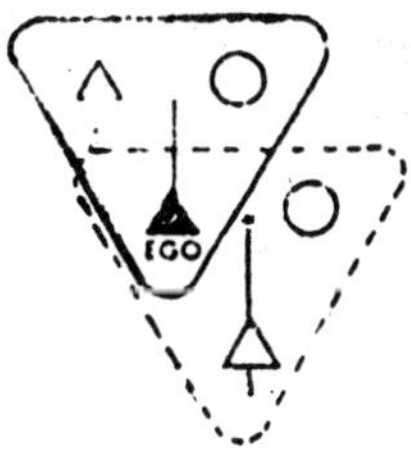

—Family of orientation

—Family of procration

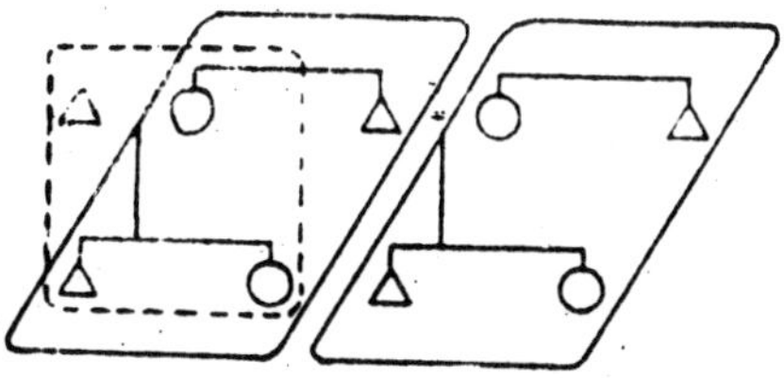

—Conjugal family

—Consanguineal family

III Composite Conjugal

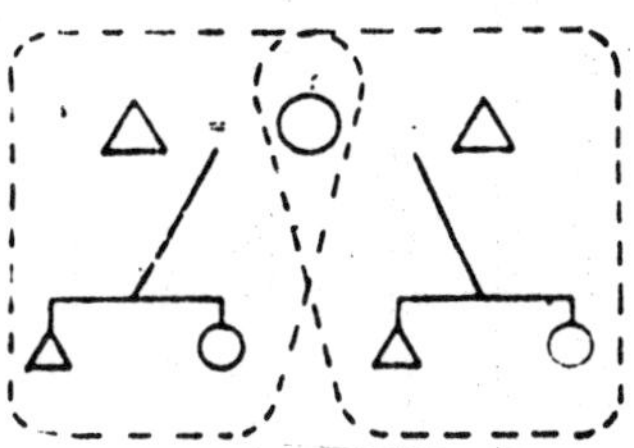

(a) A polyandrous composite family

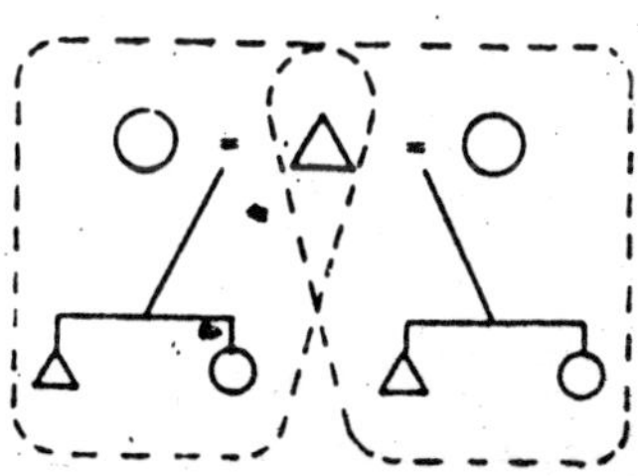

(b) A polygynous composite family

Dotted lines indicate conjugal family segments

IV. Composite unilineal or extended family

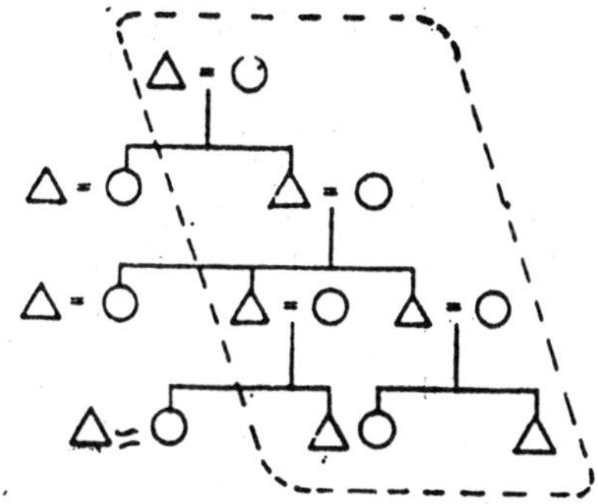

(a) A patrilineal extended family

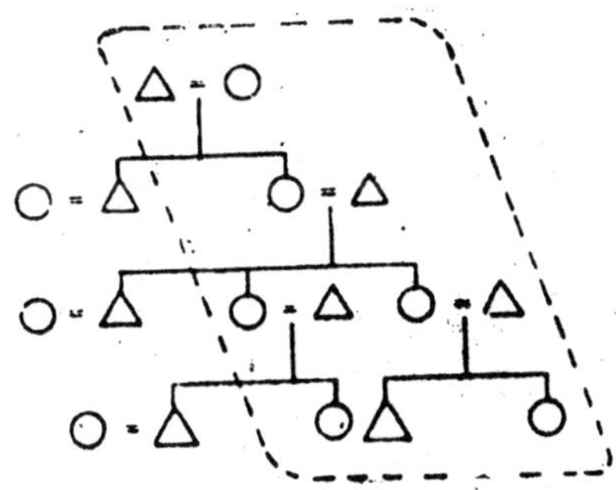

(b) A matrilineal extended family

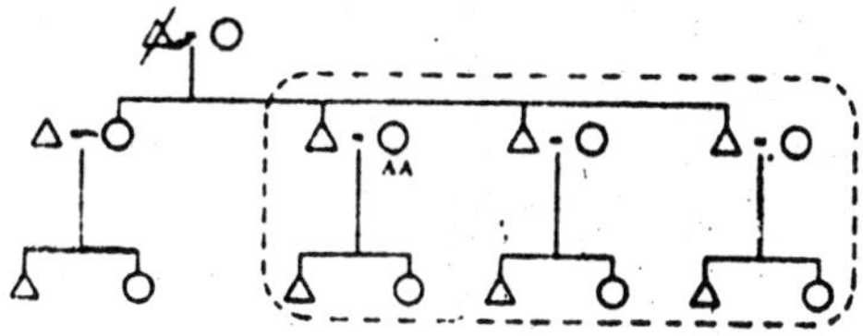

(c) Joint family

Developmental/Processual Approach

The third dimension of the study of family is its dynamic nature which is studied by bringing the "time factor" into family and clustered groups. This approach is called the "development cycles" in family. It refers to a series of stages passed through by any family; it is analogous to the individual life cycle. The three phases most often cited are expansion (from marriage of parents to completion of their families of procreation), dispersion (or fission, beginning with the first marriage of all children), and replacement (marked by the death of parents and replacement in the social structure by families of offspring). The timing, rights, and roles of the members at various stages differ from culture to culture. As the size and composition of the domestic group changes, so do the rights, duties and expectations of its members in relation to one another (Fortes, 1958).

Some Studies on the Development Cycles

Although our immediate purpose is not to present review of past works on the topic under consideration we may refer to the studies of Goody (1958), Freeman (1958), Gulliver (1953, 1964), Levine (1964), Harris (1964), Kopytoff (1964), Smith (1956), Hammel (1961), Otterbein (1970), Symes (1972), Coale (1965), Martin (1973, 1994), Shah (1974), and others.

Above studies present various methods to study developmental cycles in domestic groups (family/household). Some of them have recognized the relevant variables such as demography and economy that control the cyclings of (phases/paths) of domestic groups. Thus the growing concern with developmental cycles represents the beginning of a recognition that every society has characteristic demographic properties and processes; and that these manifest in the functioning of domestic group. In other words, the changing economic and domestic inter-relationship among the members of a group are a function of a number of variables. These include the number of people in the group, their sexes, age intervals separating them, and the distribution of economic resources among the people. It is, therefore, pertinent to enquire into the specific ways in which these variables control the forms and phases in the developmental cycles of the domestic group, an area largely ignored by above investigators.

With this aim I carried out a field study on a small semi-agricultural tribe of south Bihar over a period of two years (Korwa and Palamu) and have demonstrated as to how Korwa domestic group, their patterning and development are reflected through the distribution of surviving sons, their relative ages, their ages relative to their fathers and distribution of economic resources such as land, forest, etc (see Srivastava, 1969, 1979, 1994). The processual (formal) model of domestic group emphasizes that a consideration of demographic and economic variables is absolutely essential if we are to go beyond description of social structure.

The Nature of Korwa Domestic Group

A domestic group, as used in the present study, refers to a group of people related by marriage, filiation and siblingship, who form a common reproductive, consumption, production and resource holding unit. The people forming such a unit live in the same house/adjacent buildings, but it is not always the case that same people will cooperate in all of these ways. Thus, with reference to the Korwa society, some members form a single consumption, production and resource holding group, but not a single reproductive unit. In still other cases, members form a common resource holding group, but go their separate ways with respect to everything else. Finally, the types of activities which unite the members of a domestic group often change through time. The crucial points are: why do some domestic groups have one production unit but two or more reproductive and consumption units? Or, more fundamentally, what controls the developmental cycles of domestic group?

Below I intend to offer answers to the above problems: why, how and when cyclings of domestic group?

The Field Investigation

The Korwa, the people of interest, who number a little over twenty-five thousand, are chiefly found in the southern part of the state of Bihar (Palamau district), India. After an extensive reconnaissance of the northern parts of Palamau, three Korwa villages of the Chainpur block were chosen as a site for an intensive study. Altogether a total of eleven months were spent in the field.

Techniques employed for the collection of data included participant-observation and interviews. A census, including genealogies, was of prime importance. Interviews were conducted in Sadani (the *lingua franca* of tribal Chotanagpur-south Bihar), Korwa and Hindi languages.

Originally, the members of this tribe were said to be dependent on swidden cultivation. Now one seldom finds them engaged in this form of cultivation, for swidden has been replaced by more intensive plough agriculture. Today the Korwa of the northern part of Palamau are settled cultivators. Like many tribal groups of the area, the Korwa live in small villages which differ in layout, size, and composition. The total population of the Korwa of the three villages investigated was 428 (221 males, 207 females).

The Developmental Cycle in Domestic Groups

A Korwa man along with his wife and sexually immature children occupy a building in which they sleep and in which meals are cooked. This is the place where the man and his wife spend most of their day-to-day life. This grouping is what the Korwa call a *ghar* which I have translated as a reproductive group. A Korwa dwelling is called a *dera* and is identified by a few tangible features—walls, thatched roof, poles, and hedges. Inside the dwelling is a hearth which is used both to cook food and to warm the dwellers. The Korwa call this a *chulha.* The major activities around the hearth involve cleaning, grooming, and caring for the young, the preparation and consumption of food, entertainment, and adult sexual activities.

The man is the head of the dwelling unit in his roles as husband and father. He is the controller of the resources (land, tools, etc.) that provide the economic bases for the group. As head of the dwelling unit, he represents and acts on behalf of his dependents in relations with other domestic groups and their heads. At this stage of the development, the social group, led by the husband and wife. is a reproductive, consumption, production and resource-owning group. By virtue of these four criteria, a group is a *kothari*—domestic group.

With the passage of time, such a domestic group acquires more members. This happens as the head's children grown older and progress into adulthood and parenthood. When a son is 18 years old, he is expected to find a mate. The prevalent forms of obtaining a mate are "bride price" and "suitor service." The former is a practice of paying for the bride both in cash and in kind to the father or brother (if the father is dead) of the bride. My analysis of 100 marriages shows both bride price and bride service occurring with nearly equal frequency.

Whether the son continues to stay with his natal group or with the wife's natal group, within a few years he sets up his own consumption unit *(chulha)* within the main *kothari.* This involves building a new house or room and cooking at a separate hearth. The average age of the son at this time is 22 years.

At this point the junior couple (son/son-in-law and his spouse) forms a separate reproductive and consumption unit, but remains part of the senior couple's production-resource holding unit; they are still members of the senior couple's *kothari* (domestic groups).

At this stage of development a *kothari* may include one or more reproductive and consumption units, but it remains as the single production resource owning group. The married coresident son (son-in-law) as an independent consumption unit continues working with the senior man as a common production-resource owning group; the occasion arises when this consumption unit may become an independent production unit in the sense that the junior couple's agricultural activities are independent of the senior man's activities. In other words, the senior man no longer controls the economic decisions of the junior couple which now has formed its own production unit and which shares the *kothari* lands with the senior man.

The situation continues until the senior man dies or retires from the *kothari* resource management. The average age of the son when this occurs is 30 years. Thus the developmental cycle in the *kothari* with one son is completed when the coresident married son (or son-in-law) becomes *kothari* head.

The course of the developmental sequence becomes more complex with two coresident sons in a *kothari*. When the second son marries and lives with the wife under the sponsorship of his father, a third reproductive unit is added to the *kothari*. (The first is that of the *kothari* head, the second is that of the first son, the third is that of the newly married younger son.) For consumption and production purposes, the younger son depends on the sponsoring group (father). After a few years the younger son adds his own *chulha* to the *kothari;* the *kothari* has now three consumption units. For the production purposes, the younger son is still with his father. When he establishes his own production unit, like his elder brother, he no longer remains under the economic control of his father. As long as the senior man is active and vigorous, he maintains control over the resources of the *kothari*. Independent production units may continue, but soon after the death of the senior man the production units of the sons become two separate groups, each managing its own resources; each is now a *kothari*.

My analysis of 59 *kothari* revealed 11 ways in which three units of *kothari* are organized. Of the 59 *kothari*, 46 have two or more reproductive units; 36 of the 46 with two or more reproductive units also have two or more consumption units. Of the 36 *kothari* containing two or more consumption units, 15 have two production units.

The Demographic Base of the Korwa Domestic Groups

Obviously, demographic variables are among those things which control how *kotharis* are organized. The most important demographic variables are the distribution of sons among the fathers (heads of domestic groups), the ages of fathers and sons, age intervals between the fathers and sons, and age intervals between the sons. Important in shaping these variables are age at marriage and the males' fertility and survivorship schedules.

Using a method developed by Coale (1965) I calculated the fertility schedule for the male population from the data on birth of male offsprings and ages of their fathers. According to this, the mean number of ever born sons for age groups, 20-24, 25-29, 30-34, 35-39, 40-44 and 45-49 years are 0.3, 2.2, 3.0, 4.1, 3.9 and 4.1 respectively. For the problem at hand we are mainly interested in knowing the fertility pattern of the males of completed fertility, that is, males of 50 years old and older. Because Brass' method does not provide corrected figures for age groups beyond 50 years, I took the mean number of the surviving sons of males of 50 years and up and related this empirical distribution to those of a standardized distribution. Using the Chi-square Goodness-of-fit test the empirical distribution very closely approximates a Poisson distribution (P>0.90, df. 5) for the mean of 4.1. I then took the individual figures of 4.1 to get the expected distribution of ever born sons of males of completed fertility. The individual terms in the Poisson distribution of the mean value for 4.1 are .017 (0), .068(1), .140(2), .190(3), .195(4), .160(5), .109(6), .064(7), .033(8), and .015(9).

To determine the probabilities of having one or more sons who survive to various ages, we need to know the survivorship schedules. For this I followed Weiss' method which consists of tabulation of the male population in terms of age groups and division of the number of males of a given age group by its preceding age group (Weiss, 1973).

Thus from the fertility and survivorship schedules we determine the probable number of male offsprings who survive to ages 18, 22 and 30 years. We are interested in these age groups for the reason noted earlier. This calculation involves the following steps.

First, we found out the interpolated individual value of survivorship *(p)* from my survivorship Table for age 18, 22 and 30 years. These ages were obtained by subtracting each survivorship value from one (q=1-p). Second, following binomial theorem* we expanded each of the interpolated survivorship values upto five (beyond five the outcome was zero). Third, the expansion for each value was multiplied by the respective probability of occurrence which was found from the Poisson distribution of a mean value for 4.11. Finally, all values for zero, one, two upto five sons were summed respectively. Probabilities thus obtained are presented in Table 3.1.

It lists the probabilities of reproductive success for a male of completed fertility in terms of the number of surviving sons. The first value noted in column 4 of Table 3.1 indicates that 22.9 per cent of males should have no son surviving to age 18 but dying before the age 22. Taking another value and phrasing it in a different way, the probability is .028 that a male will have two sons who live to age 18, but only one of whom will survive to age 22 and then to age 30 as well.

What Table 3.1 tells us is the potential paths of development for Korwa

* The formula is $P_n\ (p + q)^n$ where n is the number of sons, P_n is the probability of sons being born, p is the probability of survivorships and q is the probability of death.

TABLE 3.1 : Probable Number of Male Offsprings Surviving to Ages 18, 22 and 30 Years of Males of Completed Fertility

Number of Male Offsprings to Ages			Probabilities (P)
18	22	30	
0	0	0	.229
1	0	0	.025
1	1	0	.048
1	1	1	.269
2	0	0	.001
2	1	0	.004
2	1	1	.028
2	2	0	.009
2	2	1	.051
2	2	2	.156
3	2	1	.006
3	2	2	.019
3	3	1	.006
3	3	2	.035
3	3	3	.171
4	4	3	.011
4	4	4	.017
5	5	3	.001
5	5	4	.003
5	5	5	.004

domestic groups. If we look at the population over time, or in retrospect, approximately 35 per cent of the adult males will have a son who survives long enough to marry, establish a consumption unit, becomes economically independent (as a head of a production unit) and perhaps succeeds his father as head of the domestic group. Approximately 21 per cent of the men will have two sons who survive this long and 8 per cent will have three. But, for economic reasons, some of these surviving sons leave their natal groups and join their wives' natal groups when the latter have no surviving sons. Thus, to estimate the probable lines of development for the Korwa domestic groups, we must consider Korwa economy.

The Economic Bases of the Korwa Domestic Groups

A detailed study of resources available to the Korwa and their population and work force reveals that they spend approximately 52 per cent of their total available time (40,474 man-days) on food producing tasks (growing paddy by both broadcast and transplanting methods in their fields) and income seeking tasks (wage labour). Of the 20,877 mandays actually spent, about 56 per cent are directly engaged in agriculture and 44 per cent on other tasks.

Examination of food production and food requirements of individual groups shows that 13 domestic groups produced 70.99 per cent of their food requirements. The production of 9 groups falls in the range of 50 to 69 per cent, 7 in 30 to 49 per cent, and production of 6 groups is under 30 per cent. The percentages of food requirements produced is a function of the amount and quality of lands available to a group and the size of the group. The domestic groups which produce more than their requirements have relatively better balanced land-man ratios than those which do not meet their requirements. What induces sons to stay with their fathers is the lands and their productivity, and not the wage labour (a Korwa may work as a wage labourer whether he is in his natal village or he is in his wife's village). In other words, the critical factor is land. Table 3.2 illustrates the connection between the probability of a son remaining at home and the productive capacity of the lands.

Note that (overall) as the percentage of food requirement increases, so does the percentage of sons who remain in residence. The critical point seems to be at 50 per cent of food requirements produced. Among those

TABLE 3.2 : Distribution of Number of Kothari by their respective Percentages of Subsistence Requirements produced and the Number of Surviving Sons (18 Years Old and Older)

Percentage of Requirements Produced	# Kothari	# Sons 18 Yrs Old & Older					# Sons 18 Yrs Old & Older at Natal Kothari		% Sons Present at Natal Kothari	% Sons not living at Natal Kothari
		0	1	2	3	4	1	2		
Under 20	4	1	1	2	-	-	2	-	.40	.60
20-39	2	-	-	2	-	-	1	-	.25	.75
40-49	7	2	3	-	2	-	3	1	.55	.45
50-69	9	6	-	2	1	-	1	2	.71	.29
70-99	13	6	2	1	3	1	2	5	.70	.30
100-175	8	4	-	4	-	-	2	2	.75	.25
Total	43	19	6	11	6	1	11	10	.62	.38

groups which obtain 50 per cent or more of their subsistence from agriculture, about 28 per cent of the sons leave. Among those which get less than 50 per cent of their requirements from agriculture, the rate of loss is at least double.

Interaction between Demography and Economy

Earlier I sought to show that the distribution of fertility among males and rates of male survivorship could be combined so as to allow calculation of the probable distribution of sons surviving to 18, 22 and 30 years of age. For instance, I indicated that we should expect that over a period of time only 8.3 per cent of males could hope to raise three sons to 30 years of age, only 21 per cent would raise even two, and 35 per cent would raise just one (calculated from Table 3.1). The materials in Table 3.2 suggest that, due to the distribution of and general level of agricultural resources, some of these men, including men with just one son, will lose sons to wealthier *kothari.* In the census population, one man in ten with only one son had that son leave. Of the men who raised two sons, three in ten lost one due to economic reasons. Half of the men who raised three sons lost one of them, and the other half lost two.

If these rates can be extrapolated and be applied to the theoretical distribution of sons living to 30 years of age, we would expect the following over the long run:

(1) .422 of the males will develop their domestic groups and bequeath their lands to one son;
(2) .185 of the males will develop their domestic groups through two sons;
(3) .354 of the males will not be able to raise a son but .86 of them will be able to raise a daughter and attract a son-in-law. Hence, .304 of the males will form their domestic groups and bequeath their lands to a son-in-law;
(4) .090 of all the males will be unable to raise or hold a son, hence their domestic groups will die with them.

Concluding Remarks

In this study my concern has been to specify precisely the various forms of domestic groups and their relative frequencies over time and to show these to be the outcome of a few fundamental demographic and economic variables. I have also sought to show something of how these domestic groups cycle and how their patterning and development over time reflect the distribution of surviving sons, their relative ages, their ages relative to their fathers, and the distribution of lands. I recognize that I have only begun to explore the relations between these variables and the cycling of domestic groups. In future I would like to pursue in greater depth the mathematical computations which will allow me to estimate the number of *kothari* and their probable sizes and composition for any given moment in time (Martin, 1973, 1994). At this point I am satisfied with specifying the relative frequencies of types of *kothari* over time and emphasized the point that a consideration of demographic and economic variables is absolutely essential if we are to go beyond structural descriptions of domestic group (see also Srivastava, 1994).

REFERENCES

Buchler, I.R., and H.A. Selby. 1968. *Kinship and Social Organization: An Introduction to Method and Theory*. New York. The Macmillan Company.

Coale, Ansley J. 1965. "Estimates of Average Size of Household", (pp. 64-68) in M.J. Levy *et al.* (eds.) *Aspects of the Analysis of the Family Structure*. New Jersey: Prentice Hall, Inc.

Davenport, William. 1961. "The Family System of Jamaica", *Social and Economic Studies*, 10: 420-454.

Fortes, Meyer. 1949a. *The Web of Kinship among the Tallensi* (the Second Part of an Analysis of the Social Structure of a Tranns-Volta Tribe). London: Oxford University Press.

—. 1949b. "Time and Social Structure; an Ashanti Case Study," in M. Fortes (ed.) *Social Structure Studies Presented to A.R. Radcliffe-Brown*. New York: Russell and Russell.

—. 1958. "Introduction" (pp. 1-14) in Jack Goody (ed.) *The Developmental Cycle in Domestic Groups*. Cambridge: The Cambridge University Press.

Freeman, J.D. 1958. "The Family System of the Iban of Borneo", in Jack Goody (ed.), *The Developmental Cycle in Domestic Groups*. Cambridge: The Cambridge University Press.

Goodenough, Ward H. 1970. *Description and Comparison in Cultural Anthropology*. Chicago: Aldine Publishing Company.

Goody, Jack (ed.). 1958a. *The Developmental Cycle in Domestic Groups*. Cambridge: The Cambridge University Press.

Gulliver, P.H. 1955. *The Family Herds a Study of Two Pastoral Tribes in Central Africa, the Jie and Turkana*. London: Routledge and Kegan Paul.

—. 1964. "The Arusha Family", (pp. 197-229) in Robert F. Gray and P.H. Gulliver (eds.). *Family Estate in Africa Studies in the Role of Property in Family Structure and Lineage Continuity*. London: Routledge and Kegan Paul.

Hammel, E.A. 1961. "The Family Cycle in Coastal Peruvian Slum and Village", *American Anthropologist*, 63: 989-1005.

Harris, Alfred, and Grace Harris. 1964. "Property and the Cycle of Domestic Groups in Taita," (pp. 117-155) in Robert F. Gray and P.H. Gulliver (eds.), *Family Estate in Africa Studies in the Role of Property in Family Structure and Lineage Continuity*. London: Routledge and Kegan Paul.

—. Kopytoff, Igor. 1964. The Family and Lineage Among the Suku of the Congo", (pp. 83-116) in Robert F. Gray and P.H. Gulliver (eds.), *Family Estate in Africa Studies in the Role of Property in Family Structure and Lineage Continuity*. London: Routledge and Kegan Paul.

Levine, Robert A. 1964. "The Gussi Family", (pp. 63-82) in Robert F. Gray and P.H. Gulliver (eds.), *The Family Estate in Africa*. London: Routledge and Kegan Paul.

Malinowski, B. 1913 (1963). *The Family among the Australian Aborigines: A Sociological*

Study. New York.

Martin, John F. 1973. "On the Estimation of the Sizes of Local Groups in an Hunting Gathering Environment," *American Anthropology,* 75:1448-1468.

—. 1994. "Changing Sex Ratios among the Hava Supai Indians", *Current Anthropology,* 35 (4).

Murdock, George Peter. 1949. *Social Structure.* New York: The Macmillan Company.

Otterbein, Keith F. 1970. "The Developmental Cycle of the Andros Household a Diachronic Analysis," *American Anthropologist,* 72: 142-1419.

Shah, A.M. 1974. *The Household Dimension of the Family in India.* (A Field Study in a Gujarat Village and a Review of Other Studies). Berkeley: The University of California Press.

Smith, Raymong T. 1956. *The Negro Family in British Guiana.* London: Routledge and Kegan Paul.

Srivastava, A.R.N. 1969. Society and Economy Among the Korwa of Palamau; A Study in Change, Unpublished Master Thesis, North Carolina: Wake Forest University.

—. 1979. The *Development Dimension of Domestic Group in India: An Anthropological analysis of Demography and Economy of a Tribe of Central India.* New Delhi: Books Today.

—. 1994: .On Social Structure and Demography," *Current Anthropology.* 35(5).

Symes, David. 1972. "Farm Household and Farm Performance, a Study of Twentieth Century Changes in Ballyferriter. Southwest Ireland," *Ethnology* X11: 25-38.

Weiss, Kenneth M. 1973. "Demographic Models for Anthropology," *Memories of the Society for American Archaeology,* Number 27.

SECTION II

ETHNICITY, UPRISING AND REVIVALISM

FOUR

THE REBIRTH OF A NATION
The Winnebago Tribe of Nebraska and Managed Ethnicity

PETER T. SUZUKI

An intriguing concept frequently used but one often left undefined or ill defined in much of social science literature is ethnicity. One reason for this is because the analyst more often than not assumes that a group under question which the analyst is interested in possesses ethnicity in-as-much as the analyst who is circumscribing the group already has set it apart as an ethnic group (e.g. Parrillo, 1997: 42-45 *et passim:* Romanucci and DeVos, 1995). Unfortunately, this type of circular thinking does injustice not only to the reader but to social science in general, particularly in failing to advance *ethnicity as a theoretical concept.*

This essay attempts to obviate this pitfall by looking closely at what *ideally* constitutes ethnicity, applying its constituent elements to a specific group, and offering some theoretical issues.

The position taken in this paper concerning ethnicity is that in the *ideal case,* the following features are present for a group distinguished as being ethnic. It is important that the group have *physical boundaries.* They might range from large national borders whose integrity is defended by armed forces to regional or local ones (e.g. a town or village) within a large setting such as the nation state.

High on the list of desiderata would be a *common language* or *mode of communication* for the group in question. Such a system is the basic for the necessary exchanging of ideas and meeting of the minds within the group and is a *sine qua non* of ethnicity. Of importance to developing ethnicity would be a fair degree of constant *face-to-face interaction.* Hypothetically, owing to modern technology and mass media, this component of ethnicity could be facilitated and maintained with a minimum of physical contact.

Whether the individuals within the group have a *sense of identity* that ties them together cannot be gainsaid as an important component. With this, solidarity and a sense of meaning and purpose can be achieved.

A *common history* would assist the group in strengthening the bond among its members.

Pervading many of the features noted above would be a set of *commonly shared values.* The values often cohere around an identifiable religious system practiced by the group or imbued within the family or kin group.

Reinforcing a sense of solidarity would be certain *regular rites, rituals, and ceremonies.*

A specific group may satisfy all the criteria above but its sense of identity and unity may be weak or non-existent. This is by way of remarking that like any other set of criteria in defining a situation, not everything is always perfectly clear-cut and well structured. It follows, thus, that a sense of identity for a group may range from *languid* to *moderate* to *fervid*. Contemporary examples are the Germans of the Yorktown section of Manhattan, Japanese, and Tamils of Sri Lanka, respectively. A good case could be made of groups that, at one time, possessed all the attributes save a sense of ethnicity; such would be the many Indian tribes who, shortly after having been placed on reservations, were a very dispirited people.

The salience of the criteria delineated is that commonality of a physical attribute such as race is *not* necessarily a requisite feature. Thus, hypothetically, a collection of people with a unique occupation could be an ethnic group. To help clarify this last statement, consider the following illustration: Wall street brokers. Geographically, be definition they are situated in the Wall Street area of Manhattan, New York, where the New York Stock Exchange is located. To this extent, the boundaries are physically delimited. Their *language* is unique to the degree that the average citizen on the street hardly knows the meaning of such arcane terms as "puts," "calls," "junk bonds", etc. in addition to the unfathomable (for the outsider) sign language used by those in the Exchange to signal selling and buying, and monikers, acronyms, abbreviations, and jargon for certain terms and procedures.

The floor of the Stock Exchange itself, "The Pit," would be the arena of most frequent physical *face-to-face interaction,* while the history of Wall Street, including the crash of 1929, is probably well known to most brokers. Should they be asked, for example, by an official U.S. Census Bureau census taker, "What do you do for a living?," virtually all of them would identify themselves as Wall Street brokers, and probably quite proudly so. The profit-making motive by buying and selling stocks, bonds, and commodities would be the commonly shared values of those affiliated with the New York Stock Exchange. The shouts of joy and jubilation when the gong closing the Exchange at the end of an extraordinarily good market day, when many stocks have risen precipitously in price, and the sounding of the gong may be seen as important rituals, in addition to certain *celebrations* held before the Exchange closes for the Christmas Holiday season.

Note the following: those in the Exchange are of various races (historically, this was not the case, of course, before the policy of Affirmative Action and Equal Opportunity had been implemented, when Caucasian males were the sole brokers). Presently, much of the communication takes place via computers but communication nonetheless takes place with the special language of Wall Street. The history may or may not be accurate as certain myths might embellish it, but knowledge of the history of Wall Street, strong or dim, depending on the individual, is, nevertheless known (and, in the case of Wall Street, formalized through history books written on the topic).

The point to be drawn from the case depicted above, however exaggerated it might be in applying the features that ideally consitute ethnicity, is that ethnicity is a rich concept whose theoretical power as an explanatory mechanism has not been fully appreciated. It may be an evanescent force or one of a lasting nature; it can be developed, shaped, and manipulated; and it can be used for good or evil.

Therefore, to cite examples that would elucidate the observations in the previous paragraph, a well-defined ethnic group in the United States, Japanese Americans in California, over time have been losing their ethnicity owing to what Milton Gorden (1964) has identified as key in assimilation, viz. structural assimilation through extensive intermarriage with members of the Caucasian race. In this case, ethnicity is an evanescent force for this group as one of the most important elements of ethnicity is the sense of identity or solidarity members of this group feel *qua* Japanese Americans.

On the other hand, the Black Panthers and the Symbionese Liberation Army, militant Black groups that were active in the 1960's and early 1970's in the U.S., attempted to manipulate a perceived ethnicity among America's Blacks for their own selfish ends (Hearst, 1982). On the contemporary international scene, the recent events in Yugoslavia point up a tragic case of the former communists under Serbian President Slobodan Milosevic having whipped up ethnicity among Serbs in Croatia and Bosnia and then supplied them with arms. The results are well known. Parenthetically, Milosevic's policy went forth despite massive protests in Belgrade on June 28, 1992, when 100,000 took to the streets against him and his communist followers for having illegally annulled election results that would have weakened those in power considerably. It would not be far fetched to conclude that the Milosevic case exemplifies how ethnicity can be used for evil ends.

The position taken in this paper is that, despite fairly rigorous criteria in delimiting an ethnic group, owing to various situations in which ethnicity as such appears, it makes sense to disaggregate ethnicity into coherent *types*.

The examples briefly touched on previously constitute *managed ethnicity*.

Most commonly under this rubric, those in power or authority consciously attempt to mould and/or use ethnicity to achieve specific ends. As was remarked for the likes of the Black Panthers and the Serbian president, the ends have proven disastrous. It is superfluous to add that this may not always be the case. The conclusion to be drawn is the following: there are gradations and sub-types within managed ethnicity, as will be shown in the discussion which centers around the Winnebago Tribe of Nebraska. For lack of a better term, another type of ethnicity is *natural-historical ethnicity*. This is the more common form insofaras historical circumstances have taken place to fashion a group that ends up being an ethnic group with all the attributes, including ethnicity. Some obvious examples are the many (but not all) American Indian tribes, Flemings of Belgium, Bosnians, French Canadians, Hasidic Jews of Brooklyn, New York (vs. other American Jews), *et al.*

Shifting now to the main topic of this paper, the Winnebago Tribe of Nebraska, the succeeding pages will examine some dynamic forces that have been taking place on the reservation and to contextualize them in a framework of ethnicity etched in the previous passage of this essay. After a brief overview of some general observations about the Winnebago Tribe of Nebraska, including its history, the study will proceed to an examination of the basis for the rebirth of this nation, that is to say, ethnicity of the managed kind.

The Winnebago Reservation is situated approximately 80 miles from the city of Omaha, Nebraska's largest city, and is only some eight miles from another reservation, that of the Omaha Tribe of Nebraska (see Map 4.1). In driving from the City of Omaha to the Winnebago Reservation, the driver will know immediately when he/she is entering the reservation as there will be a large sign notifying the driver that he/she is entering it.

Ho-Chungra is the name the people of Winnebago give themselves, and is a term that translates to mean "People of the Parent Speech". They are a Siouan-speaking tribe originally from the State of Wisconsin, where today the Wisconsin branch numbers a little more than 5,000. The Nebraska Winnebagos settled in this state's reservation in 1865 on a land purchased from their friends and allies, the Omahas (Smith, 1996).

The census takers of the U.S. Census Bureau tallied 1,156 as the official count of those living on the Winnebago Reservation in 1990.

The reservation itself was established, and most of its present boundaries drawn, in 1865. Of the 95,545 acres of the original reservation, non-Indian--virtually all Whites—own 71 per cent of it. The land in the hands of Winnebagos presently amounts to 40,000 acres, either tribally or individually owned (the vast majority is individually owned).

In modern times, the federal policy that sank to a nadir regarding treatment of Indian nations was in 1953 when the Termination Act was passed to end the U.S. Government's relations with Indian tribes (Suzuki,

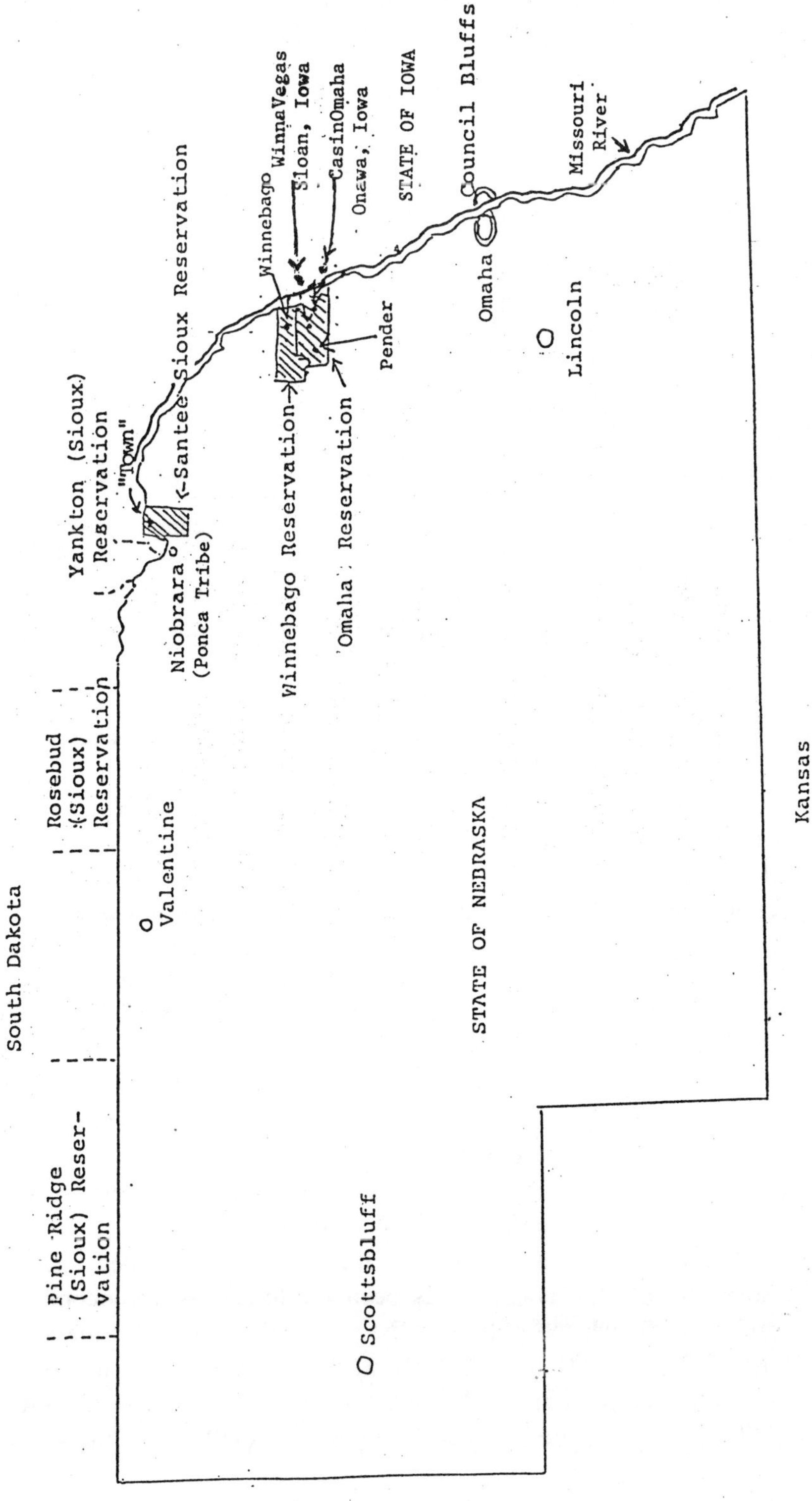
South Dakota
Pine Ridge (Sioux) Reservation
Rosebud (Sioux) Reservation
Yankton (Sioux) Reservation
"Town"
Santee Sioux Reservation
Niobrara
(Ponca Tribe)
Valentine
Scottsbluff
Winnebago
WinnaVegas
Sloan, Iowa
CasinOmaha
Onawa, Iowa
STATE OF IOWA
Council Bluffs
Missouri River
Winnebago Reservation
Omaha Reservation
Pender
Omaha
Lincoln
STATE OF NEBRASKA
Kansas

1996). A total of one-hundred and eight tribes were indeed detribalized until President Richard Nixon put an end to this policy in 1970, and declared a new policy, one which is still in place, that of self-determination. The psychological effect of termination on Indian peoples was devastating, as can be imagined. This includes those who were not terminated but were on the list of the Bureau of Indian Affairs to undergo the process in short order; the Winnebago Tribe of Nebraska was one of these.

A good case which underscores how desolating the Termination Act was and the fear that it engendered can be seen concerning the Winnebago reaction to retrocession. This term refers to the States' transfer of jurisdictional powers over civil and criminal cases on Indian reservations back to the tribes via the federal government. In 1968, when retrocession became possible in Nebraska, the Omaha Tribe--which had not been on the short list to be terminated--unhesitatingly jumped at the chance to exercise what they considered to be a significant sovereignty issue and established a tribal court and police organization on the reservation. The Winnebagos, on the other, took a different position. Owing to what they felt relatively content with what would take place, they had the federal government take over the judicial and police functions, functions that, prior to retrocession, were handled by the State of Nebraska (Suzuki, 1992).

The key issue in retrocession is sovereignty, which is the sense that a tribe feels to be autonomous of the federal government and exercises that right whenever possible. Jurisdiction over issues related to the reservation and policing the reservation are seen as fundamental to exercising sovereignty. Whereas the Omaha Tribe was not in any better financial position to assume their criminal justice system, notwithstanding this, they took over. As in all retrocession cases, the federal government was there to assist with funds during the transition. The stated reason for the Winnebago Tribe not to assume control on the reservation after 1968 did not square with the facts, as the real reason was that the tribe felt not organized well enough to take on the added responsibilities that retrocession entailed.

In the mid-1970's, the Tribe felt confident and strong enough to retrocede but were not granted that right. In 1985 they tried again, and after a lengthy hearing before the legislative body of the State of Nebraska, assumed partial retrocession starting on July 1, 1986. As a result, the BIA came to provide the law enforcement and judicial services on the reservation.

A sense of physical and psychological enclosure, demarcated since times immemorial by distinct borders, has been reinforced as a concomitant of retrocession. Although the police on the reservation are under the aegis of the Bureau of Indian Affairs (BIA), all are Native Americans, and the same may be said of the personnel affiliated with the tribal court system (Anon., 1996a). The village on the reservation is where virtually all of the agencies, office buildings, churches, and schools are. This is where the most frequent face-to-face interaction takes place.

The feeling of confidence of the Tribe in retroceding may have had its roots in a change of investment strategy that marked the beginning of the 1980's, one that would yield handsome dividends. Caught up in the then prevailing philosophy of Reaganomics, in the beginning of that decade saw the establishment of the Winnebago Enterprise Board, which "realized that the development of business would create jobs and stimulate the economy and (therefore) set about finding and establishing . . . businesses" (Snake *et al.,* 1985: 4). As a result, in mid-1983, a small store, Heritage Foods, was founded, one which turned a profit in 1985. One year after Heritage Foods opened, a Philips 66 gasoline station next to it opened for business; so too a small eatery under the roof of the store. In June 1992, the Heritage Foods Store, a vastly expanded supermarket from the original store, started greeting its customers.

Shortly before the gas station started providing fuel to cars and trucks, the Tribe undertook its largest investment project: Winn-A-Bingo, with high-stakes prizes offered for its games of chance, welcomed gamblers on a parcel of Winnebago land on the Iowa side of the Missouri River, near Sloan, just off an important north-south highway in Western Iowa, Interstate 29 (see Map 4.1). All of these enterprises were funded by the private sector, loans from banks and investors, and support from the federal government.

Although the bingo hall proved to be a profitable venture, there were some problems with the outside management firm that had been contracted to operate the games (it skimmed profits that were not due to the firm). Winn-A-Bingo experienced closure in 1988 and remained in that status until 1990; then on April 30, 1992, the tribe opened WinnaVegas, a casino with games similar to those found in Las Vegas that included a large restaurant after its move to the former bingo hall in March of 1993. Although a Las Vegas–type casino established by the Omaha Tribe of Nebraska only some 20, miles south of Winna Vegas (see Map 4.1) had its grand opening on July 22, 1992, both casinos did very well financially. (In 1995, two large casinos in Council Bluffs, the city across the Missouri River from Omaha, put out the welcome mat thereby lowering the $600,000 to a million dollar a month profit that each tribal casino on Interstate 29 had been registering. Earlier, Bluffs Run Casino with nothing but slot machines had opened and was also providing stiff competition for the Indian enterprises.)

All told, of the 360 employed at Winna Vegas, 141 (39.2%) are tribal members. A positive effect of these new enterprises has been a drop in the unemployment rate from approximately 70 to 45 per cent (Mullen, 1993: 15). A profit of $14 million was recorded from the casino operations in the fiscal year that ended in September 1995 (Shanahan, 1995).

With the newly acquired wealth, diversification has been the investment strategy, as the Winnebago Tribe viewed the steady profits from the casino to be of a short-term nature. Indeed, by 1995, the profits had dropped 22 per cent (Smiley, 1995). In September 1994, Ho-Chunk Inc., an investment arm of the tribe, was established with $1.5 million to get it going. Ho-Chunk itself is an umbrella for its four subsidiaries. Under HCI Hospitality, the main development subsidiary, are a 53-unit hotel near WinnaVegas (opened in August 1995), Rodeway Inn, the Ramada Inn with its 67 units in the City of Omaha (its first guests were accommodated in June 1996), and the 64-unit Ramada Limited in Lincoln, Nebraska (its opening date was November 5, 1996). A complex of apartments in Omaha also has been a target of Ho-Chunk's investments, while another hotel near Omaha's airport is in the works. And the cities of Ft. Collins, Colorado; San Diego, California, Yakima, Washington; and Salt Lake City, Utah, are now seeing construction of hotels by the Winnebago Tribe in consort with a firm in South Dakota.

The Tribe and the South Dakota firm are also planning to build a minimal on the reservation and are investing in an apartment complex in Houston.

Constructing and operating of hotels comes under HCI Hospitality wehreas HCI Real Estate is that arm of Ho-Chunk which has been investing in the real estate ventures noted. The two other subsidiaries of Ho-Chunk, Inc. are HCI Leasing, for the purpose of leasing equipment to casinos, and HCI Investment, for investments in stocks, bonds, mutual funds, etc. Annually, Ho-Chunk receives 20 per cent of casino profits for its investments, and another 30 per cent is provided for HCI investment activities.

Profits are also being plowed into land that was once owned by the Tribe for there now is a buy-back policy. The tribe has set a goal of 1,000 acres a year as buy back, and $400,000 is banked for this purpose. Individual tribal members have also profited by receipt of an annual $599 each year of the three years, 1994, 1995, and 1996; for those under 18 the money is put into a trust fund until they are of age (Hammel, 1994: 2; Blackwood, 1996; Dorr, 1997).

Aside from individual payments, tribal members are also benefiting from improved health-care services and scholarships thanks to casino profits. The number of youths attending college or vocational school on scholarships from casino profits has increased to around 45 in the past few years, which is almost double the number that could be counted prior to the success of the casino (Dorr, 1996).

The litany of positive effects based upon the casino's success has not been confined to the tangible items listed in the previous sections.

A common language and a sense of common history, distinguished as features of ethnicity, are being played out in the following ways on the reservation today. Owing to the pervasive use of English, this tongue has been the common means of communication on the reservation in modern times. In this regard, then, the tribe is not different from its surrounding white communities. However, there is now a concerted effort to "revive" the language by teaching *Hocak*—the official name of the language—at all levels of the school system, including the community college.

A significant policy of the tribal newspaper, *Winnebago Indian News,* is the following enunciated by its editor, David Morgan:

> *"The Native American Studies"* is a new section for the *Winnebago Indian News.* It is an education section designed to educate readers about or to reinforce every aspect of *Native American Culture* (Original italics) (Morgan, 1996: 6).[1]

Since the inception of this section, there has been a weekly column entitled "Hocak Language Lessons" with, typically, a vocabularly list of native and English terms.[2] The history section started with a detailed article, "Treaty with the Winnebago, 1828." Since then, articles in the history section have dealt with fishing rights, those from the tribe who had attended the Carlisle Indian School, Carlisle, Pennsylvania, and for the past eleven months there has been a series on the history of the split of the Nebraska Winnebagos from their Wisconsin branch. Photos from the tribe's archival collection also may be found on these pages and in other sections.

Another example of institution-building within the reservation may be seen in the recent move by the Winnebago Tribe to establish their own community college. In 1979, Congress passed Public Law (PL) 95-471, the Tribally Controlled Community College Act. The Nebraska Indian Community College (NICC), which had been in existence—although under a different name—since 1973, became eligible to receive federal aid under PL 95 as did a number of other Indian community colleges across the nation. NICC comprised community colleges on Nebraska's three Indian reservations that worked cooperatively under the NICC umbrella until 1996. The Winnebago Community College pulled out of this association, renamed its college Little Priest Tribal College (in honour of a revered tribal chief of the past), and started its own programme in the fall semester of 1996. The reason for pursuing this policy lay with the tribal council's belief that the tribe could better control its own destiny independent of NICC, better serve its people, and could pursue more freely the development of courses that were geared to Winnebago language, history, and culture than under the old NICC structure.

Although it has not shown a profit yet, competing for headlines with WinnaVegas and Ho-Chunk's new hotels has been the Winnebago Bison Project. Begun in 1994, and headed by Louis LaRose, a former tribal chairman, the tribe now has a herd of more than 50 bisons, the traditional animal of the

Great Plains, in a large fenced refuge on the reservation. The ultimate goal of this investment is to sell buffalo meat, which is much leaner than beef, and make it an economically profitable enterprise (Hammel, 1996; LaRose, 1997; PBS, 1997). In the "Mission Statement," what is most revealing about the project is that its main goal is "cultural and spiritual revitalization" (Winnebago Tribal Council, 1996). That the people of this tribe were of one mind regarding this goal was brought out prior to the issuance of the "Mission Statement," which was distributed in the fall. In the summer of 1996, a survey of tribal members was taken (the sample size was 264): "The Bison Refuge was seen as most important for its *cultural* significance. . . (by the respondents)" (italics added) Szymanski, 1996). It would be fair to state that there is great public support for the project even though it could be some time before the ledger books will show finances in the black (LaRose, 1997).

Equally exciting for the tribe is the construction of a new hospital in the near future (the present one was built in 1938) and the streamlining of social services so that they will be more efficiently and expeditiously provided (Winnebago Mental Health Center, 1996).

Undergirding all of these notable changes, and projected changes, on the reservation is the annual pow-wow (an Algonquian term for "conjurer"). The 1997 pow-wow, to be held at its usual time at the end of July, will be this tribe's one-hundred thirty-first. It is a joyous occasion when many tribes throughout the nation gather to take part in the celebration in this four-day event. It is a renewal ceremony, when the unity of the Tribe is concretely expressed through prayers, music, dances, speeches, feasts, give-aways, games, inter-tribal dancing contests, and special rites (e.g. flag raising) (Anon., 1989).

Conclusion

There are some dramatic changes taking place on the Winnebago Reservation in Nebraska, and these are exciting times for the people. The Winnebago nation is seeing a rebirth, to a large extent because of the changing economy brought about by Winna Vegas. To describe the changes as "dramatic" is not overstating the case. Consider this only seven years ago, an outside consultant group, from Washington, D.C., assessing the economic situation of the Winnebagos, noted the following: "There is a visible sadness among the Winnebago people" (The Madison Public Affairs Group, 1990:14). One would be hard pressed to describe the people on the reservation in the same way today owing to the optimism that pervades them. There is indeed a palpable tingling sense of anticipation of positive change in the air, and this is understandable given what has been taking place in the past few years.[3]

Like any picture, there are flaws that must be taken into account. There is the perennial and pervasive problem of alcoholism and substance abuse, and a newly emergent one is that of youth gangs on the reservation. Moreover, there is a major housing shortage resulting in a homeless population, and poverty is still a real concern (Anon., 1996b; Burbach, 1996).

Withal, what has been taking place in the past few years can be seen as a minimum an adumbration of the rebirth of this nation.

In re-examining the criteria established that would mark a group off as ethnic—with the Winnebagos in the crucible—there is no gainsaying the existence of well *recognized physical borders* marking off the reservation, *face-to-face interactions* (especially in the village of Winnebago), a common mode of communication (English), *rites and ceremonies* (the pow-wow and attendant activities), and a *common history.* What is significant is that a greater sense of *solidarity* and *identity* as Winnebago is being engendered by such things as the attempt at revitalizing the language, imbuing the people with a sense of common history through the pages of *Winnebago Indian News,* the Bison Project, the Little Priest Tribal College, and the modernization projects (the new hospital and the streamlining of social services). Furthermore, an unanticipated consequence of disbursing annually an amount of money from the casino profits to those tribal members who can prove their affiliation by means of the tribal enrollment card has had the effect of providing those who may have been indifferent to tribal identity to enhance their sense of identity, if for no other reason than to claim their disbursement checks.

All told, a common set of *shared values,* which holds that these people are unique and indeed constitute an identifiable tribe, is emerging, a core that constitutes the rebirth of this nation. With what has been delineated in the previous paragraph, the final conclusion to be drawn is that Winnebago Tribe of Nebraska satisfied all the criteria of an ethnic group.

Because of the approaches and policies that have been taken by the Tribe as chronicled in these pages, the theoretical model that fits most appropriately Winnebago ethnicity would be *indirectly managed ethnicity.* This term is fitting for what has been transpiring on the Winnebago Reservation because some of the events that are assisting in solidifying the Winnebagos, although initiated by the tribal council and other authorities, were fortuitous happenstances that were or are being undertaken because the times called for them. Disbursement of casino profits to individual tribal members, plans for the construction of a new hospital, the development of Little Priest Tribal Community College, and the Bison Project come to mind. One would not be accused of overstating the situation to state that a number of forces are coming together for the Winnebago Tribe of Nebraska that are sparking a new sense of confidence and pride in their tribe *qua* nation. At this juncture, it would be accurate to state that the Winnebagos have a moderate degree of ethnicity, but one that has been growing from an inchoate one. The Tribe itself has put its rebirth in these words—against which there is no argument—as part of a longer formal statement reaffirming their sovereignty: "The vibrant . . . culture . . . (is) flourishing. Our traditions . . . are the indispensable underpinnings for tribal policy" (Winnebago Tribal Council, 1991).

Quite in contrast to the Winnebago case, *directly managed ethnicity* is exemplified by the situations cited earlier in this essay, by such people as the president of Yugoslavia. In this type of condition, quite frequently those in power and authority positions attempt to manipulate and guide the people's sense of solidarity or identity for self-aggrandizement or hegemonic purposes.

To recapitulate, three degrees of ethnicity have been distinguished: languid, moderate, and fervid, and two types of ethnicities noted: natural-historical and managed. In the last-named category are the directly and indirectly managed ethnicities.

The theory of the degrees of ethnicity and the types of ethnicities posited in this paper—in conjunction with the criteria that one must seek in circumscribing whether a group is ethnic or not–should provide better conceptual thinking regarding ethnic group and ethnicity than is presently found in the social science literature.

Acknowledgements

I gratefully acknowledge the following persons on the Winnebago Reservation who have been of great assistance to me over the years and have always graciously welcomed me: Jean Balille, Pearl Bigfire, John Blackhawk, Scott Johnson, Jerome LaPointe, Louis LaRose, David Morgan, Lance Morgan, Fern Norris, the late Reuben Snake, Jr., Ki Tecumsah, Kathy Stout, and Anital Little Walker. I also thank the Winnebago people for their hospitality and kindness.

I bear sole responsibility for all statements in this paper.

NOTES

1. David Morgan: a former student of mine who had just completed a course on Native Americans that I had taught.
2. Native terms for the people, "Ho-Chunk," and their cognates are gaining greater currency among the people. On the status of the language programme, see, Anon., 1997.
3. One measure of mental well-being on the reservation is the absence of suicides or attempted suicides among any age group in the past five years (Interview with Fern Norris, Winnebago Mental Health Center, among other times, February 14, 1997: October 11, 1996.

REFERENCES

Anon. 1989. "History of (the pow-wow) Celebration", *Winnebago Indian News*, July 27, p. 1.

—. 1996a. "Winnebago Supreme Court Justices Sworn in", *Winnebago Indian News*, March 2, p. 1.

—. 1996b. "Town Still has Homelessness, Poverty", *Winnebago Indian News*, Dec. 7, p. 4.

—. 1997. "Hocak Wazijaci Language and Culture Program", *Winnebago Indian News*, February 15, p. 2.

Blackwood, K. 1996. "Four Tribes Mount Efforts for Economic Development", *Omaha World-Herald*, September, 23, p. 9+.

Burbach, C. 1996. "Winnebago Urged to Face Gang Problem", *Omaha World-Herald*, April 13, p. 23 (evening ed.).

Dorr, R. 1997. "Midlands Tribes see some Growth", *Omaha World Herald*, January 27, p. 1 (morning ed.).

Gordon, M. 1964. *Assimilation in American Life*. New York: Oxford University Press.

Hammel, P. 1994. "Tribes Buying Back Property", *Omaha World-Herald*, March 28, p. 1-A.

—. 1996. "Tribes Try Comeback with a Mainstay Buffalo", *Omaha World-Herald*, November 1, p. 21 (evening ed.)

Hearst, P. 1982. *Every Secret Thing*. Garden City: Doubleday.

LaRose, L. 1997. Series of interviews, the latest was on February.

Madison Public Affairs Group, 1990. *Economic Development and the Winnebago Tribe*. Washington, D.C.: The Madison Public Affairs Group (Typescript).

Mullen, K., 1993. "Casino's Move Gives Customers Breathing Room", *Omaha World-Herald*, March 17, p. 13-B+.

Parrillo, V.N. 1997. *Strangers to These Shores: Race and Ethnic Relations in the United States*. Boston: Allyn & Bacon.

PBS (Public Broadcasting Station). 1997. *Louis LaRose and the Winnebago Bison Program*. Television Interview, a 30-minute program shown on February 14.

Romanucci-Ross, L. and G. Devos (eds.). 1995. *Ethnic Identity*. 3rd ed. Walnut Greek: Altamira.

Shanahan, D. 1995. "Winnebago Tribe Thinks Gambling well will go dry", *Omaha World-Herald*, October 11, p. 1 (evening ed.).

Smiley, J. 1995. "WinnaVegas casino has 22 per cent decline", *Omaha World-Herald*, April 27, p. 13 (evening ed.).

Smith, D.L. 1996. *Ho-Chunk of Nebraska*. Winnebago: Ho-Chunk Historical Society.

Snake, R.A., Jr., D.M. Vandall, R. Benesh and R. Davison. 1985. *The Winnebago Tribe of Nebraska*. Minneapolis: Bolger.

Suzuki, P. 1992. "Retroscession and Jurisdictional Issues Facing the Omaha Tribe of Nebraska", *Man & Life*, 18: 1-10.

—. 1996. "Pan-Indianism, Ethnicity, and the Omaha Tribe of Nebraska", in G. Pfeffer and D.K. Behera (ed.), *Contemporary Society: Tribal Studies*, 1: 103-114.

Syzmanski, M.B. 1996. "Land Management Results of 1996 Summer Survey", *Winnebago Indian News*, December 21, p. 7.

Winnebago Mental Health Center. 1996. "Reorganization Chart" (typescript), Winnebago.

Winnebago Tribal Council, 1991. "Critical Issues in Federal Indian Policy", *Winnebago Indian News*, June 16, p. 7.

Winnebago Tribal Council. 1996. "The Winnebago Bison Project: Mission Statement", (typescript), Winnebago.

FIVE

ETHNICITY AND IDENTITY
Preliminary Study of Varâmeen

SOHEILA SHAHSHAHANI

Introduction

In this paper we will study a city close to Tehran which is extremely rich in its ethnic component. The three prevalent ideologies of the state, religion and communism have all tried to attenuate the importance and functionality of ethnicity. Thus ethnicity has been losing colour and importance. It is no longer the all-encompassing human environment in which one is born, to choose one's spouse, speak its language, eat its food and wear its clothing and fights to keep its identity through self-affirmation in disputes. Yet, ethnicity continues to be a buffer to protect individuals, it provides them with a network of social relations, it is the ground for self-realization and shared imagination, but it is not itself an aim. In order to find the ethnic identity of Varâmeen, we shall look into its history, its subsistence, everyday culture, and the imagination of its people.

Varâmeen Area: Brief Geography and History

The city of Varâmeen located in a township (šahrestân) by the same name is located in Tehran Province (Ostân). It is 40 kilometres southeast of Tehran and it covers 130,000 hectares of agricultural pasture land with 65000 hectares of soil classed good for agriculture. It sprawls over an area between 51 degrees from 30 to 55 seconds East, and 35 degrees from 5 to 28 seconds North.

What is very peculiar about the location of Varâmeen is its north-south frontiers. On the north there is the mountainous Damâvand region, and in the south there is the desert. Its elevation from the sea level is from 915 to 165 metres. There is, therefore, a north-south sloping of the landscape. Mount Damâvand with an elevation of 5671 metres from the sea level is snow capped all year round. Therefore, the basic source of river water available to Varâmeen is the Jâjrud River. Besides there are still many different ancient "quânts" and deep wells in the area. In the south, the land is not arable, it is used seasonally at best by transhuming nomadic tribes. The temperature differs 57 degrees from the hottest summer to the coldest winter days: 43°C in summer and –14°C in winter. Its annual rainfall varies between 100-250 millimeters a year.

The History of Varâmeen like the history of a number of Iranian cities is millennial. Varâmeen is close to the city of Rey, an important archeological centre. It is believed that "Varena" and "Raka" in the Vendidad (part of Zoroastrian religious text) relate to Varâmeen and Rey: Varena was the fourteenth country created by Ahuramazda, it is the birth place of King Fereydun *(Avesta,* reprint 1370: 663), one of the most important mythical kings of ancient Persia.

During the Islamic period, this city was one of a cluster of cities of central Iranian plain, Qom, Sâveh, Kâšân, Varâmeen and Sâri which were the stronghold of shi'ite Islam (Vaziri in Zeide Abolhasan, 1374:10). In 804 A.D. the Califa Hârun al-Rašid came to Eranbuye a village near Varâmeen for the burial of two erudites Mohammad ibn-Hasan Sheibani and Abol Hasan al-Nahvi, and he had exclaimed. "Today I buried jurisprudence and Syntax at Eranbuye" (Vaziri 1358: 8) referring to the respective knowledge of each man. In the 12th century Varâmeen is noted for its population and prosperity *(ibid:* 17) and in the 15th century it is ceramics and mosaics which attract great attention.

Sa'id Vaziri, contemporary historian of Varâmeen published a book called *Ahsan ol-Akbar* (1374) by Mohammad ibn al-Olume al-Varâmeeni. According to Vaziri this book writtten in 1434 was the first Persian Book (not Arabic) that in good and fluent language related the life history of the twelve Imams (1374: 4). The mosques of Varâmeen and Pišvâ date to the ninth century.

More important than a traditional history of Varâmeen, it is the history of various people we find in this area that concern us here. This huge plain hosts more variety of people than its original inhabitants. During the Safavid period the capital of Iran was Isfahan. The heads of the Iranian state realized that Varâmeen was an extended area which could host a considerable number of people. This could serve a few purposes: In north-western Iran the increasing Turk and Kurd population was felt as a threat to the Central Government. Tapper's distinction between "state" and "empire" on the problem of minorities, brings the general attitude of the Safavid kings toward these populations into focus,

> "a state does not recognize the existence or operation of any semi-independent or autonomous polities within its territory, while an empire by definition does, being interested less in political control than in economic security and income" (Tapper, 1988: 25)

Although the Safavid kings could not tolerate strong minority groups which could threat the existence of Central Government, it was through their dislocation that decreased their threat to political hegemony of their empire. The Safavids could not totally annihilate a large group of pastoral nomads who were a minority group by their distinctions with the surrounding group, they tolerated them and their power and population up to a certain degree. Beyond that, they dispersed them through policies of dislocation. A group could be divided by sending one part with a leader to a frontier territory, or it was exiled into a territory less with positive political aim, rather more for punishment or simply for retaining part of a reserve political and military power at hand in case of eventual need. In any event, from an emic point of view a small group was forced to leave its original territory, which kept political allegiance to the king because it was separated from its own central power. And because of the legitimacy of the position of the king, and it continued its existence in reserve for future service to the central government.

Pastoral Nomadic Populations

Who were the groups which were brought to this area? The Kurds, Lors, Turks and Arabs. These identify general linguistic categories used for pastoral nomadic tribes who were displaced from southern, central, western and north-western Iran to this territory. Various anthropologists have showed sensitivity to the categories under which populations are studied, whether they are tribal studies or ethnic studies and we are faced with this problem at the outset trying to identify the different groups:

> "Interest in ethnicity among anthropologists has indeed burgeoned . . . ., with the general shift in the discipline away from tribal towards urban and multi-cultural studies, and a shift in theoretical interests from group to network, from states to transaction, from structure to process . . . , and from function to meaning" (Tapper paraphrazing others, 1988: 22).

In other words, the populations who were moved to the area were of pastoral-nomadic tribes; studying them today, we will use the term "ethnic groups." While the discipline has shifted its attention, the means of subsistence of people under study has changed also. Trying to identify the people of Varâmeen, let us look closer at the history of its pastoral nomadic populations: Kurds, Lors, Turks and Arabs.

Kurds

The following subdivision of Kurds were displaced by Royal Degree at the peak of the Safavide era: Seil Separânlu (known Sil Supur), Pâzuki, Siâh Mansuri, Čegeni, Qaraĉurânlu, Kordbaçe. According to Tavahodi the Kurds came from Azerbâijan and Mahâbâd willingly to an area close to Rey . . . where they found best arable land. Azerbâijân and Kurdistân could not contain such a large transhumant population. A considerable number of them were sedentarized in the area. South Caucasia was lost to the Ottoman Turks, thus thc summer quarters of Qarabâq, Širavan, Ganjeh, Naxjavân and Aras River borders were no longer available to these tribes. As a result the Turkish tribes of Qâjâr, Ostânlu, and Afšâr and some Kurds of Azerbâijân area were confined within the Iranian Azerbâijân area. Overpopulation caused dispute over water and territory. Shâh Abâs Safavid worried about the situation and the threat such a power could eventually pose to his thrown, he cunningly promised them excellent land for agriculture, husbandry, and transhumance should they move to Varâmeen and some neighbouring area.

The Pâzuki are reported to have had ebbs and flows in their chieftainship from 1501, the date Shâh Esmâ'il was enthrowned (Mardux, 1371: 367-9) till the end of the century when their main chieftainship was dispersed (Field, 1939:133 per ed) and some families moved to the Varâmeen area. Then we have the Siâh Mansuri who had an important history of chivalry during the Safavid period. It was with skillful ruse and the use of the long-lasting method of lies and promises practiced by the kings of Iran, that Shâh Abbâs was able to deceive their chief Dowlatyâr Xân and brought this Kurdish power under his control (Mardux, 1371: 431-3). It is logical to deduce that they were brought to the area in punishment. In contrast, the Seil (Separânlu) Supur Kurds were apparently given land in the area in recompense for their chivalrous acts in 1603 against the Ottoman empire. They were part of the Shâhsavan" confederacy, loyal to the Safavid king Shâh Abbâs (Tavahodi, 1359:505). They spoke Turkish and at times they are known as Turks. There are three small Kurd tribes in the area: the Burbur, Larney and Kordbaçe. The exact origin of their exodus and time of arrival to the area is not clearly known. What is certain is that it occurred during the reign of Nâder Shâh (1735-47). They came either from western Iran (Kermansah region) or from the south (Fars province). The origin of the Larney is questionable, yet they came to Varâmeen before Nâser ed-Din Sâh's reign. The last pastoral nomadic group is the Kordbace. They had come to the area during the Safavid period.

Lor

Who are the Lor population of Varâmeen? Basically two groups are here: the Hadâvand and the Baxtiyâri. The first group being part of Lor-e Kuçak (small lor), they are by far the more numerous tribal population of the area. They are from Lorestân province in the western Zâgros mountains. Their exodus from

Lorestân occurred during the reign of the only Lor king of Iran, Karim Xân-e Zand, (the others being either Turk or Persian). He reigned from 1749 to 1779. People claim the population came here through his decision, another view is that he moved them to the Fars province, close to his capital city Širâz, and they were moved to this area by the following dynasty more precisely by Aqa Mohammad Xân-eQâjâr. They numbered 600 families when they arrived in Varâmeen area.

The Baxtiyâri Lor were moved to this area during three eras. There were important figures in the large tribe of the Baxtiyâri and who were forcibly moved to the area to separate these leaders from the main tribe, and have the rest obey the central government, be it the Zandieh, or the Qâjâr dynasty.

Turks

Who were the Turks who were moved to the area? They were either from the north-western Iran or from the southern province of Fars. Those who came from the north were first the Qâjâr who formed a dynasty, and the Osanlu, the Kangarlu, the Shâhsavan, and the Karxane Yusofi, and the ones from Fars were the Qâsqâ'yi, the Nafar and the Lašni and Xalaj.

We first encounter the Qâjâr in the 12th and 13th century. They were originally inhabitants of Caucasia and at this time they moved to Syria. Some of them returned in later years, but the Safavid moved them to various parts of Iran including Varâmeen. During the reign of the Safavids and Zandieh, they were among the powerful tribes of Iran. They were important in the army and had the governorship of certain provinces.

The coronation of Âqâ Mohammad Xân and the intention of forming a next dynasty in Iran needed the cooperation of various tribes in this area: the Turk, Kurd (Pâzuki), and Arab joined forces to strengthen Aqâ Mohammad Xân at the beginning (Amini, 1368: 22). Âqâ Mohammad Xân the first king of the Qâjâr dynasty was coronated although under a large tree and with a copper crown—in this very area (Amini, 1368: 23). So the presence of the Qâjâr in Varâmeen played an important role in the history of the whole country. The Qâjâr having an important base and population here, they chose Tehran as their capital (Vaziri, 1358: 52). Thus Tehran being the capital is due to its closeness to Varâmeen!

Varâmeen is a vast rich valley the king could count on for its products for nourishing his army. Later in history, about the end of the Qâjâr period, the kings depended on this area's adherants in order to enhance their reign in the country. The village Jamalabad had the royal stable. Eastern and south-eastern Varâmeen was host to the royal family on their hunting expeditions.

The Osânlu in 500-1000 households were moved to the area by Âqâ Mohammad Xân in order to be a buffer against the Turkmans in the north who could easily raid the area. The Kangarlu left Iravan area because of Russian-Iranian war which ended in Russian victory and loss of territory by Iran. The Shâhsavan tribal confederacy were inhabitants of the Azerbâijân province; part of them moved to Saveh area south-west of Tehran, during Nâder Shâh's reign and they were moved to Varâmeen by Qâjâr kings. Kârxâne Yusofi (there is no hint as to the meaning of this peculiar name: "Yusofi factory") were brought here either from Kermânšâh or from Zanjân both in western Iran.

The Turkish tribes coming from Fârs are few in number and scant in importance. The Qašqâ'yi must have come after 1880's. The Nafar, although part of the Xamse confederacy (the Arab Bâsseri were part of it) were Turkish speaking and we know of 1000 men of this tribe participating along with other royalist tribes against the Constitutional Movement of Iran. Nothing on the origin or the date of displacement of Lasni and Xalaj is known.

Arabs

Now we come to the final group the Arabs, who were basically two large tribes: the Miš Mast and the Koti. The Miš Mast Arabs were among the tribes who came to Iran up to Khorâsân province in the north-east and settled there. They continued their tribal life in the area and two of their chiefs figure among Nâder Shâh's generals. Nâder Shah gave the governorship of Kermânšâh to one of them. During Qâjâr period the Miš Mast were settled in Varâmeen area. The Koti have their origin in the country Omân. During the first centuries after Arab invasion, they were moved to Khuzistan, and Fârs provinces in the south. During Nâser ed-Din Shâh's period they were moved to this area. They are the last group along with the Hadâvand Lor to retain what remained of pastoral nomadic life.

A look at the ethnic map of Iran shows that all the basic ethnic groups of Iran are represented in Varâmeen except for the Baluch. Besides some small groups who were brought from Khorâssân who were themselves originally from western Iran, no eastern ethnic group is among them. Historically the reason could be wars with the Ottoman empire and Russia in previous centuries.

Another important point we should make about ethnic maps, and this paper helps to show it too, is their relative importance. The movement of human populations makes their boundaries very questionable. Even their centrality is tantamount if a total population is moved from place to place. If important figures are removed from the centre, a weakening of ethnic identity follows. It is, therefore, with great care and relativism that one uses these maps. For every period of Iranian history an ethnic map should be provided. Different historical periods give varying importance to such identification of people. Scientific work is not devoid of political colour in identifying people according to ethnicity (See Orywall, 1988: 35).

Needless to say we believe in a context oriented, situational approach to ethnicity, one which is defined in space and time.

> "The essence of ethnonyms and of conceptions of ethnicity is that they cannot be pinned down 'scientifically' by maps, by lists of traits and attributes, but that they are essentially ambiguous and shifting materials for the construction and manipulation of identity, by actors, by others, by administrators and by social researchers." (Tapper, 1988: 21)

Having presented the history of various pastoral nomadic groups we have seen different reasons for which these people occupied this area: Some came forcibly, some in order to save their lives. Some by positive and some by negative decree. But it should be noted that from the perspective of the central government (see above quotations from Tapper) it was not only for economic security, but for political control that governments decided to move them. The contemporary relationship of the state to tribal population becomes very clear in this area: The central governments need the tribes: they need their army (there was no organized army till the 20th century and the army constituted of armed men from various tribes and villages), their tax and their herds as provision.

But they could not tolerate their becoming too numerous, and too powerful. This was seen as a threat to central government. From the perspective of tribesmen, life was not tied to a particular area. Lack of pasture land and water and poor chieftainship means death. Therefore, if one moves with one's household and preferably one's lineage and larger subdivision with a large enough number of tribes-people, so that future marriages could take place endogamously, then migration would be more bearable. Although marriage can be exogamous in Iran, yet it is preferable not to give one's daughter outside the group. Given that the figures for an emigrating population was 500 households, this shows that a group who moved had the possibility of living self-sufficiently as far as marriage was concerned for some time. Thus going to another area with good pastures is not a problem. One is used to moving. But a difficulty which might rise is the neighbouring populations. In this area all of a sudden one had neighbours of different languages and origins. We do not have much data on how they regulated their problems of occupation of territory during transhumance and when settled in the summer or winter quarters. We only know that they occupied the environment according to royal decree.

According to documents from late Qâjâr period, Varâmeen was divided into 5 parts (Amini, 1368:51-3). We can deduce from the names of the areas that the tribal populations who were most successful and numerous in the area gave their name to their corresponding land. The five were Behnâm-e Arab,

Behnâm-e Seilsupur, Behnâm-e Pâzuki, Qâjar and Burbur. They each had a definite area allocated to them: The Arabs were mostly in the southern and south-eastern area close to the desert. The Seilsupur were more in the western area; the Qâjâr were more in the northern area; the Pâzuki in the north and north-western area; the Burbur were mostly in the northern and north-eastern areas.

Rural Background

So far we have dealt with the urban and tribai history of this area. But we have also mentioned that its land was important for agriculture. It is evident that there was a rural life in this area also. We know the ethnic origin of a few villages, we know that the inhabitants of a number of these villages were the pastoral nomads who settled down. It is interesting to note that the pressure of ethnic population of the area was such that the local population calls itself Tâjik, that is the term used by non-Persians for Persians. We shall be very brief on the ethnic constitution of the rural population. We cannot ignore this issue as today Varâmeen is nothing but an amalgam of rural constituencies.

We have an interesting historical source from 1872 (Ettehâdieh, 1993) on villages owned by the Central Government ("Xâlese"). It gives statistics on the population, number of people in each family, tax in kind and in money, number of herd, situation of the villages and its irrigation system, etc. The total number of villages are 33 (in Amini : 63, the number is reported to be 52). In one column we find ethnic reference for the villages. But that of only twelve are mentioned. Looking at the list we find no Arab ethnic identity for these royal villages. The tribes mentioned are Hadâvand, Baxtiyâri, Kordbaçe, Loreini and Shâhsavan. We thus see the major Kurd, Turk, and Arabs not among villages belonging to the government. They were either continuing their pastoral nomadic life, or had settled in villages owned by share holders. In any event the condition of villages and their irrigation system is reported to be dilapidating. The Qâjâr royal family were the biggest land owners of Varâmeen. During the whole period we hear of Varâmeen providing wheat and barley, and cucumbers and melons in season to the capital.

Is the ethnic identity of rural population always tribal or local? We have a number of distinct villages which have their origins in the other side of the desert, i.e. as far as Yazd. The cities or their corresponding rural areas which gave emigrants to Varâmeen were Kâšân, Isfahân, Zavâreh, Ardestân. Yazd and Šahr-e Bâbak. With the exception of Kâšân, the others left their territory because of famine. The Kâši were exiled to the area. They were originally the followers of Nâyab Hossein-e Kâši, a rebel group who were defeated in 1909. Asgar Âbâd in central Varâmeen is the name of the village built by the Yazdi.

One point on religion should be noted before we move to today's panorama:

As we mentioned at the beginning, Varâmeen and the smaller city of Pišvâ were important Shi'ite centres, and the majority of the local population are Shi'ite Moslems. What about the incoming ethnic groups? Were they all Shi'ite and Moslems? The Seil Supur Kurds were Sunni, belonging to an order called Ahle-Haq. There are some Sunni in Quhe, and some Hanafi in Anbarbuye. This is besides the Sunni Afqan population whom we have not yet discussed. There were some Bahâ'yi in the area, but no Christians, Jews or Zoroastrians are reported to have lived in the region.

We had to indulge in this long historical search in order to show the multiplicity of ethnic presence in this area today. People refer to their past in order to define their identity. In every group there are a few individuals who know the topic well and at certain occasions discuss it. Some have made the effort of going back to the place from which they believe they have come in order to find their origins and their relatives. Finally the rationale of historian, S. Vaziri to write the history of Varâmeen has been to give a sense of pride to the young. He has done this through discussing historical figures and monuments.

Measures of Change from Above

Now let us move toward the present, and see what were the most important elements of change, and how they affected the ethnic groups, the relationship between them, and their relationship to their environment. By the end of Qâjâr period, that is the end of the century, this area was in a decadent situation. The Arab and Qâjâr populations were royalist, the Baxtyiari were constitutionalist and they had both gone to Tehran with their corresponding armies. The religious element was also strong particularly in the city of Pišvâ. With the establishment of the Pahlavi regime, the "xale^e" villages (villages belonging to the government or royal family) were practically transferred to the Pahlavi royal family. In 1963 land reform measures distributed them to peasants or share holders.

From 1935 brick factories which were prohibited to function in southern Tehran because of pollution, they were given permission to operate in northern Varâmeen area in Palašt. A factory of military ammunitions was established in Parçin near Palašt. Vegetable oil and sugar refinery were other important industrial centres in Varâmeen.

The new railroad which was centered in southern Tehran and came to the city of Rey, passed through Varâmeen to go to the holy city of Mashad in the northeast of Iran. The Tehran-Isfahân road which went through Rey, and thus Varâmeen, could easily have correspondence through it, lost importance, because two different highways were constructed which joined Tehrân to Isfahân via Qom and Sâveh.

In the 1940's the Point Four project of the American president Mr.

Truman touched the area: it concerned on the one hand agriculture and on the other education. It set up a training school in Mâmâzan, the net result of which was according to a high school teacher, "The end of cotton production in Fe:lestân which was an important product exported for its excellence . . ., and training of peasants to cultivate the seeds which the educators were bringing to the area. Second there was the selection of intelligent students and training them to take political responsibilities on local and national level, i.e., become village chiefs or work in government offices. The best students were selected and sent for a year of training to the U.S. One example was Dr. Sâm who started as head of the education bureau in Varâmeen, then became head of the Four Point training school, and later became minister of education." They also had a journal called *The Life of Varâmeen.*

This same period was important for the activities of the pro-Russian communist party called the Tudeh. The area having a growing working population in industry, it was fit for political activity. The interest of people in education was another propicious ground for the Tudeh party. Their "anti-feudal" ideology was appreciated by anyone who had felt the yoke of the land owners. The Tudeyi were cunning enough not to attack religion or personal religious activity of people. They therefore penetrated the area, and a few important figures of this party came from Varâmeen. In the 1963 anti-Shah religious uprisings, a group of manifestors marched from Varâmeen into Tehran. They are known as a hard-core group armed to the teeth, who are ready to attack if necessary, and ready to sacrifice if the cause is just.

At the same time, the situation of the city of Tehrân has changed a great deal. Not only has it become a capital with its ever increasing population and its need for products from Varâmeen, but it also needs Varâmeen source of water. The Jâjrud river which was divided into 80 riverines and was the major source of water for this vast area, now flows behind the Latiân Dam to provide part of the tap water for part of the ten million or more people who inhabit Tehran mega-city. Water level of the area goes down 80 centimeters annually. In the Palašt area a total lowering of 250 meters water level is reported (Sâlehi, 1373: 30). Already today certain villages do not receive any of the Jâjrud river water. Certain southern villages do not have access to potable water even through wells. Therefore, certain villages of the southern region are deserted *(ibid;* 30). No wonder from 284 villages of Varâmeen township only 193 have inhabitants *(Farhang-e Abâdiha,* 1373: XX).

Naturally there is a desertification and a change in irrigation system. There is a definite move towards cash crop, from barley and wheat to vegetables, cucumbers, tomatoes, melons and watermelons and today flower production is taking over. There is a 9 per cent decrease in percentage of farmers of the area. This means there is a definite shift from subsistence to market economy.

What has happened to the pastoral nomads of the area? There is sporadic transhumance of Arab or Hadâvand Lor shepherds who take their herd in the summer to limited allowed pasture lands in the Lâr valley and in the winter in Siâh Kuh area. There is some grazing in the vicinity of the villages. Feeding the animals on harvested fields is also practiced. But herding is now commercialized. The army has the biggest production unit in Jalil Abâd and uses its products for the army. Ten complex of industrial herding existed before the Revolution of 1979, now there are 40 such centres, and they provide the milk, mutton and beef for the capital and the Varâmeen area. The feed for the animals is mostly from the same area (Sâlehi, 1373: 121-7). Two most important herding complexes belong to Arabs in the southern village of Jâvâd Abâd.

The chicken production with 450 units in 1984 and 245 in the beginning of 1990, although it is taking up the best agricultural land of Xorrein village of the Siâmansuri, is a very dependent industry. The chicken and all their feed and medication is imported, i.e. "99 per cent of industry" (Sâlehi, 1373: 128).

One symbol of modernization of Iran is new housing. How is Varâmeen in this regard? Given that the previous rural and urban architecture of the area was reported to have been in a state of ruin at the end of the Qâjâr period, and secondly given that a large population was transhumant or lacked a settled tradition, and thirdly that there was multi-culturalism, thus there is not a single style in home building. The impression one gets today is even more incoherent. There is no definite well-defined architecture structure. What has been built today is according to pre-fabricated models of rural and urban housing and by personal whim. For the general usage of Varâmeen villagers three space units are missing which effect negatively their rural life: a large storage, a stable, and then a bread oven. Therefore, people have to buy their bread in the majority of villages, and they cannot keep a few cows to supply them with dairy products, and they do not have the space to store their agricultural products (Sâlehi, 1373: 118).

Identity of Various Ethnic Groups

Today Varâmeen township divided into three sections, Palašt, Central and Jâvâd Âbâd (compare with previous ethnic names) boasts of five towns: Mâmâzan, Palašt, Pišvâ, Qaraçak and Varâmeen. Mâmâzan and Palašt are in the northern industrial area, closest to the Tehran-Mašhad highway. Pišva is the religious centre. Varâmeen is the capital, important for government offices, business, health and educational centres. Qaraçak village which had only 23 households some 40 years ago and was sold for about $25000 at that time, has more than 200,000 people today. What is important about Qaraçak is that it is the closest town to southern Tehran. A new highway joins Tehran to Varâmeen and the railroad has stations in Qaraçak. This town has thus become an inexpensive suburb for Tehran.

Looking at the population of Varâmeen, we can see the following statistical trends: from 1966 to 1976, there is an increase of 19.3 per cent for the population of the township, while in 1966 the urban population was 20 per cent and in 1991 it has increased to 54.15 per cent of the population. There has also been an increase of 20 per cent (from 46 to 66%) in population born in other provinces: from 3 to 16 per cent from other provinces, and from other countries from 1.6 to 8.6 per cent (Sâlehi, 1373: 82, 87, & 102).

Given all the changes mentioned above, it is no exaggeration to say that Varâmeen has faced an upheaval. Now we have to scan through these changes and focus on our topic of ethnicity. In this panorama of Varâmeen, what does ethnicity mean?

To look at the ethnic question of a nation-wide basis we quote from Mojab and Hassanpour. They look critically at the perspective of the Pahlavis and even before them at Iran's Constitution and say:

> "The first Constitution (1906) depicted Iran as a nation-state with one official language, Persian, and a centralized political structure. Although the Constitutional Revolution was brutally suppressed in 1911, the formation of a nation-state based on the Persian language and national identity remained on the agenda. Even before the fall of the Qajar dynasty, the prime minister issued a decree in 1923 proscribing the use of non-Persian languages, Turkish and Kurdish, in the schools of Azerbâijan and Kurdistan. The Pahlavi monarchy (1925-79) combined extreme violence with extensive propaganda in order to build the nation-state of Iran, one nation, one language, and one centralized secular state . . . The state machinery, especially the educational system and the media was used to Persianize non-Persians . . . The Pahlavi state, especially under Reza Shah, conducted genocide, ethnocide and linguicide in order to Persianize the non-Persians" (1995: 231-2).

In this atmosphere where the religion, state law, and opposition's creed (Tudeh communist ideology) either tried to destroy ethnic traits or believed in their equality and did not insist on differences, how could we still find Lor, Kurd, Turk or Arab in Varâmeen? Today when we drive in the area, the name of stores, the family name of physicians posted on their doors, a number of street names clearly bear ethnic identity.

In comparing a list of terminology on kinship (48 words) that I have filled out with members of various language groups. I must admit that I had to ask to speak with a person of the older generation to get the terms right. People of even 35-40 years of age did not know all the corresponding terminology. The younger generation can understand, but they cannot speak the language of their ethnic group. The most complete list belongs to the Afqâns, the last immigrants to the area. Thus time is an important element in having people forget or not learn their language or dialect under the specific conditions noted above.

Also, the difference in clothing of various groups is a matter of memory. Grandparents who have passed away used to wear different clothing. It is rarely that we see an old Arab woman wrap a kerchief around her forehead and tie it in the back. Today's uniformity of women's clothing hides even more all differences. Men's clothing changed already earlier.

Concerning food, we get some shades of differences. If one has guests from outside the lineage, certain well-known Persian dishes are presented: the most common is chicken and rice and barberries (zerešk) with saffron. All over the country during the past ten years this has become the dish for guests: Quick to make and appreciated by young and old alike.

On the occasion of mourning ceremonies also one specific Persian dish (xorešte qeime) is widespread. What marks the food of ethnic groups shows in their private day to day meals and possibly their wedding dishes. It should be noted that for weddings only invited people stay for a meal, while for mourning ceremonies people come and stay for meals by their own volition. What limits their number is the abomination some people feel toward eating the deceased one's meal ("qazâ morde"). For mourning, people of different ethnic groups according to neighbourhood or other ways of acquaintanceship share tear shedding, but joyful ceremony of weddings is through invitation and lineage.

Religious mourning ceremonies have an ethnic centre, because most groups have their central shrine or they have a sanctified object (such as an "alam") within a shrine or simply a sanctified tree. On these occasions people of every ethnic group feel obliged to go to their own sanctuary. Every Thursday people who have had recent deaths in the family may go to their cemetery in very small groups. They may go to their local mosque also.

Thus an individual's mourning ceremony is attended by different ethnic groups, it is inter-ethnic. Sorrow is shared by everyone. But marriages and religious group ceremonies are intra-ethnic. The latter has lineage boundary, the former has not. Therefore, religious mourning ceremonies are the most popular inter-ethnic gatherings.

We noted above that the food on wedding ceremonies may have an ethnic identity, but for music apparently the Arabs of Varâmeen provided the musical ambiance for different ethnic groups. The Azerbâijân Turks had their own musicians, as did the Hadavand. The Tâjik of Varâmeen, just like the people of all central Iran who do not have honourable regard toward music, and have generally small Jewish groups to play music, have the tribal population or more exclusively the Arabs play at musical occasions. The dancing practised is either the kerchief dance for women or stick dance for men, performed by the young of various ethnic groups. Today tape recorders and cassettes have an important transmitting role to play.

Looking at the kinship relationship of the lineage of the individuals I interviewed, I noted at least 70 per cent of marriages within lineage and I heard often that they are marrying more and more with non-kin. This marriage with non-kin has brought lots of changes to the wedding ceremony and all that it entails, from the first proposal visits, till the last "pâgošâ", the invitation of the couple to her parent's house.

In mixed (inter-ethnic) marriages compromising is often observed. Whatever the variation, the basic theme of "xâstegâri" (the proposal ceremony), "aqd" (the religious civil ceremony), and "arusi" (the wedding, the most important part of which is the moving of bride's dowry to the groom's house and her own relocation, "Pâtaxti" (the gift giving ceremony by all relatives and friends), and "pâgošâ" is followed.

Why does marriage outside the ethnic group practiced? The example is set by those who succeed in education or in their profession, then through marriage with someone outside the kin, preferably living in a place considered better than Varâmeen (Karaj, Šemirân, Tehran) the man becomes settled at her place of residence and through her kinship structure gets support professionally. Through such marriage he expects a better life than if he had married a woman of his own kin. If a large number of men from a lineage practice such opportunistic marriages, it would logically follow that the rule of not giving a daughter outside the kin (but bringing wives within the kin), will be obliterated. Girls marry outside the lineage or even outside the ethnic group in order to prevent their celibacy. This means that marriage is not a private act of social and psychological importance only, it has political and economic function to perform. As a household cannot conceive of its success in a Varâmeen local scene anymore, it finds a broader perspective than its previous boundaries.

Do the individuals in a lineage of ethnic group help each other professionally? In Iran it is general practice to help close kin once one gets established somewhere or when one works in a stable profession. Do the Varâmeeni do this? I often hear "No!" The members of Kârxâne-Yusofi have succeeded in providing many experts in the medical profession and in banking, but this needed individual effort. One often hears that if one Varâmeeni succeeds in a profession, he would not invite close kin to follow. "If one Rasti arrives here, in a few years we find a cluster of them. But the Varâmeeni are 'qowm be bad'. They would not take a kin's hand for success." A Burbur Kurd who is experiencing his children leaving the household says.

"With progress and better conditions ("emkânât") ethnic traits

> disappear. Those who are educated speak in a different way. (He does not mean just language, but also topics of conversation and meaning.) The 'should's' and 'should not's' have also changed, differences have grown. When there are differences people just do not see each other anymore, because better conditions allow for separate lives. They do not work together, they do not need each other. Brothers do not see each other anymore."

An element from the indigenous way of life which helped to establish atomization of the family is disputes. Not only is it theoretically important to consider dispute and marriage as two mechanisms of social cohesion, it happens to be also the paramount trait to the Varâmeeni. On the first day of my visit to Varâmeen my informant who has served in the local armed forces and is also my student, asked me with some excitement, "Did you see those guys on the motor-cycle with the branches?" "Yes I did, what were they? Were they going to plant them?" "No," he says a bit wearily "they were sour cherry branches?" "Oh, were they?" And I remembered the phrase "The logic of sour cherry branches" meaning the power of the stronger man. Branches of the sour cherry tree ("âlbâlu") must be kept in every house. Today they may be hidden in closets, but they should be there in case a fight breaks out. These are the first weapons which are used. Afterwards, fights can graduate to knives and even to "qame", a sabre like metallic weapon used particularly on the day of "Âšurâ" (on the tenth day of the holy month of Moharram) in a few cities of Iran. They are ceremonious objects generally inherited by the family, and the person using them knows how to do so artfully, so that when he hits himself on the head, he bleeds, but nothing really dangerous happens to him. This is acted out in a procession, because of vows or in continuation of family oath, at dawn before sunrise. In Varâmeen "qame" is used as the most dangerous cold weapon in fights. The head of the bureau of justice in Varâmeen tells me that an enormous number of knives and "qame" were confiscated from the people coming to the courts. "But they do not stab to kill, they stab to win. Once there was a man who had dealt 47 cuts from neck to abdomen to his opponent. They can be very artful about it. This is a show of manliness for them." And we may add, thus not a crime. They fight to prove their power, their point of view, they fight to show their identity as member of their lineage.

Fights occur mostly over land, water and family honour. Before the land reform (1963) land owners were very often responsible for instigating discord, so that they could reign better. Today we have fewer fights over land and water, but more important than the issue is how a fight starts and who is responsible for it. Who hit the first blow is less important than the actual course of the fight and the show of supporters on each side plus the final victory. A young man whose father was killed when he was a child, took revenge in his adulthood. An automobile accident started a fight. "If the feeling of revenge gets takes root, there is no way out. They must fight it out. Then just a phone call or an errand to relatives, and they certainly come!"

What is the relationship of people who fight? "Strangers do not fight," so it is relatives who fight. In front of strangers and other ethnic groups one cannot lose face, but with relatives tensions give way to violence.

People of certain villages are known for getting into fights such as Šowrân, Jalil Âbâd, Rostam Âbâd, Tarand, Bâq Xavas, Javâd Âbâd, Toqân Kohnegel and the new city of Qaraçak. I heard it said many times that the rural Yazdi in the village of Asgar Abad have not even one suit at the courts. But the Kurds, Lors, Turks, and Arabs with their pastoral nomadic background and tradition of chivalry have all experienced disputes in profusion and profundity. People were always apologetic when it came to speaking about disputes. One reason for it is that if fighting is with lethal weapons, it is defined as a crime. Therefore, fighting as a means of defining identity and ethnicity becomes a negative instrument, a self-defeating one. Fights involve men who are generally between 15-25 years of age, and they may last from a few hours up to a generation, as mentioned above. An old Kangarlu admits that lots of disputes concerned honour, "One who is a stranger needs respect; if he feels disrespected he is touchy, he easily gets into fights to show his power and following." Those feelings are definitely related to the insecurity of a man within rivalrous ethnic groups. No wonder that Qaraçak with the largest Afqân population and Jalil Âbâd with Afqân and Irâqi population have higher crime rates. (No statistics are available, but this is based on statements from the officials of the bureau of justice in Varâmeen.)

How does a fight end? By the mediation of the elders ("riš sefid") or by the legal system or both. Noland writing on two villages close to Varâmeen says, ". . . the main factors in choosing the mode of settlement in these two Iranian communities is the kinship obligation" (1978: 198). An old respected man from the Hadâvand Lor says to me proverbially: "A broken arm is tied around one's neck" ("daste šekasteh vabâle gardaneh"), meaning "a lineage is responsible for a fight, it has to take care of its members."

The relationship between disputes and lineage brings the case of Afqâns into focus. Dispute-rich Qaraçak is nicknamed "Kâbol." Jalil Âbâd has an Afqân population. Although these immigrants are engaged in the most strenuous jobs in brick factories, in chicken and herding industries, they are regarded as tough men, who commit "criminal acts of profoundest degree," attested by the head of the Bureau of Justice. These immigrants are mostly bachelors or, to the utmost, have their nuclear family with them. They do not have the "ris sefid" of their lineage with them, thus they do not have elder members of their community present, individuals whom they would respect and follow in difficult circumstances.

Kinship structure has been a buffer to withstand the shocks of modernization. On "moneyscape" gaining importance (term more inclusive and parallel to Appadurai's, 1991) and all that is entails, would kinship structure which in turn is placed within an ethnic structure, still be able to exist? A retired high school teacher tells me, "Sharing in one religion, being educated under the same roof" softens people towards each other and destroys demarcating lines of ethnicity.

The example of Varâmeen shows us that inter-ethnic disputes are not great in frequency, but within ethnic groups (intra-ethnic) disputes are common. This exposes problems of identity, which could weaken family ties, while it is only within the kinship structure that one could get family support to pass crises of identity. But if disputes cause dispersion, then they lose their cohesive function; that is, if it is not the family but the legal system that ends them, and if the kinship relations do not become strengthened through their necessity in later professional life, then there would be pressure on them to be weakened.

In case of Varâmeen, we have seen that people do not rely on kinship as a way of obtaining a job and support in professional life, and thus people do not make an effort to incontestably keep family ties. Therefore, kinship is now losing importance more than what was reported in 1978 by Noland's research. The change is not yet complete, as we do not find the individual able totally to depend on his professional life. The fact that a Varâmeeni often has two jobs, one at a government civil office or in the military, along with some agricultural, herding or trading activity, this shows his attempt to keep both the traditional support and modern way of income. The same is true with dispute settlement: both kinship and court solution methods are being used.

As to relationship towards the environment, the ethnic groups were adjusted to their environment in particular endemic way: one through their pastoral nomadic way of existence, another through their rural life style. The changes in the environment are now decided by the central government through large projects such as the Latian Dam, or by changing pasture lands to national parks, or the polluting effects of brick, oil or sugar factories. These changes have affected the ethnic groups' relationship to the environment, but it is not possible to consider that without examining also government policies and actions in the given area. This makes it evident that any study of ethnic groups must be situational and contextual.

The Role of Imagination

Before the conclusion I would like to quote from Arjun Appadurai's brilliant article "Global Ethnoscapes: Notes and Queries for a Transnational Anthropology":

> "There is an urgent need to focus on the cultural dynamics of what is now called deterritorialization. This term applies not only to obvious examples such as transational corporations, and money markets, but also to ethnic groups, sectarian movements and political formations, which increasingly operate in ways that transcend specific territorial boundaries . . . what a new style of ethnography can do is to capture the impact of deterritorialization on the imaginative resources of lived experience, local experiences . . . the beginnings of an answer . . . lie in a fresh approach to the role of the imagination in social life" (1991: 192 & 196).

I find this element of imagination a necessary part of everyday life of a Varâmeeni, if not of an Iranian. The element of hope which has always been part of Iranian life-world is what can explain the life force during very difficult periods. Today I find it beautifully portrayed by an Afqân, a man from the Iranian plain, an immigrant the weakest person in the Varâmeen ethnic landscape. However, before considering him, let us give two other examples: One from a Lor and the other from a Tâjik. Mr. Širakvand, a Hadâvand Lor who retired after thirty years of teaching, started to learn calligraphy, at the age of 59. He soon proved to be an excellent calligrapher and he has set up a centres for teaching this art. He is very proud that one of his students, a 16 years old Hadâvand girl was able to receive a national prize. So we see that the medium of expression is national although kinship is there also.

Once Mr. S. Vaziri came to Tehran University. He heard two students speak with Varâmeeni accent. He asked them where they were from. They would not admit they were from Varâmeen. Later they confessed they were not proud of being Varâmeeni, because it did not give any particular positive identity to them. This incited Mr. Vaziri to unravel the history of Varâmeen, as related before, and not on ethnic groups. Now we come to our last example: Mr. Abdolqadir Rasin has a university degree and before coming to Iran was teaching literature at Herat University. He is in Iran ever since he came twelve years ago, living with his wife and four children in a small house. He leaves his four crates of fruits, which he sells daily, to his trusted neighbour and leads us to his house. The food he offers us, the clothing of the different members of his family, the furnishings of the rooms, even the names of his children are Iranian (Fereydun, Farangis, Parisâ and Behruz). He discusses in truly beautiful and refreshing terms and phrazes his experience as an immigrant. It is very difficult for him to be a fruit-seller, "I asked them to let me teach at a grade school" he says, and he was refused. He finds the crime rate among Afqâns so high before because the Iranian workers would not accept an Afqân worker. Now the rate has declined. He thinks the Afqân has now proved that he respects the law. He pays his bills on time. He has good social relations with landlords, neighbours, customers. For the Afqân, this area is very good because there is no class differences among people. They are all poor. He has his house, equipped with electricity, gas, telephone, and his children go to school. This is ideal for him to be able to have his children go to school. Education is the means of success for the next generation. His only hope is to return to Afqânistan ("del ânjâst"), but he thinks that he has gained a great deal as an immigrant: The Afqans came here with nothing. Now they are experts in construction, in stone and brick work, in agriculture and animal husbandry. At school the children are doing very well. It does not matter which power (ethnic or political) will reign in Afqânistan, "When we return, we will take our ideas and our art with us and with this we will rebuild our country."

Conclusion

In this paper we have focused on a small area of Iran which is a conglomeration of various ethnic groups of the country and thus can be a reflection of the whole. This city like so many others in Iran, has a nexus of an ancient city. The rest is a multitude of previous rural, and pastoral nomadic populations who have settled to create a new urban form. These populations define themselves through their history, subsistence and through their culture of everyday life. These elements join to form a whole picture of ethnic identity. Imagination to build a better future needs a sense of pride in history of geographical location. In everyday life this belonging to a particular place is portrayed in forms of behaviour at particular events, specially in ceremonies and in disputes. Better future is a positive incentive for all people specially those in situations of distress.

The people of Varâmeen as people of many areas in Iran and the world have the experience of deterritorialization. Here we see this situation most clearly portrayed by the Afqan who is the latest arrival in the area. He has a sense of shame in regard to this compatriots who do what is illegal, which is seen magnified in the area to set them aside as an ethnic group: it causes a feeling of racism against them. In self-defense, he is very conservative and law-abiding in his own attitudes to prove himself to the host area as a responsible citizen. He is very thankful for his present way of life as he compares himself to his compatriots in Afqanistan. He looks forward to a future when he and his children will build a better home-country due to accomplishment during displacement.

The deterritorialized share a common imagination for the future, as more and more people are living within this category. It remains to be seen with rural exodus, with sedentarization and immigration to urban areas, how large a portion of urban living today in Iran can be categorized under this rubric and what role imagination will play in pushing people forward in their multiple distressful situations.

REFERENCES

Amini, Mohammad. 1368. *Tarixe ejtema'yi-e varâmeen dar dowre-ye qâjâr* (Social Histor, of Varâmeen during the Qajar Period), Tehran: Sahami am.

Appadurai, Arjun. 1991. "Global Ethnoscapes: Notes and Queries for a Transnational Anthropology", in R.G. Fos (ed.), *Recapturing Anthropology*. Santa Fe, School of American Research Advanced Seminar Series.

Avesta. 1370. (reprint) vol. 2. Tehran: Morvarid Publisher.

Cahen, Michel. 1994. *Ethnicite Politique*, L'Harmattan.

Edgerton, Robert B. 1965. "Cultural' vs. 'Ecological' Factors in the Expression of Values, Attitudes, and Personality Characteristics", *American Anthropologist*, 67.

Ekvall, Robert B. 1983. *Fields on the Hoof.* Waveland Press.

Ettehadieh, M. 1993. "The Xalese of Varameen", *IJMES*, 25. (England).

Farhang-e Abâdi â-ye Kesvar (Iran's Rural Census). 1367. *Sarsomâriye Omumiye Kesar.* Tehran Province, Vol. 1&2.

Field, Henry. 1343. *Contributions to the Anthropology of Iran* (original edition 1939) Persian edition. Tehran: Ebne Sina Publisher.

Mardux Ruhani, B. 1371. *Tarixe Mashâhire Kord.* Tehran: Sorush.

Mojab, S. and A. Hassanpour. 1995: "The Politics of Nationality and Ethnic Diversity," in S. Rahman (ed.), *Iran After the Revolution.* London.

Orywal, E. 1988. "Conceptual and Methodological Considerations", in *Le Fait Ethnique en Iran et en Afghanistan*, Paris,

Salehi, Xadije Homaye. 1373. A Survey of Varameen from an Agricultural Perspective, doctorate thesis, Azad University.

Tapper, R. 1988. "Ethnicity, Order and Meaning in the Anthropology of Iran and Afghanistan," in *Le Fair Ethnique en Iran et en Afghanistan*, Paris,

Tavahodi, Kalim-Ollah. 1359. *Historical Exodus of the Kurd.*

Vaziri, Sa'id. 1358. *Tarixe Varâmeen* (The History of Varameen). Varâmeen.

Zeide Abolhasan. 1374. *Ahsân ol-Kebâr*, edited by Vaziri, Sa'id, Varâmeen: Azad University Press.

N.B.: The Iranian years in A.D. in order they appear in the "References" are: 1368=1989/ 1370=1991/1367=1988/1343=1964/1371=1992/1373=1994/1359=1980/1358=1979/ 1374=1995.

SIX

THE TRIBES OF INDIA
Patterns and Problems of Identity

MANIS KUMAR RAHA

India is a vast country with different ethnic situations, diverse cultural patterns, different religious faiths and varied world views and idealogies. Any one who travels from Kashmir to Kanyakumari or from Rann of Kutch in the West to Arunachal Pradesh in the north-eastern realize it fully (Raha and Ghosh, 1998: 18). The people here—"belong to different castes, creeds, sects, and religious groups. They have different social systems, languages, and cultural patterns. They survive with different livelihood patterns, different social orders, world views and with multiple religious faiths" (Raha, 1996: X).

Undoubtedly, India is a country of strong heterogeneity of languages, religions and ideologies (Raha and Ghosh 1998: 18).

But in spite of these diversities the people of India have been living together and interacting with one another for centuries. These contacts with one another since times immemorial have helped them to establish a vast network of relations and strong bonds basd on faith and oneness. Though various invasions in different periods of history massacred the life of the Indians, still those added new diversities to the already existing ones. These unique diversities of India most probably prompted Pandit Jawaharlal Nehru to state that "the diversity of India is tremendous; it is obvious, it lies on the surface and anybody can see it. It concerns itself with physical appearances as well as with mental habits and traits" (1986: 61).

> "No doubt these unmatched diversities have made India a unique one in the global arena, but these diversities are superficial as there lies an under current of unity everywhere. Here in spite of great diversities the

Indians are found to live in the midst of harmony having both cohesions and conflicts. Here diversities are found to co-exist with unities" (Raha 1996: X).

India with an area of 3,287,263 sq. kms has accommodated a total of 844,324,222 individuals (excluding the population of Jammu & Kashmir), according to 1991 census. Of the total population 8 per cent are Scheduled Tribes and 16.73 per cent are Scheduled Castes. The country has allowed 4635 communities (including 3742 castes and 427 Scheduled Tribes) to live in harmony in its 26 states and 6 union territories. This big country has 190 religions and 1652 mother tongues.

This vast tract of land has varied ecological zones. From the snow clad rugged unkept mountanious region to the coastal areas, from deserts in the west to the islands in the seas, from plains and plateau areas to deep forests, almost all sorts of ecological conditions prevail here. And Indians are found to live in all such varied ecological set–ups. There are places where there is heavy rainfall which often creates flood. Simultaneously, places are there where people do not experience any rainfall for years. Places are there also where people live at a temperature much below zero at least during half of the years, at the same time in some places they get exhausted due to scorching sun during major part of the year. It reveals that people of India live in a diverse ecological and environmental conditions.

Like the varied ecological conditions, different racial elements are also found to present here. All the four major racial elements, viz. caucasoid, mongoloid, australoid and negroid, have been accommodated in this country. While the mongoloids are found in the northern, north-western and north-eastern fringes of the country, the negroids are found in the Bay Islands. The caucasoids are mostly found to inhabit in the northern and western parts and the australoids in the central and southern India.

As already stated there are 1652 languages and dialects in India of which 1549 are of Indian origin and the rest are non-Indian languages. These languages and dialects as spoken by the people of India belonging to four major linguistic groups like Indo-Aryan, Dravidian, Mundari and Tibeto-Burman. The Indo-Aryan languages are spoken mostly in the northern and north-western part of India. Dravidian is spoken mostly in central, southern and eastern parts of India. Mundari language is the mother tongue of many groups of central and eastern India. Many people living in Himalayan region speak in Tibeto-Burman language. Of course, there are some other minor languages and also some languages which have not been properly classified.

Similarly, like the ecological diversities we also find cultural heterogeneity in this sub-continent. People remain engaged in different occupations from simplest hunting and food gathering to the very complex profession. While the Jarawa and the Sentinalese in the Bay Islands hunt, fish and gather honey, fruits, roots, tubers, etc. to fulfil their hunger, the Gujjar and the Gaddi in the Himalayas move with flocks of sheep, goat or cattle to earn their livelihood. The shifting cultivation, terrace cultivation and settled cultivation are found to be practised by different people. Similarly, many people are found to reside in the urban centres or industrial towns to remain engaged in modern complex professions.

The people of India also have varied types of social organization. Both matrilineal and patrilineal societies are found here. Different marriage forms, kinship systems, rules of inheritance, ritual patterns and so on co-exist in Indian soil.

The movement of people from one place to another by way of trade and business, pilgrimage, invasions, war, calamities, etc. has given them chance to come in close contact with their brethren in other parts since the dawn of civilization. These movements have increased in the modern era. These have no doubt set in the cultural flow enabling people of our country to imbibe cultural traits one another.

In spite of all these diversities and unity, there lies some conflicting situations in India. One such situation is in relation to the identity of various ethnic groups of India. In the following pages I have discussed in brief the question of the tribal identity.

The Tribal Population in India

In India there are 67,758,380 tribals forming 8.08 per cent of the total population of the country (1991 Census). They were 6.82 per cent of Indian population in 1971 and 7.76 per cent in 1981 census. These tribal people are distributed in almost all states and union territories except Haryana, Punjab, Chandigarh, Delhi and Pondicherry. In these states and union territories they are found to be settled in varied number; somewhere they form the majority while in some other places they are insignificant in number. The largest number of the tribals are found in Mizoram where they constitute 94.75 per cent of the total population. Similarly, in Lakshadweep they have formed almost the whole population (93.15%). They are in overwhelming majority in Nagaland (87.70%), Meghalaya (86.52%), Arunachal Pradesh (63.65%) and Dadra and Nagar Haveli (78.99%). But in some states and union territories they share a small part of the total population. For example in Uttar Pradesh the Scheduled Tribes form only 0.20 per cent of the total population. In the same way in Tamil Nadu (1.03%), Kerala (1.10%), Himachal Pradesh (4.22%), Karnataka (4.26%), West Bengal (5.59%) and also in some other states and union territories they are found in very small number. The tribal population is smallest in Goa where only 376 of them are found to live.

Analyzing the position of the Scheduled Tribes of different states and union territories in terms of the total Scheduled Tribe population of India, it is seen that Madhya Pradesh has the highest number of the Scheduled Tribe population forming 22.73 per cent of the total tribal population of India. Maharashtra (10.80%), Orissa (10.38%), Bihar (9.78%), Gujarat (9.10%), Rajasthan (8.08%) and West Bengal (5.62%) come in the following order. Some of the states and union territories where Scheduled Tribes form overwhelming majority of the total population, actually contribute very small part to that of the total Scheduled Tribes of India. For example the Scheduled Tribes of Mizoram form 0.96 per cent, Lakshadweep 0.07 per cent, Nagaland 1.56 per cent, Meghalaya 2.24 per cent, Arunachal Pradesh 0.81 per cent and Dadra and Nagar Haveli 0.16 per cent of the total Scheduled Tribe population in India.

As already said there are 427 Scheduled Tribes in India. Some of these tribes are quite large in number such as the Gond, Bhil, Santal, Oraon, Munda, while some others have very low population, viz. the Onge, Great Andamanese, Toto, Raji.

Ethnic and Ethnicity

Webster's Third New International Dictionary (1967) defines the term "ethnic" as the "community of physical and mental traits possessed by the members of a group as a product of their common cultural tradition or indicates the racial, cultural ties of peoples with specific group of exotic primitive culture." Ethnic has been referred to as the group of people having common cultural characteristics in Charles Winick's *Dictionary of Anthropology* (1964: 193). Barth (1969) identifies ethnic as categories of ascription, the identification of which is made by the actors themselves. The members of an ethnic group generally identify themselves on the basis of certain bio-genetical and cultural features which distinguish themselves from the others (Danda, 1991: 51).

> "On the other hand ethnicity "stands for the ethnic quality or affiliation of a group bearing different meaning in varied situational contexts . . . Thus, race/sub-race, tribe/sub-tribe, caste/sub-caste, class/sub-class, language/dialect, religion/faith, sect/sub-sect, territoriality, nationality, degree of aristocracy, and at times levels of techno-cultural efficiency have all been used sometimes singularly or in various combinations to delineate ethnicity" (Danda, 1991: 51).

Types of Tribal Identity

As already stated that India in her vast tract of land with varied ecological niches has given shelter to a large number of tribal groups. The basic characters of these groups is "the peculiar system of endogamy combined with exogamy, running through the whole system" (Chattopadhyay, 1994: 108). Each tribal group has its own identity by which the members are known to themselves and/or to the outsiders. But often it is seen that some of the tribal groups have multiple identities or their identity is overlapped by some other identity imposed on them. With the heavy migration of population from one place to another, people of one place come in contact with those of the other places. Again a number of invasions have forced the tribal groups of a place to come in contact with the invaded force and later on get new identity from the invaded force. Similarly, the foreign rulers imposed some new identity on some of the ethnic groups. In the same line, movement of people from one place to another for various purposes, viz. pilgrimage, migration for livelihood, bring people from one place closer to those of another. For all these reasons people having their traditional ascribed identity which they acquired by birth, also get additional identity. "There are instances of the identity being assigned to groups or individuals by some extraneous agencies like authority in power. Such identity may or may not agree to the peoples' self ascription of the same" (Danda, 1991: 51-52). In certain cases the imposed identity has become more important and dominant one, and thereby overshadowing the original identity of the groups. As such many communities are now known by the imposed identity given to them by the outsiders. "Possibility of people's switching over from one ethnic identity to another even in day to day life is not only common but frequent" (Danda, 1991: 52).

Against the backdrop the identities of the tribal groups may be classified into the following categories:

Ascribed Identity

All ethnic groups have their own identity which was traditionally ascribed to them. With this traditional identity they have been introduced to the people outside their own group. For example the Rabha are known by the term the Rabha. The Koli are known as the Koli. Similarly, the Garo are known as the Garo and the Sherpa as the Sherpa. The Manikfan of Lakshadweep are referred to as the Manikfan.

Self-Imposed Identity

As already said some tribal groups have acquired a new name and identified them by that new name for some reasons. They have identified themselves by a new name and like that people far and near also identify them with this newly acquired name. A section of the Munda, a Scheduled Tribe inhabiting

South 24-parganas, adopted "Murari", presumably a caste name for their section and recorded this new identity in the official documents mainly for the interest of easy transfer of land. It may be said that there is no separate community known as Murari in this region, and that those Munda people who recorded their name as the Murari in certain documents, were by no means different from the other Mundas in the same area (Danda and Raha, 1962: 77).

Similarly, in certain areas of West Bengal the Kumarbhag Paharia, after suppressing their own ethnic identity, started claiming themselves to be the Malpaharia, a Scheduled Tribe, in order to gain certain constitutional facilities. The Mikir of Assam now preferred themselves to be called as the "Karbi" which they have adopted for the fulfilment of their socio-political aspirations. In the same way, the Abor of Arunachal Pradesh call themselves Adi (Hill people) and like to be identified by that name as they consider their previous identity (Abor) as a derogatory one. The Dafla for the same reason discarded their earlier identity and accepted a new name "Nishing" meaning hill people (Raha and Mahato, 1985: 19-20)

Imposed Identity

The movement of people in different forms bring a section of the people nearer to another. And once they come closer to one another some of the groups give new names to identify some other communities who in a later period of time come to be identified by the new names given to them. For example, the Santal prefer to refer themselves as Hor but the non-Santals call them as the Santal, and they are quite well known by this term (Danda, 1991: 52).

Similar is the case with the Mishing. Though they prefer to be identified by the name Mishing, yet they are popularly known by the imposed name Miri given to them by the plains-Assamese (Das, 1989: 201).

The present day Jarawa of the south and middle Andamans have their own traditional name. The "Jarawa" is not the original community name. According to Radcliffe-Brown (1964: 10-15) the word "Jarawa" is apparently derived from the *Aka-bea* language of the Great Andamanese which means "stranger to the country". At present they are popularly known by this term and their original identity has not been known to others.

The Lhota normally call themselves "Kyon". However, the Assamese have given them the name "Lhota" and they are popularly known by the name given to them by the Assamese (Das, 1989: 209).

Spatial and Territorial Identity

Often many tribal groups in India have got their identity from the region or the place they inhabit. This spatial or territorial identity become dominant, and their own ethnic identity becomes secondary. The inhabitants of Kinnaur are known as the Kinnaura or Kinner and it includes the Khosia (or Rajput or Kanet), the Lohar, the Badhi or Auras, the Koli and the Nangalu (Raha and Mahato, 1985: 19; Raha, 1987: 330; 1995: 81). Same is the case with the Jaunsaries of Jaunsar-Bowar region of Dehra Dun district, Uttar Pradesh. Danda (1991: 52) believes that the Santal is a territorial identity of a group of people.

Multiple Identity

The perception of identity of a group varies according to time and space (Danda, 1991: 52). Further a group may have different identities at the same time. For example a citizen of India could be a Bengali, a Hindu, a Kayastha and so on (Danda, 1991: 52).

The Nagesia of Madhya Pradesh who are known as the Kishan in Bihar and the Lambadi in Andhra Pradesh have been popularly known as *Banjara* in Maharashtra and Gujarat (Danda, 1991: 57).

The Malasar of Palghat (Kerala) and Coimbatore (Tamil Nadu) are also referred to as Malsar, Malayar and Malasir. Thurston (1909) has mentioned Malai Malasar (who live on hills), Malasar (who lives on slopes and plains) and Kadir and Eravallen as groups among the Malasar (Singh, 1994: 730).

The Sugali, a pastoral tribal community of Andhra Pradesh are also known as Lambadi and Sugalollu. Their counterparts in Telangana and coastal Andhra Pradesh are referred to as the Lambadi.

The Barda of Maharashtra and Gujarat are also known as the Barea Bhil, and sometimes as the Khandeshi Bhil. They have also other names such as the Lunia or Lahiliya Bhil.

The Hakkipikki, a trapper and seller tribe of Karnataka also call themselves as the Raj Pardhi. They are also known as the Vahgri in Gujarat. The people in Nilgiri call them the Guddi Bethe. In the Hindi and Hindusthani speaking regions, this tribe is known as Mel-Shikari (Mann, 1980: 6).

The Oraons who migrated to Sundarban areas (southern most part of Bengal) to clear the virgin forests about hundred and fifty years ago and settled there, are also known as the "Sardar". The local people gave them this name.

Constitutional Identity

With the promulgation of the Constitution of India in 1950, a number of ethnic groups have also got some new identity. Many of them have been identified as the Scheduled Tribes, while a large number as the Scheduled Castes. Almost all the states and union territories have a list of Scheduled Tribes and/or Scheduled Castes. So a group marked as the Scheduled Tribe in a state and/or union territory may also have the same constitutional status in some other states and/or union territories. On the other hand, there may be some other groups marked as the Scheduled Tribes only in one state or union territory even though they are found to inhabit in some other states or union territories without being scheduled.

Common Identity

Sometimes two or more tribal groups are known by a common name. That means two or more tribes are identified by a common name. Here the case of the Sugali of Andhra Pradesh may be cited. These people are also known as the Lambadi. Again the Nagesia in Madhya Pradesh are also known as Lambadi in Andhra Pradesh (Danda, 1991: 57).

Identity Markers

Each and every ethnic group or community of this world has its own identity, a name, by which it maintains its ethnic boundary. Every ethnic group tries to keep a stable identity as it helps maintaining the solidarity and integrity of the ethnic group. Sometimes it is difficult to maintain a stable identity and also group boundary by some ethnic groups as some disruptive forces try to destabilize the ethnic group and its boundary. However, they are some markers for ethnic identity, some important markers are as follows:

1. *Ascribed:* Every ethnic group in this world has a name which gives the ethnic group a definite identity. The Raji has the name Raji, the Garo has Garo, the Meithei has the name Meithei, the Baiga has Baiga, the Keer has Keer, the Dhodia has Dhodia, the Bhunjia has Bhunjia and so on. These ethnic groups/tribal groups are identified by the name they have ascribed.
2. *Racial:* In India the ethnic groups may be divided into caucasoid, mongoloid, negroid and australoid. Ethnic groups living in northern and northwestern parts of India may be grouped under caucasoid. People living in the Himalayan region such as the Bhotia, Lepcha, Jad, Kinnaura, Khamti, Khampa and others are mongoloids. The

four tribal groups living in the Bay Islands namely the Great Andamanese, the Onge, the Jarawa, and the Sentinalese belong to negroid group. A large number of tribal groups living in central, eastern and southern India come under the australoid racial stock. Some of them are the Santal, Munda, Korwa, Kodaku, Nagesia, Gond, Bhil and others.

3. *Cultural:* Culture is one of the basic elements by which an ethnic group can be identified. Each and every ethnic group has its own cultural characteristics which are not commonly found among other ethnic groups. In this regard culture of an ethnic group may be considered as the identity formation factor. In fact when the question of identity of an ethnic group is examined, one looks into the culture of that group and by co-relating various cultural traits including language, religion and world view, one traces out the identity of that group. On the other hand, when a group loses its culture due to contact with a mega culture or by some other ways, and adopts cultural traits from another culture, the former may be stamped as losing its cultural identity. They may have kept their identity by the name only. This is also true for certain tribal groups of our country. For example the Rabhas of Western Duars due to their long contact with the neighbouring Rajbansi, the most dominant caste group of the area, and due to their strong aspiration to enter into the caste fold, have adopted the "culture" of the Rajbansis replacing majority of their cultural traits. It is now very difficult to distinguish the culture of the Rajbansis and Rabha. Through a definite reformative movement for entering into the Hindufold which started as early as 1939, the Rabhas adopted Hinduism after performing a number of *yagna* and other associated rituals. They imbibed the local Rajbansi culture and started employing Brahmin and Barbar. (Raha *et al.*, 1978: 50-55; Raha, 1973: 102). On the other hand, groups of Oraons who were brought to Sunderban (southern fringe of Bengal) about one hundred and fifty years ago to clear the virgin forests and then allowed to settle there, have adopted the culture of the local people by giving up their age old customs and manners. Now it is difficult to distinguish their culture from that of the local caste groups who have definitely developed a regional culture having many distinct features not available outside the region. The Organs and some other tribal groups migrated from Chataragpur areas have gradually accepted this regional culture by abandoning their own cultural traits as a part of their survival strategy (Das and Raha, 1963; Raha, 1965: 361-368).

On the other hand, the Santals of the same region have still retained their cultural identity even in very adverse situations because of their strong sense of solidarity.

4. *Territorial*: Territory is also an important identity marker. A large number of ethnic groups in India have accepted the spatial identity. The people of Kinnaur district of Himachal Pradesh who belong to different ethnic groups, are known as the Kinnaura or Kinner. The Nicobarese have obtained this identity as they live in the Nicobar group of islands. The Sentinalese are known as the Sentinalese because they live in north Sentinnel Island of Andaman and Nicobar Islands. The people of Pangi valley in Chamba district, Himachal Pradesh are known as the Pangawala. The Khasi and the Garo are identified by the area they live (Khasi and Garo Hills respectively). The Ladakhi have received their identity from the area (Ladakh) they inhabit. Being inhabitants of the Jaintia Hills, the Jaintia are identified by the name Jaintia (Deb Roy, 1984: 81-82) The Kadar of Kerala are known as Kadar because they are forest dwellers (Kadar = forest). Thus it is seen that identification can also be made from the place of original habitation.
5. *Historical/Mythological Figure:* Sometimes a community is identified by the name of some historical or mythological figure. The Chaudhri or Choudhra of Gujarat call themselves as the Ravalia after the last Rajput ruler Patel Raval. The Karwar of Madhya Pradesh on the other hand, believe that their tribal identity has been derived from Kaurava of *Mahabharata,* and so they consider themselves as the descendants of one of the Kauravas (Singh, 1994: 484). The Saunta of Madhya Pradesh trace their origin to a mythological king, Balak Lodha, son of Burha Saunta. The Pando of Madhya Pradesh and Maharashtra consider themselves as the descendants of the Pandavas of *Mahabharata.*
6. *Common Ancestry:* In North-East India some tribes took up a new identity because they had a common ancestry. The Zemeis, the Liangmeis and the Rongmeis believed in a myth of their common ancestry. Following this myth, the leaders of these three groups got the opportunity to combine themselves into a single group and took a new identity Zeliangrong, by prefixing each of these three group names (Das, 1989: 199).
7. *Profession:* In India there are tribal groups who got their name from the profession they were engaged in. The Bakarwal are a pastoral nomadic Scheduled Tribe of Jammu and Kashmir. The term Bakarwal has been derived from the word Bakriwale, meaning herder and rearer of sheep and goat (Singh, 1994: 82) or from the word *Bakri-Charana* meaning grazing of goats (Maity, 1992: 344). Similarly, the Lohara

or Lohra, a Scheduled Tribe of West Bengal and Bihar, derived their name from the word *Loha* that means iron. Professionally they are blacksmiths. The Kisan got their tribal name from their profession (cultivation). In the same way the Halba derived their identity from *Hal* meaning plough. Their primary occupation is agriculture (Singh, 1994: 384-385).

8. *Natural Objects:* Some of the tribal groups have derived their names from different geographical bodies like hill or mountain, river, forest, etc. The Gadaba who are found to reside in Orissa, Andhra Pradesh and Madhya Pradesh, have derived their identity from the river Godavari (Singh, 1994: 264). The Dhanka, a Scheduled Tribe of Gujarat, Maharashtra and Rajasthan, derived their name from the Persian word *"dang"* meaning hill. They are hill dwellers *(ibid:* 232). Similarly, the Garo prefer to be identified as the Mande or Achik which means hillmen or hill dwellers. The Dhokpa or Brokpa of Jammu and Kashmir have been given the said name as they were grass land dwellers (Dhokpa-grass land). The Korwa of Madhya Pradesh have derived their tribal name from Kodera, a particular species of tree.

Problems of Identity: Some Cases

Ethnic identity is not always a stable one. It sometimes changes and group takes up a new identity for some specific reasons. In most of the cases the transformation of identity of any ethnic group rests on the strategy of convenience (Danda, 1991: 120) and also their strong desire for achieving certain social status or facilities or benefits. This often makes the question of identity highly intricate, if not multiple *(ibid:* 120) Therefore "for determination of ethnic identity, a close attention to the basic processes of identity transformation seems essential since the question of identity as a whole depends upon the nature and character of processes" *(ibid:* 120).

I would like to cite some cases below which will give evidence that for certain reasons some ethnic groups changed their original ethnic identity and took up a new one.

The Munda-Murari Case

In West Bengal and possibly in most of the States and Union Territories the alienation of land of the tribal people is a serious problem. In order to check the alienation of tribal land and to safeguard the interest of the tribals the

Bengal Tenancy Act 1885 (modified varsion of 1954) Chapter-VIII AP-140 provides that "no transfer by an aboriginal land holder *raiyat* or under-*raiyat* of his right in his tenure or holding or in any portion thereof by private sale, gift or will, mortgage, lease or any contract or agreement shall be valid to any extent" (Raha, 1964: 22). In order to sale the land to other tribals prior permission of the Collector is essential. Now some persons of the District of 24-Parganas, West Bengal, after declaring themselves as belonging to the Murari, Nagbansi, Murari or Kompat Murari community, have manipulated the situation in their favour. Though the names of these communities were not included in the notified list, yet these names are really synonyms of the Munda which is a notified tribe for the purpose of this Act" *(ibid:* 22).

The question of identity of these people with the Munda was of prime importance since it involved right over the land of a number of persons. After thorough study of the published records, collection of evidences from different areas, scrutiny of documentary evidences, study of the social customs relating to migration and social organization with reference to genealogies, language tests, etc., it was found that these people who declared themselves as the Murari with or without the additional appellations like Kompat and Nagbansi, were none but the Munda. Risley considers Murari as a corruption form of Mundari, sometimes used outside Chotanagpur as synonym for the Munda (1891: 109), again both the term Nagbanshi (Risley, 1891: 121) and Kompat (Dalton, 1872: 165) are title of the Munda. The Munda on their migration to the Sunderban about hundred and fifty years ago to clear the virgin forest and then settled there, considered Murari as a derogatory term during some part of their life in the Sundarban. So in order to retain the social prestige "the synonym Murari was suppressed." After independence they dug up the same derogatory term for the easy transfer of land. Later on realizing the facilities under Constitution of India granted to the Scheduled Tribe and also the provision under the said Bengal Tenancy Act they were willing to get back the land already sold. And therefore, this group of people changed their identity more than once for some specific reasons.

The Kinnaur Case

Kinnaura is one of the eight Scheduled Tribes found in Himachal Pradesh. They have their concentration in the district of Kinnaur. Again some other ethnic groups of this district like the Lohar, the Badhi or Aras, the Koli and the Nangalu have been declared as the Scheduled Castes. Though by Kinnaura it normally means the Kanet or Khas or the Rajput, still all the inhabitants of Kinnaur including the Scheduled Tribes and Scheduled Castes are considered as the Kinnaura. At the beginning there was a big confusion as the Koli, the Lohar, the Badhi and the Nangalu, who were declared as Scheduled Castes, also claimed facilities of the Scheduled Tribe as they wanted them to be considered as the Kinnaura being the inhabitants of the district of Kinnaur. The confusion as to whether they would be considered as the Scheduled Tribes or Scheduled Castes continued for a long time. In some cases they were treated as the Scheduled Tribes and in some other as Scheduled Castes (Raha and Mahato, 1985; Kapoor, 1971).

This confusion also puzzled the government officials who eventually stated that, all the non-migrant natural inhabitants of these two districts (Lahaul-Spiti and Kinnaur) can claim themselves as the Scheduled Tribes under Government of India, Ministry of Home Affairs Scheduled Castes and Scheduled Tribes List Modification under 1956." (Singh, 1972: 2).

Therefore, an individual could either return himself/herself as a member of Scheduled Tribe or as a Scheduled Caste. The same authority felt that decrease of Scheduled Caste population from 1961 (11,133) to 1971 (9669) and increase of Scheduled Tribe population from 1961 (25,667) to 1971 (34,090) may be one of the reasons for this.

The Rabha Case

The Rabhas have been recognised as a Scheduled Tribe in West Bengal since 1959. Prior to 1959 they were considered as one of the Scheduled Castes of West Bengal. Interestingly enough in 1931 census they were regarded as Depressed Class (Porter, 1933: 239). Again in 1911 Census they were recorded as a Backward Class (O'Malley, 1913: 183). Thus it is seen that statutory identity of the Rabha fluctuated from time to time.

Again the Rabha being a matrilineal group were also confused as the Garo. Sunders in his settlement report mistook the Rabha as the Garo (1895: 72-79).

The Purum Case

The Purum "one of the most widely discussed communities in anthropological literature" (Danda, 1991: 105) belong to the old Kuki Tribe. McCulloch considered the Purum as an independent tribe belonging to the Kuki stock though he could see the resemblance of the Purum with the Chote in physical appearances and in some cultural traits (1858: 64-65). But Brown treated them as a sub-division of the Kom tribe (1873: 53-55).

When T.C. Das studied the Purum in 1936 he found 305 Purums. But in 1951 and 1961 their strength got reduced to 43 and 82 respectively. 1971 census could not record any Purum. In 1975 when Das Gupta undertook a study he could trace out the significant reduction in the Purum population and increase of the Chote population from 1951 to 1975. While in 1931 the

Purum population was 305 and the Chote population was 250, in 1951 the Purums reduced to 43 and Chote increase to 695. In 1961 Purum population was 82 but the Chote was 1035. In 1971 and 1975 no Purum was found but the Chote population increased to 1905 and 1464 respectively. The reason has clearly been studied by Das Gupta and others:

> "To come back to the Purum case, we know that all the Purum villages have this prefix because Purum is the type of land in which they inhabit though the villagers call themselves as Chote. To the Meitai or any village group, Chote or Purum Tampak may be known as only Purum, and this might have resulted in confusion for others" (1985: 53).

But Danda was not quite satisfied with the arguments given by Das Gupta. He thinks:

> "Although some of the observers of the Purum situation raised issues like self-identity and ascribed identity and tended to argue that Purum is actually a label assigned to the Chote by others, there cannot be any denial of the fact that Purum as such as a concept exists" (1991: 115).

Considering various factors responsible for the change of identity of the Purums, Danda writes:

> "Thus the self-perpetuating Purum system when exposed to various solidarity movements, the Purums should not normally have any difficulty in assuming new identities without discarding the old" (1991: 117).

Mishing-Miri Case

The Mishing are one of the major tribal groups of upper Assam. Though they identify themselves as the "Mishing" but the non-tribal plains Assamese call them by the term "Miri" (Pegu, 1956: 4 *cf* Mipun, 1993: 17; Bhandari, 1992: 23). So they are popularly known as the Miri. The term Miri has been used for the Mishing by the Assamese since they came in contact with them in the remote past (Bhandari, 1992: 23). They are also listed in the list of Scheduled Tribes as the Miri. The term Miri has, however, caused some confusion in the proper identification of the Mishing who regard it to be a misnomer (Bhandari, 1984: 79-80). The term "Miri" normally used to designate other tribal communities inhabiting the hills of the north-east frontier regions between the Gorge of the Subansiri river and the Siyang river in Arunachal Pradesh (Das, 1987: 202). Even the ethnic groups like the Sarak, Panibotia, Tarbotia, Ghasi, and the Ghaghasis were also accepted as Hill Miri (Dalton,

1949: 423). But these ethnic groups are closely related to the Dafla rather than to the Mishing, the latter being close to the Adi group.

Conflicting Situation

It is seen that each and every ethnic group has an identity and it tries to retain it. However, under some compelling situations this identity often varies. (i) Some ethnic groups change their traditional identity for some reasons, (ii) some other shift their identity temporarily for some other reasons and then again revert back to their traditional identity, (iii) and the members of some other groups retain their traditional identity ignoring the allurement for changing their identity for certain benefits or pressure. The Rabhas of North Bengal have identified themselves with the Rajbansis for getting a position in the local Hindu caste hierarchy; the Oraons of Sundarban have accepted a new identity as the Sardars for the same reason. A group of the Panr declared them as the Munda in order to avail Scheduled Tribe facilities. For the same reason a group of the Kalindi Dom, a sub-caste of the Doms, declared themselves as the Oraon (Raha, 1965: 21-24).

With the spread of literacy and also activities of the Christian missionaries some tribes started considering themselves as superior to others. Therefore, in order to level them distinct from others, those tribes accepted a new identity rejecting their age old identity. The Lushai are one such tribe.

> "The Lushais are the first who became conscious of such a situation and disassociated themselves from the blanket term "Kuki" by adopting a new name "Mizo". During a course of time the Mizo became a prestigious and powerful group which attracted some other groups like the Hmar Poi, Relte, Lakher and also to some extent the Darlong to join their fold" (Sree Krishan, 1995: 274).

As an example of the second group we may cite the case of the Bhotia of Munsiari Tehsil of Pithoragarh district. Till mid-fifties they went on imbibing some cultural traits from the local Kumaoni Hindus in order to secure a place in the caste hierarchy. But after mid-fifties when they could realize that the Scheduled Tribes get a number of benefits, and they were a Scheduled Tribe, they started giving up many Hindu cultural traits which they imbibed from the local Hindu groups in their process of Hinduization. Now they are reverting back to their traditional way of life, recovering many traditional norms which they once gave up or rejected. This revivalism of cultural identity is due to their need for statutory facilities (Raha and Das, 1981).

To give another example of the Second category we may cite the case of some old Kuki tribes like the Aimal, Anal, Chowthe, Chiru, Kalhen, Kom, Lamkang, Purum (now Chowthe) and the Moyon-Monsong (said to be a faction of the Anal). These tribal groups on becoming conscious of the superiority and dominance of the New Kuki (Thadou) group, also gave up, in a similar way, their age-old Kuki identity and adopted the name "Naga" to identify themselves (Sree Krishan, 1995: 274). But later on when these old Kuki groups claiming Naga identity were not accepted as the Naga by the Naga people and also by other fellow people, they became disillusioned. Some of these people like the Aimol, Chiru, Chowthe, Kolhen, Kom and the Lumkang took up a new identity of "Komrem" after giving up their newly acquired identity of "Naga". Again with the establishment of Mizoram as a union territory, the tribal groups like the Hmar, Poi, Relte, Lakher and the Darlong reverted back to their respective clan identity which they had before the new identity of "Naga" *(ibid:* 274).

In the third category we may include the Rabhas of West Bengal. Though they were influenced by the Rajbansis and got impregnated with the Rajbansi cultural traits, still they retained their Rabha identity. Similarly, those Santals who were taken to Sunderbans (southernmost part of Bengal) more than one hundred and fifty years ago to clear the virgin forests there, were compelled to adopt regional culture for their survival. At present culturally they do not have much similarity with their brethren inhabiting in Bihar. Still they identify themselves as Santal.

Varification of Identity

The presence of different forms of identities, particularly multiple identities, among some tribes and change of identity for various reasons among some other tribal groups, often create confusion and develop conflicting situation. And it becomes sometimes difficult to trace out proper identity of these tribal people.

Again some tribal groups like to retain multiple identities. All these have created a very conflicting situation so far as the ethnic identity is concerned. Therefore, a fresh look into the proper identification of the tribal groups is required in case of some such conflicting cases. To my mind varification of identity is essential in the following cases (Raha, 1965).

(i) Identification of a tribal group or a part of or sub-group within or an individual belonging to such tribal group that has forgotten its own identity or known by some other synonym or pseudonym;

(ii) identification of certain tribal groups or part of or sub-groups within such tribal groups those have suppressed willingly their original identity and have taken the identity of some other tribal groups for specific reason;

(iii) identification of certain tribal groups or part of or sub-group within such tribal groups or some individuals of such tribal groups those have been imposed a new identity by a group or some other groups; and

(iv) assessment of the backwardness of certain tribal groups desirous of their inclusion in or exclusion from the list of the Scheduled Tribe.

Basu Mullick rightly asserts that the "identity does not become a problem in the history of a people until their identity is being questioned or threatened by others" (1993:5-6). Agitation develops when identity of any group is threatened as with the identity the members of a group have a strong emotional attachment and behind the identity of any group some ideology always works. Therefore, Ideology as an expression of "Identity always contains a criticism of how power is distributed, and advocates a redistribution of powers. Ideology and identity are always a political reality . . ." (Basu Mullick, 1993: 12).

It is thus seen that search for the identity of the people sometimes "implies a demand for a redistribution of political power" *(ibid:* 12). The demand of the Adibasi Mahasabha in Bihar in late thirty's for the creation of a separate state after taking the advantage of political fluidity of the region was because of the confused identity and status of the indigenous tribal people. This demand ultimately helped them to the rise of the Jharkhand Party (Danda, 1991: 176-177).

> "Concern for protection of language, culture, and identity and resistance against oppression and over-exploitation were conspicuously menifested in the native force behind Jharkhand movement" *(ibid:* 184).

Possibly the movements in Nagaland and Mizoram and also in some other areas can be attributed to the same reasons.

It is therefore clear that identity of any group is very important for its members. Though they may change it, yet they may restore to agitative means when their identity is threatened.

REFERENCES

Barth, Fredrik. 1969. *Ethnic Groups and Boundaries,* London: George Allen & Unwin.

Basu Mullick, S. 1993. "Indigeonous peoples of India: Identity Crisis and Search for a New Identity", in S. Basu Millick, Edwin Jaydas, Anto Akkara and Anita Joydas (eds.), *Indigenous Identity Crisis and Reawakening.* Delhi: Navdin Prakashan Kendra.

Brown, R. 1873. *Statistical Account of the Native State of Manipur and the Hill Territory under its Rule.* Calcutta: Superintendent of Government Printing.

Chattopadhyay, K. P. 1994. *History of Indian Social Organization: An Easays in Social Anthropology.* Calcutta: K.P. Bagchi & Co.

Dalton, E. T. 1872. *Descriptive Ethnology of Bengal.* Calcutta: Superintendent of Government Printing.

Danda, A.K. 1991. *Ethnicity in India.* New Delhi: Inter-India Publications.

—. 1996 "Ethnicity and Nationality: Some Thematical Issues", *Journal of the Asiatic Society,* XXXVII: I.

Danda, A.K. and M.K. Raha. 1962. *Ethnic Identity, Ethnicity and Social Stratification in North-East India.* New Delhi: Inter-India Publications.

Das, T.C. 1945. *The Purum: An old Kuki Tribe of Manipur.* Calcutta: University of Calcutta.

Das Gupta, B.K. *et al.* 1985. *Purum (Chote) Revisited,* Calcutta: Anthropological Survey of India.

Das, A.K. and M.K. Raha. 1963. *The Oraons of Sundarban,* Calcutta: Cultural Research Institute.

Deb Roy, H.L. 1984. "The Dominating Motives in Jaintia Religious life", in S. Karotemprel (ed.), *Tribes of North-East India.* Calcutta: Firma K. L. Mukhopadhyay.

Ghose T.K. 1992. "Social Stratification in Lahul", in M.K. Raha (ed.), *The Himalayas and the Himalayans.* Calcutta: Anthropological Survey of India.

Gokhale-Chatterjee, S. 1987. "Stratification and Change in the Contemporary Ladakhi Society", in M.K. Raha (ed.), *The Himalayan Heritage.* Delhi: Gian Publishing House.

Kapoor, D.D. 1971. "People of Kinnaru-An essay in the problem of the Tribe", in K.S. Singh (ed.), *Tribal Situation in India.* Simla: Indian Institute of Advanced Studies.

Mann, R.S. 1986. *The Ladakhi,* Calcutta. Anthropological Survey of India.

McCulloch, W. 1885 (1959). "Account of the Valley of Munnipore and the Hill Tribes with Comparative Vocabulary of the Munnipore and other Languages", Selection from the Records of the Govt. of India No. 27, Calcutta: Bengal Printing Press.

Maity, S. 1992. "Pastoral Economy and Territorial Organization among the Bakarwals of Jammu and Kashmir", in M. K. Raha (ed.), *The Himalayas and The Himalayans.* Calcutta: Anthropological Survey of India.

Nehru, Jawaharlal. 1986. *The Discovery of India.* New Delhi: Jawaharlal Memorial Fund.

Radcliffe-Brown, R.R. 1964. *The Andaman Islanders,* New York: The Free Press.

Raha, M.K. 1965. "A Short note on Ethnic identity", *Bulletin of Cultural Research Institute,* IV

—. 1973. "The Rabhas of Western Duars: A structural Analysis of a Changing Matrilineal Society, *Bulletin of Cultural Research Institute.* X: 102.

—. 1978. "Stratification and Religion in a Himalayan Society", In James P. Fisher (ed.), *Himalayan Anthropology.* The Hague: Mouton & Co.

—. 1987. "The Khandan System of the Kinnaura of the Western Himalayas", in M.K. Raha (ed.), *The Himalayan Heritage.* Delhi: Gian Publishing House.

—. 1987. *Matriliny to Patriliny: A Study of the Rabha Society.* New Delhi: Gian Publishing House.

—. 1989 a. "Andaman Tribals: Problems of Survival", in M.K. Raha (ed.), *Tribal India: Problem, Development Prospect.* Vol-I. New Delhi: Gian Publishing House.

—. 1989 b. "The Himalayan Nomads and Their Economy", *Man in Asia,* II: I

—. 1995. "Society and Religion in Kinnaur", in M.K. Raha (ed.), *The People of the Himalayas.* Calcutta: Anthropological Survey of India.

—. 1996. "Introduction", In M.K. Raha (ed.), *Dimensions of Human Society and Culture.* New Delhi: Gyan Publishing House.

Raha, M.K. and J.C. Das. 1981. "Divergent Trend of Transformation among the Kumaon Bhotia in C. Von Furer-Haimendrof (ed.), *The Asian Highland Societies: An Anthropological Perspective*. New Delhi: Sterling Publisher.

Raha, M.K. and A. K. Ghosh (eds.) 1998. *North-East India: The Human Interface*. New Delhi: Gyan Publishing House.

Raha, M.K. and S.N. Mahato. 1985. *The Kinnaurese of the Himalayas*. Calcutta: Anthropological Survey of India.

Risley, H.M. 1891. *Tribes and Castes of Bengal*. Vol.-II, Calcutta: Bengal Secretariat Press.

Singh, K. S. (ed.) 1994. *The Scheduled Tribes*, New Delhi: Anthropological Survey of India & Oxford University Press.

Singh, R.C.P. 1965. *District Handbook: Kinnaur District, Himachal Pradesh*. Census 1961, Simla.

Shree Krishan. 1995. "Language Identity and Linguistic Situation along the North-eastern Border", in M.K. Raha (ed.), *The People of the Himalayas*. Calcutta: Anthropological Survey of India.

Winnick, C. 1964. *Dictionary of Anthropology*. New Jersey: Littlefield Adams & Co.

SEVEN

TRIBAL ETHNICITY IN SANTAL PARGANAS
An Anthropo-Historical Appraisal

R. M. SARKAR

The concept of ethnicity in human society is an old phenomenon and its roles in the shaping of the behaviour-patterns of the people in the diversified levels of living are significant. Various population groups in the world have been characteristically seen in variegated ethnic identities based on specific socio-economic, political as well as religious sentiments. Ethnicity in human communities in the ancient period developed on the basis of economic group formation and the nature and extent of exploitation of the natural resources for livelihood. Later on that particular group formation was related to the other factors like historical, psychological and political aspects. Ethnicity is effectually emerged due to the interactions between various cultural groups working in the perspective of a specific socio-cultural milieu. Sometimes ethnicity is rooted to the cultural distinctiveness—the reciprocal action-oriented situations amongst the different cultural groups give rise to ethnic groups. The trend of self identification of the human groups is as old as human civilization. The traditional norms and ideologies of various ethnic groups concerned are the core elements of the concept of ethnicity and by these an ethnic group maintains its distinctiveness. This perspective of social sameness is a dynamic process which is subject to change and transformation as per changing context of the country in which the ethnic groups have been and are being nurtured through the ages. In the study and analysis of the ethnic groups and their working behaviours it has been seen that various social inequalities based on unequal shares in exercise of power, wealth and prestige symbols are conspicuous in many ethnic groups. In recent years there has been rapid growth of the concept of ethnic identities. It is seen that ethno-cultural mobilization and ethnic agitation have become a continuous process. The launching of various ethnic movements especially tribal movements in India has exerted tremendous influence on the socio-political sphere. Ethnic unrest is the outcome of exploitation in inter-ethnic and even intra-ethnic groups. The roots, nature and conditions of ethnic unrest are not necessarily the same, and these differ from situation to situation as well as from region to region. The ethnic identity and its changing process is dependent on the nature of political forces. Thus after India's independence the pattern of ethnic identification has taken a completely different issue. In the post-independence development the democratic set-up of the country has caused a great deal in the emergence of socio-political consciousness. This consciousness has given birth to the idea of cultural revivalism amongst different ethnic groups.

Ethnicity results from the different causes. It may have resulted due to the cultural arrogance of the majority population group in a society or there are reasons for the emergence of ethnicity when one group is exploited and undermined as well as suppressed by the more powerful group. Besides, the prejudice of a particular human group may function categorically in the formation of an ethnic group. It has been seen through the ups and downs of history that the ethnic groups many a time are afraid of wiping out of their cultural existence and identity situation. The inequality of economic distribution and other benefits of development most of the time mobilize the affected group to create a basis for protest centering round ethnic background. Ethnic identity in relation to human communities may be based on both biological and cultural affairs. Practically the term "ethnic" directly relates to race–the division of mankind with specific heritable biological traits. A group of people with some common biological features generally form an in-group and the people belonging to it possess a strongly "we-feeling". They are closely related to each other in happiness and sorrows, in fears and frustrations as well as in scarcity and prosperity.

Ethnicity is specifically a multi-disciplinary phenomenon in human totalistic life. The problems of ethnicity can thus be viewed from different angles and naturally there may be diversified methodological principles in the study of ethnicity. As because ethnicity in social perspective is developed round the united appeal of the ethnic group concerned to establish its proper claim and also to resist various injustice and negligence that the group faces in course of its day to day life, so it has become, of late, a specific tool for studying various social sentiments, patterns of their interactions as well as the emergence and growth of various integrated socio-political movements. Ethnicity has, therefore, become an important global issue in the study and analysis of the interacting patterns of the world population. In recent time, a large number of instances of ethnic tensions and conflicts has been seen in the different parts of the world the causes of which are multifarious. In the study of nature and extent of population patterns and the related affairs the ethnic situations and their reciprocal activities are needed to be analyzed in the background of the socio-political settings of the country concerned. In a vast, heterogeneous and tradition-bound country like India problems relating to ethnicity have now become a very delicate issue. It results varied unfortunate situations in the day to day life of the country. It is not only the problem of the minorities, but it may create problematic situations in the way of life of the majorities also. Whatever may be the fact, the problem relating to ethnicity needs proper anthropological evaluation in the background of multidimensional activities of human groups. Its formation, character and interactions should be understood in the background of changing socio-political situations of the country. Ethnicity in India is in a rapid process of development as well as change and, therefore, it is high time that the attention of the scholars should be drawn towards this specific social phenomenon to evaluate and understand it properly to cope with the unfavourable situations rooted to the evil effects of ethnicity.

Tribal India is highly characterized by the instant emergence and speedy development of ethnicity. There have been many instances of socio-political processes which crystallized the joint claim for tribal autonomy and to demarcate the specific tribal territory. A number of social scientists have researched on different dimensions of tribal ethnicity in Indian context. Here mention may be made of Sarkar, S.S., 1938; Jha, 1964; Sen *et al.,* 1969; Sarkar, R.M., 1971, 1986, 1993a, 1993b; Sen, 1972; Dhan, 1977; Singh, 1977; Das, 1987; Dube, 1997; Sachchidanand, 1997, etc. who have made some useful contribution in this regard. During the colonial period the tribal people in consequence of multiple reasons felt their identity crises and were compelled to be united to raise their joint voices against oppressions, ill-treatment and indifference of the rulers of the country in their domain of life. The tribal people in India since times immemorial have been enjoying the different resources of the country without any sort of obstruction or protest made by others. They thought themselves as the masters of the territories concerned where they had been living. Thus when the colonial government started imposing a number of restrictions through the establishment of their respective ethnic identities, the tribal people living in the hilly tracts and forest infested regions unitedly communicated their protest which was reflected through their modes of behaviour. The colonial government took all possible steps to show indifference to the cause of the tribals and they readily applied the trend of isolationism. When in 1873 the "inner line" was imposed by the then government in the hilly tribal concentrated areas of the north-eastern regions of India the entry of the non-tribal peoples into the hilly tribal areas was stopped causing dissociation in the close link between the tribal and the non-tribal people. In addition to this several administrative measures were also adopted by the colonial administration and as a result of those the tribals were totally isolated from the rest of the people of India. Besides the north-eastern Indian tribal regions, attempts were also made by the colonial government to seclude the other tribal concentrated hilly and forested regions of the central as well as south India following the same principle. This particular course of action very naturally retarded and even stopped the social and political developments that were taking place in other parts of India. Being cut off from the principal territory and at the same time due to the objectionable legislations imposed by the then rulers there developed a situation which narrowed down their freedom of exploiting natural surroundings and resources. In course of time that situational context did a great deal in the creation of discontent among the tribal people who through a pattern of ethno-social formation could publicize their identity and placed their respective ethnic norms and close link of these with the land and environment. Many of the tribes of north-eastern region of India long before the country's independence started agitation for their safety and protection from the intruders. There were many instances of ethnic-cultural mobilization and ethnic movement which were launched by the tribal groups separately to lodge their protest against the trends disintegrating their cultural traditions caused by the imposition of various restrictions in their life-style. History reveals that a number of tribes in Assam came forward as the forceful factors in the ethnic politics of the territory. Some of the changed tribal groups wanted *desanskritization* of their behaviour-patterns through the effective launching of movements. They started a rapid process of *retribalization* of the customs and traditions which helped a lot in the building of broad-based ethno-political movements. After independence the ethnic movements of the tribal groups became accelerated as the people have been afraid of their cultural, linguistic as well as economic existence and they very naturally have developed a trend of separatism to keep them protected from the clutches of outside influences and administrative pressure. In this way the tribal people at the different tribal concentrated regions of India have started agitation to save their interest through the presentation of the respective ethnic identities as well as formation of ethnic-political groups to place their demands to honour the tribal interest.

In Central India the Kols revolted against the oppression of the British. At the very outset the Hos of Kolhan resisted the entry of the British in their locality which, according to their tradition, was the land of Singbonga—the Supreme deity of the Hos. When British came to power in that area the Hos were put under the direct control of the zamindars and ultimately they were fallen in the cluthces of the money-lenders. Being harassed by the joint tyranny of the zamindars and the money-lenders the Hos developed a group-protest in which their ethnic situation in the background of Kolhan region was clearly depicted. It was a sort of ethnicity that developed in them as back as 1931. On the basis of that ethnic-political set-up the Hos united in a common front to save their interest as an ethnic group intimately related to a tradition-bound territory. This ethno-territorial philosophy of the Hos caused a great deal in fighting out their cause in the sphere of their totalistic life. The Kol insurrection constituted a wide-spread struggle for establishing the right cause in relation to the Hos and a number of neighbouring tribes. In these uprisings tribal sentiment was nurtured to a large extent and amongst the tribals involved a wave of ethnicity reigned the whole situation. The Birsa movement of 1895 constituted a concrete example of ethno-political upsurge among the Mundas of Chotanagpur to put a firm resistance on the large scale conversion of the Mundas to Christianity. It was an allurement given by the Christian missionaries that on becoming Christians the Mundas would be relieved of their oppression from the hands of zamindars and money lenders. But it was far from reality. A tribal leader from among the Mundas, named Birsa, gave the Mundas an ethnic stability through the introduction of a new religious sentiment in which there was an attempt for giving proper honour and prestige to the indigenous tribal system. Thus the ethno-religious identity of the Mundas and other neighbouring tribes as developed by Birsa Munda has resulted in the formation of an ethnic situation in which the tribals have found themselves in a close-knit perspective. The Kandh rising in Orissa, which started in 1837 and continued upto 1856, also illustrates a specific happening in the domain of ethnic assemblage clarifying the ethnic identity in the perspective of a particular traditional belief pattern. The system of Mariah, i.e. human sacrifice was the basic element of their socio-religious life on which the total Kandh society used to rotate (Padel, 1995). When the British entered into their territory characterized by inaccessible hill tracts with the dense jungle coverage, and started to stop the century-old traditional Mariah, Kandhs unitedly rose against that attempt of the British. Under the leadership of Chakra Bisoi, a Kandh tribal, all the Kandhs came close to each other identifying themselves centering round the Mariah trait. Their ethnic identity was strongly established on the nature and extent of human sacrifice which, according to their belief-pattern, was the inevitable factor for their overall existence in the midst of diversified calamities caused by the displeasure of deities who could be satisfied through human sacrifice. Thus the ethnicity of the Kandhs became expressive in their attempt to unite for that common cause though it was subsided through the direct interruption of the British. All these attempts either for resisting injustice and ill-behaviour done to the tribal people or for placing their demand in getting due attention from the ruling authorities were processed through the identity formation and focusing the ethnicity centering round the tradition-bound situations in community level. In this way it will be seen that the tribal ethnicity is a phenomenon of the long past period and since then it has been developing in different patterns and perspectives conditioned by the changing socio-political scenario of the country.

II

Tribal ethnicity in Santal Parganas has a traditional history behind it. The region Santal Parganas owes its name to the Santals in consequence of the tremendous uprising of the tribe during 1855-57. Prior to this period the region in question was known as *Damin-i-koh* or skirts of the hills. During the second half of the 18th century as well as in the early 19th century the Santals started immigrating into that region from the localities like Palamau, Hazaribagh, Chotanagpur, Cuttack, Dhalbhum, Manbhum, Midnapur, Bankura and the neighbouring Birbhum. *Damin-i-koh* was at that time covered by dense forests and the Santal after coming to that locality cleared the forests to reclaim land for cultivation. Being encouraged by the Lord William Bentinck's government and by dint of their specific industrious nature the Santals could explore the region and thereby brought it under their control. But at the very outset they, however, resisted by the Pahariyas—the original inhabitants of the Rajmahal Hills region. *Damin-i-koh* region was an extensive tract of land distributed among the three districts like Bhagalpur, Murshidabad and Birbhum. During 1837-38 the region was put under the superintendentship of James Pontet of the uncovenated civil service and he was there to look at the interest of the government through the adoption of effective measures in making favourable land settlements with the Santals and thereby collecting rent from them. Gradually the *Damin-i-koh* started developing, the Santal settlements were in the increase at the rapid pace and thus the amount of annual rent was upto the satisfaction of the government concerned. During this time the interest of the immigrated Santals was kept properly and they were perfectly happy in conducting their picturesque way of life through the exploitation of their landed properties by the raising of multiple crops. The hunting-gathering mode of life of the Santals had been transformed here fully and they became able to establish themselves as successful cultivators though hunting and gathering were not completely wiped out. To a great extent these became occasional as well as ceremonial features of action.

The Santals of *Damin-i-koh* did not come in direct confrontation with the original settlers of the Rajmahal Hills region as they were exclusively the dwellers on hill tops and practised shifting cultivation known as *Khallu*. Though from the very beginning the Pahariyas could not welcome the entrance of the Santals in the forested regions of *Damin-i-koh* because of the reason of Santals' overall and continuous effort to clear up the dense forest for reclamation of agricultural lands. That sort of deforestation was not liked by the Pahariyas as that attempt was detrimental to their isolated living condition without the encroachment of the outsiders. With this particular view point the Pahariyas put a strong resistance on the encroachment of the British into their traditional Rajmahal Hills region during the later half of the 18th century.

The Pahariyas united to form a specific mentality based on their tribal norms and traditions centering round their freedom in the Rajmahal region and their uninterrupted utilization of the forest-resources and thereby they raised the protest against the intruding foreign people. These tribal people faught against the British power, the tribal sentiments worked as the most dominating issue in that confrontation. It resulted in a series of disturbances which were readily put to an end through the use of force by the British. But it was soon realized that the application of force alone would not bring any effectual result in the solution of the problem. The struggle was based on the ethnic spirit in which the tribal values and sentiments became the most essential issue; it made the British to change their approach to the problem. They started the policy of reconciliation with the Pahariyas and gave up the way of confrontation with them.

Thus, Pahariya ethnicity was so much strong and integrated that the British realized to arrange for an effective administration in the region by appointing a Collector of Rajmahal Hills. He studied the spiritual aspect of ethnic realization of the Pahariyas as well as their united force and then he chalked out a specific policy to deal with the Pahariyas. Cleveland realized the ethnic integrity and united effort of the Pahariyas in maintaining their traditional way of life in the Rajmahal region and he thereby arranged to place the entire hill range under a uniform administration of a Hill Assembly. A large number of hill chiefs responded to that call of Cleveland and they took the oath of loyalty. Tribal chiefs were given special duty of reporting all law and order problems criminal and anti-social activities in the villages to the autorities. They were also given the power to resist peace-breaking activities. In return, they were given some amount of annual pensions.

Sometimes later Cleveland made an arrangement to withdraw the Rajmahal Hills tract from the Jurisdiction of ordinary courts. All the disputes in the life of the Pahariyas were judged under a newly constructed Hill Assembly where the hereditary hill chiefs or *Sardars* were given all the necessary power to judge. On realizing the fact of land grabbing by the zamindars and outsiders Cleveland formed the lands occupied by the Pahariyas into the government estate. The arrangement thus made by Cleaveland to save the interest of the Pahariyas, appeased them and thereby the tribal people declared the acceptance of British rule which provided them autonomy in that region. Therefore, Pahariya identity had been established and their ethnic recognition as a spirited tribal group was readily accepted by the British rulers. The total landmass in hill tract was unitedly given the name *Damin-i-Koh.* Under the Regulation of 1796 separate rules were prepared for administering that particular area as well as for conducting meeting of the Hill Assembly. Thus *Damin-i-Koh* was indentified as a non-regulation area.

The *Damin-i-Koh* experiment of Cleveland was proved to be a novel one in establishing a peaceful relation with the tumultuous Pahariya tribe. But that particular situation of creating protected land free from intruders made the Pahariyas isolated. Cleveland, on realizing this, devised a new plan to bring the Pahariyas under the direct contact of the plain people but owing to his premature death that plan could not be made practicable. Thus Pahariyas could have been able to establish their ethnic importance and their traditional connection with the Rajmahal Hills region before the British administration from the very beginning of its encroachment into the areas concerned. They did not submit to the British power at the cost of their autonomy. Rather the establishment of Hill Assembly enhanced their right over the land and gave proper prestige to their time-long association with hills and jungles of the Rajmahal region. Cleveland's effort to create *Damin-i-Koh* on behalf of the British government was the direct outcome of the ethnic uprise of the Pahariyas to save their autonomy in the Rajmahal Hills areas, so that age-old phenomenon of the linkage between land and ethnicity could be maintained without any pause. But the particular intention behind the formation of *Damin-i-Koh* did not bear required fruit as the policy underlying it was not maintained by the administrative successors of Cleveland. His Hill Assembly so carefully designed and so keenly organized to administer the Rajmahal Hills region started dying out owing to the indifference of the latter administrative officers. Thus *Damin-i-Koh* ultimately became an ordinary region.

When the British started allowing the Santals to settle permanently in the *Damin-i-Koh* region it took a new turn. The main intention of the British administration was to reclaim the dense forested *Damin-i-Koh* region to serve it for the purpose of agriculture and to do it the industrious Santals were highly welcomed to that region. A good amount of revenue collection was apprehended from that locality if the total planning became successful. James Pontet gave a practical view to that apprehension. The relevant records indicated that as early as 1851 the revenue collection of that area increased from Rs. 2000 to Rs. 43,919.00 and the Santals constituted there as large as 1473 villages (Datta, 1970). There were full-fledged development in agriculture; the Santals tried their level best to make the region highly productive in relation to different crops. The villages reached all round developments—there were inter-connecting broad roads to make free movements with the cart load of crops from the fields to homes as well as from the homes to the weekly *haats* and urban markets. The development programme of the *Damin-i-Koh* region was aimed at the following principles:

(1) It had not been possible by the British administration to bring the hill people of Rajmahal under the broad-based programme of settled cultivation as they were very wild and preferred to live on the hill top villages. Thus the Santals—the laborious and more considerate

tribe-were given shelter here in large numbers in the hope that they would be able to convert the jungle infested *Damin-i-Koh* region into an agriculture-oriented field.

(2) In arranging for settlement of the driven out Santals from the neighbourhood and far off places the British administration wanted to take possession of the concealed lands of the *Damin-i-Koh* as retained by the unscrupulous zamindars.

(3) Through the broad-based deforestation of the dense and extensive forests of the *Damin-i-Koh* and the adjoining portions the whole country could be made healthy and thereby it could be turned into a populous one to exploit the resources of the region.

(4) To get the possession of *Damin-i-Koh* through peaceful means which had been held for long years by the wild hill tribe as their hereditary property. There was a government notification towards that effect (dated 17th July, 1823) which wanted the speedy process of possession of the said land.

But in spite of various active measures taken up by the administration to make the above-noted intentions fulfilled thoroughly there developed a good many internal problems in consequence of the entailment of gross injustice on the innocent common people of that area. It became escalated in such a level that the peace-loving Santals rebelled. It was so happened that when the *Damin-i-Koh* became a prosperous land with the development of agriculture it attracted many of the non-tribal outsiders. In no time, there was an influx of outsiders who constituted a group of fortune seekers in the well developed and economically prosperous Santal villages. There were traders, money lenders, zamindars as well as people with multifarious interests. On entering into the *Damin-i-Koh* region these people approached the Santals limiting themselves as their friends and well-wishers. Their clever tricks could not be realized by the simple-minded and hospitable Santals and in no time they fell into the traps as put by the fortune-seekers so cunningly. The self-sufficient tribal economy of the Santals, which was based on barter and exchange, got disturbed through the introduction of money economy brought by the intruders. The money-lenders came forward to help the Santals in lending money but the latter owing to illiteracy and ignorance as well as utter faithfulness to the humanity became heavily exploited. They could not understand the unfortunate after-effect of borrowing money from the money-lenders. The interest of the borrowed money was so complicated that the debtor gradually started losing everything—his agricultural products, agricultural lands, implements and bullocks, and even household utensils. But still the debt continued through generations. The trading groups composed of Bengali and up-country merchants exploited the Santals during the purchase of crops, vegetables, milk, ghee at the village *haat* as well as from the Santal houses. Those greedy merchants used to purchase various products from the Santals in the falsified weights and measures which those simple-minded Santals could not understand. The payments were made in such a small amount that in return of their production the Santals received practically nothing. Thus gradually they were economically ruined. It was very difficult for the oppressed Santals to seek justice in the courts of law as those places were dominated by the agents of the zamindars, money-lenders and merchants. Moreover, it was practically difficult for them to present the evidence of oppression and fraud committed to them by the unscrupulous persons. The Santals of *Damin-i-Koh* were thus in a hazardous situation and their misfortune knew no bound. There was no body to save them, none to give consolation in their plight. What was conspicuously unfortunate was that the officials of British government who were engaged to look into the condition of the harassed Santals were exclusively purchased by the zamindars and influential money lenders and those officers were always ready to hold the Santals as guilty. The police personnel also were engaged to make the innocent Santals guilty of thefts and other criminal activities. The British government took indifferent attitude and tried to avoid the situation. From all the levels the Santals had been receiving unjust treatment which made those tribal people frustrated with the whole administrative set-up. In addition to those oppression, the Europeans employed in the railway construction work in the vicinity of the *Damin-i-Koh* region frequently entered in the Santal villages by the side of the railway tracks to take away fowls, drucks, goats from the households without paying anything, and lastly when those European employees ill-treated two Santal women through abducting them, the Santals became furious and they immediately decided to teach a good lesson to all classes of oppressors and miscreants. The Santal uprising during 1855-57, to lodge a strong protest against the ill-treatment and dishonour caused to the Santals by the outsiders for no fault of the innocent tribe, was the direct outcome of the instant development of ethnicity which was conditioned by multiple interests.

III

The growth of ethnicity among the Santals as back as 1855 is not only unique in the tribal history of India but it is spontaneous as in this issue it surpasses all the ethnic movements of the country. Faced by the situation it grew automatically and abruptly from the tribal feeling of strong sentiment and valued prestige. It was a sort of struggle not only for economic existence but also for the spiritual entity. The analysis of the events that occurred during the Santal uprising supplies the relevant data in considering that only the spirit of ethnicity was at the root in organizing such a broad-based and integrated protest against all the oppressors to the Santal community including the indifferent attitude of the powerful British Raj. The tribal sentiment got excessively hurt when the simple-minded people were cheated and it reached its maximum at the insulting behaviour of European railway workers to the womenfolk of the Santals. The police officer's (Maheshlal Daroga) evil activity during his investigation into a case of theft in the locality greatly injured the tribal emotion and rich philosophy when a few Santals had been deceitfully marked as thieves and were thereby taken under arrest. The government's indifferent attitude towards those unjust activities and unlawful harassment could not be accepted by the Santals in free mind. All those situations were not only unfortunate but also sufficiently injured the tribal dignity and ethics. Those were enough to intensify the discontent of the Santals.

The ethnic sentiments of the Santals became conspicuous through the mysterious happening from the supernatural world. As a staunch believer in the supernaturalism the Santal community during the period of crisis in their existence level very naturally received a supernatural indication for the future course of action. This supernaturalism bound all of them with the Santali movement—the feeling of ethnicity. Two Santal youths, named Sidhu and Kanhu, related as brothers, received divine indications through a miraculous happening by the sudden appearance of the *Thakur* (God) before them. The two other brothers, named Chand and Bhairab, joined the former in that supernatural issue. As per indication, Sidhu and Kanhu arranged for the worship of *Thakur* within the boundary of their house. That mysterious revelation was circulated gradually throughout the whole region by means of the Santal traditional symbol of *sal* (Shorea robusta) twig. It was thus the first event depicting the rise of Santal ethnicity which was at that time became very much meaningful. Being possessed by the Thakur, Sidhu and Kanhu declared the day for general gathering of all the Santals to get the divine instruction. It was 30th June 1855, as instructed by the divine power Sidhu and Kanhu announced before the large gathering of the Santals at a place named Bhaguadihi that all the Santals jointly should go out to place a challenge against the oppressors misdeeds.

The ethnicity of the Santals at that moment crystallized surrounding the *dikus*—the Bengali and up country money-lenders and traders. At the very beginning the Santals were oppressed greatly by those people and that was why their revengeful activities were directed to them. In *Damin-i-Koh* region the Santals became isolated due to the harsh and merciless behaviour patterns of all the neighbouring communities. All were cheat, tyrant and looters, and through the commitment of those evil practices they could vanish the fortune of the Santals. Thus the Santals were afraid of those outsiders—the root causes of their tyranny and unfortunate situations. Those mischievous people were kept alert by designating them as *dikus*. The term *diku* indicates non-tribal and especially those who are harmful to the tribal communities. The concept of *diku* developed long ago among this tribal community as a resultant factor in the development of ethnicity. In order to carry out the divine order, as communicated by Sidhu and Kanhu, to fight for the cause of the tribe the Santals were spirited enough to form a concerted group based on ethnic identity.

The Santals are by nature unity-oriented tribe—they have got a unique idea of social solidarity. The tribal social structure is carefully maintained by them and no haphazard social event is allowed to make an entry into it. The tribal sentiment is at the apex of everything. Thus they are always conscious about the *dikus* and even today try to maintain a distance with them so far as the social situations are concerned. During the days of Santal insurrection (called *Hul* by the Santals) the *dikus* were identified and kept off by the force of ethnicity. From the mentality and behaviour-patterns of the Santals at that time it was understood that the *dikus* did not simply mean mere non-tribal or neighbouring Hindus. The Santal villages sheltered a few artisan castes of the Hindus like Lohar, Chamar, Teli, Dom, Tanti, Kumhar, etc. who in course of time became part and parcel of those village societies. By living and working through generations these lowly Hindu caste groups developed a sort of symbiotic relationship with the Santals and therefore, they were not treated as *dikus* because of the fact that these caste groups changed many of their caste norms and accepted tribal traditions. Thus the concept of *diku* was always related to the outside oppressors who were not beneficial to the Santal community. It was to resist the *dikus* from doing oppressive activities and from cheating the simple-minded tribals the Santals devised a covering of ethnicity by deep-rooted activities of awakening the Santal community to put forward their specific identity. The Santali concept of *diku* is still forming the basis of tribal–nontribal interactions in Santal Parganas and in other region inhabited by the Santals.

The ethnicity-oriented spiritualism of the Santals could establish the truth that they had been in a severe wave of maltreatment from the neighbouring population groups and even the rulers of the country did not look into their utter misfortunes. The sense of ethnicity could make possible their severe fight with simple bows and arrows against the British power which was armed with advanced appliances of warfare. The rigid ethnicity amongst the broad-based tribal community gave birth to a new territory where their interest was promised to be kept through social legislation. The Santal areas were made into a separate non-regulation district under the Act 37 of 1855 and was known as then Santal Parganas. Thus the Santal Parganas were the end product of Santal ethnicity which was applied in deep-based circumstances. The fact of Santal ethnicity and its impact is still pulsating in the minds of the people of the affected regions even after the elapse of little less than one hundred and fifty years; various happenings are found to be reflected even today in the folklore of the region. The folksongs that have been collected at present in the affected villages in Bengal-Bihar border region still point out the dreadful days of the Santal insurrection. Out of these three songs have been presented here which pin-point the actual condition of the land and people due to the united revengeful aggression of the Santals. The first ballad indicates the actual time of insurgency and the instant assemblage of the Santals from different places on a common issue relating to the cause of their community.

> "During 1262 B.S. the violence had been born in the north from the far off places the Santals assembled there. Their unity is conspicuous, the *majhi* is characterized by firmness Santals from all the corners inhabiting in two hundred and fifty villages became united forming one unit."

Another ballad clarifies the firm determination of the Santals with free and delighted mind in favour of extending their authority over the region of their inhabitation (i.e. *Damin-i-Koh*) and to defeat the British power abruptly.

> "They decided amongst themselves with cheerful mind to establish their authoritative influence over the region they utter, 'we will snatch away the kingdom from the hands of the British after killing them'.

The next song gives an action-oriented scene of the non-tribal villages in the neighbourhood of *Damin-i-Koh.* By the tremendous attack with the accompaniment of beating of the war drums the common villagers immediately started going out of the village leaving behind their sweet homes as well as traditional occupational activities based on village industries. The pillaging of the insurgents was so serious and panicky that not only the human beings but also the powerful village goddess also fled away from her shrine.

> "They entered the village paths of Banskuli with the beating of war drums (nagara) on finding their severe appearance the people of Bansra, Muluk and Talbere villages fled away. On hearing the continuous beating of drums the goddess Kambasini became afraid and ran away."

The *hul* or the Santal unrest cannot be called as a simple localized uprising of the tribal community. Its influence made an entry into the British administrative machinery, and the British government was compelled to change its all India policy towards the tribal people. The government concerned realized the fact that in order to strengthen the root of British Kingdom in

India tribal ethnic uprising should be assessed in their own perspectives.

The ethnicity of the Santals in recent year has been developed centering round many eventful activities. As an integrating tribal community the Santals attract many social scientists because of the fact that they have changed much, at the one hand, and have been able to maintain the tribal traditions on the other. Sometimes it is seen that with the progress of time and through the acceptance of diversified patterns of life the Santals are rapidly losing their spirit of ethnicity. In many of the instances the Santals have shaken off their traditional way of living and thinking through the acceptance of industrialization. The specific quality of the Santals is that they can accept the changing situation rapidly and are able to adjust with the new situations. In Santal Pargana villages it is seen that owing to their continuous living side by side with the Hindu caste villages and through a long process of interactions in socio-economic and political horizons the Santals have developed many Hinduized beliefs and ideas. In Santal Parganas no effect of industrialization has been met with and what Martin Orans (1965) has found among the Santals of Jamshedupr industrial belt is not seen here. But in many events the Santals of Santal Parganas follow Hinduized mode of life. In most of the Santal villages in Santal Parganas especially which have deep-based connection with the Hindu villages development of Hinduized features are specifically seen. The Santal households are provided with altar of sacred *Tulsi* plant *(ocimum sanctum)* where the womenfolk regularly present burning lamp at the onset of evening. They are seen to bow down in front of the altar and following which the blowing of conch shell is done by any one of the female members. The Santal students reading in schools and colleges arrange for the worship of the goddess Saraswati on the *Sripanchami* day as the Hindus do. Following their Hindu counterparts they collect subscription with the help of printed receipt books. The worship of the goddess is done by engaging a Brahmin priest. The Santal students offer their homage to the goddess of learning through the reciting of Sanskrit incantations assisted by the Brahmin priest. But there is no reason to believe that the Santals of Santal Parganas have been converted to Hinduism. Rather there are concrete facts in favour of assessing that the Santals at the same time are highly sensitive to the indigenous traits in their way of life. Whatever may be their Hinduized beliefs and ideas, which they have adopted, they do not hesitate rather neglect to follow the traditional life situation. They have got firm faith on the *bongas;* they regularly propitiate the Santali gods and goddesses following the traditional patterns of worship and offering of sacrifices. The Santals of Santal Parganas have adopted a lot of exotic traits from the non-tribal populations with whom they have been in close economic connection. But at the same time they have got deep faith in *bongaism* and in various other indigenous belief patterns. Thus this tribal group maintains the two-way processes of philosophical principles. Hinduization and Indigenization are running side by side. They are not the whole time workers in the search of great tradition as Orans has noted in Jamshedpur or they are not in a continuous trend of coming back to the native state which Gautam (1977) has designated Santalization. In Santal Parganas the Santals always think themselves as Santals and behave like a Santal. But in course of their daily mode of life they have adopted some other traits which do not necessarily mean that these have darken their existence as Santals. Their concept of *diku* is still pulsating and working effectually in their socio-cultural and economic confrontations with the Hindu neighbours. It is an accepted fact that the Santals are very much adaptive to changing circumstances. They accept the change readily, utilize the changing factors and get benefit from these. But these are not accepted at the cost of their indigenous life-philosophy. There may be the fact that on occasions they have borrowed some Hinduized beliefs and practices but which have simply meant an adaptation of these to suit their indigenous culture (Sachchidananda, 1997). As for example, the worship of the goddess Saraswati by the Santal students is an adaptation of exotic trait of their indigenous culture. It does not disturb the traditional religious sentiments of the Santals which run smoothly with the traditional priests following the indigenous procedures.

The Jharkhand movement which took its birth in the tribal concentrated region of Chotanagpur, in the year 1911-12, was aimed at the overall welfare of the tribal people through the formation of a separate state under the name Jharkhand. The main intention of that organization was to awaken the tribal people to protect their own land and culture from the evil influence of the outsiders. The movement was led by the educated section of the tribal group having some experience in political activities and that was why it became effective from the very beginning. The party was characteristically dominated by the Christian tribals of Chotanagpur but in spite of the fact it was highly influenced by the indigenous tribal thoughts and ideas. Through the said party a united voice was raised for regional administration, better educational facilities and more employment opportunities. It also added the matter of restoration of alienated land and to take positive measures for getting the age-long exploited tribal people free from their continuous hardships. The main tribal groups supporting the Jharkhand movement were the Mundas, Oraons, Hos and Santals. But in 1968, the Santals separated themselves from the Chotanagpur tribals and formed their own party based on their own region and definite problems. The Santals of Santal Parganas nurtured a specific ethnicity which was oriented with a particular tradition created by their ancestors long ago. They thought it was befiting to design the Jharkhand movement in the line of their traditional situation. Santal Parganas as a territory is not only much valued by the Santals especially by those who have been living here but also it is understood to have created a rich philosophical pattern that is unparallel to any worldly happening; this becomes the special trend of ethnicity of the Santals in Santal Parganas. Thus the Jharkhand party, newly formed by the Santals of Santal Parganas, was named the Hul Jharkhand party and it became essentially a Santal organization. It placed a demand through the joint enterprises of its member to solve the local problems like the introduction of the Roman Scripts for the expression of Santali language as they feel if the script problem is solved the large number of literatures can be built up in Santali language which would very naturally give a special shape to the tribal identity. They also want the creation of a separate Division for the Santal Parganas as well as agricultural reforms for making an end to the tribal exploitation. Alongwith these the security of the tribal people was also demanded. The Santal Pargana based Hul Jharkhand party within four years of its formation faced another division, and the new faction became known as progressive Hul Jharkhand party. In the year 1966, formation of *Sidhu-Kanhu-Baisi* is the indicator of another concrete example of Santal ethnicity in Santal Parganas. The Baisi or the Panchayat was named after the two devoted leaders of Santal insurrection, and it was directed to take speedy and effective measures for the spread of education among the tribals, improvement of tribal economy and saving the tribal people from exploitation. There were some efforts for the expulsion of the *dikus* from the tribal area though it did not receive sufficient public support. The Santal-*diku* interactions are not being so tense now as was the case during the period of Santal insurrection. The Santals are, to a great extent, accommodative and, in course of time, they have been able to establish a sort of amicable linkage with the *dikus.* This is the changing perspective of the Santal ethnicity in Santal Parganas. Purification of Santal region by making it free from Hindu influences was also a point which was taken up in the working programme of the *Baisi.* But that situation also did not bring forth any local enthusiasm as the Santal region, they took it for granted, was not contaminated by the Hindu religious beliefs though there were some occasions of transmission of reciprocal belief-oriented traits.

After a few years Jharkhand Mukti Morcha (Liberation front) developed through the mutual understanding between the two leaders, one from Chotanagpur and the other from Santal Parganas. The leader from Santal Parganas was Sibu Soren. The *Morcha* was aimed at reviving the traditional culture and intrinsic development of agriculture as well as to provide facilities to the sons of the soil in the sphere of employment. Through a process of multifarious ground work on the development programme Sibu Soren became conspicuous. As the first stage he was working in a village in Dhanbad district, and in the later years he shifted to Dumka–the district headquarters of Santal Parganas. The functioning of the Morcha has been continuing in the line of its promise given by Sibu Soren. *Baisi* has been brought to the fore front to utilize it as people's Court. Morcha conducts different programmes meant for general well-being of the people for which the whole tribal belt in Santal Pargana is lagging far behind.

In understanding the patterns of tribal ethnicity in Santal Parganas the Santals play not only the dominant role but also the exclusive part because of the fact that other tribal group, the Pahariyas, do not like to come to the fore front. Though they put forward a stern resistance against the British encroachment in Rajmahal Hills region at the formative period of their influence, which made the British power to adopt some specific measures to make a peaceful understanding with these wild hill tribes. After coming of the Santals to that territory the Pahariyas due to their timid nature and eternal love for jungle infested life preferred to dissociate themselves and they went further interior region of the jungle covered hills. Naturally, the Santals got the total landmass favourable for the spread of their cultural patterns and the Santal Parganas ultimately became synonymous with the Santal tribe. Thus tribal ethnicity in Santal Parganas is in fact the reflection of the tribal situations of the Santals through time and space. It is characterized by cultural distinctiveness as well as close-set accommodation with contrary natured *diku* culture. There was a time when they not only disliked *dikus* but also there was a deep-rooted hatred towards the alien non-Santal communities but in consequence of long journey through the ages with the *dikus* an integrated understanding developed. It influenced the basic characteristic of the ethnicity of the Santals. The Santals in Santal Parganas are never so much vocal in warding off the non-Santals from the land which owes its name to the tribe and has been created to keep the interests of the Santals. The tribal sentiment in the Santal Pargana totalistic social situation is never harsh. The Santal villages are seen to be in an amicable bondage with the Hinduized villages characterized by various caste groups. In the socio-economic horizon of the region exclusively influenced by agriculture there is a very good understanding of caste-tribe interacting pattern. Despite all these phenomena of behavioural activities the Santals nurture a sharp identity of their own, they are always after democratic political process. In modern political activities as are reflected through the functioning principles of Jharkhand movement, the Santals in Santal Parganas show interest is following the theme of their traditional political process that is effectively democratic as designed and strictly followed by their forefathers in the remote past.

REFERENCES

Das, N.K. 1987. *Ethnic Identity, Ethnicity and Social Stratification in North-East India,* New Delhi; Inter-India Publications.

Datta, K.K., 1970. *Anti-British Plots and Movements Before 1857.* Meerut: Meenakshi Prakashan.

Dhan, R.O. 1977, "Tribal Movements in Chotonagpur", in S.C. Malik (ed.), *Dissent, Protest and Reform in Indian Civilization.* Simla: Indian Institute of Advanced Study.

Dube, S.C. 1997. "Ethnicity: Myth, History and Politics", In A.M. Shah, B.S. Baviskar and E.A. Ramaswamy (eds.), *Social Structure and Change,* Vol. 4, New Delhi: Sage Publications.

Gautam, M.K. 1977. *In Search of an Identity: The Case of the Santals of North India,* Leiden.

Jha, J.C. 1964. *Kol Insurrection in Chotanagpur,* Calcutta: Thacker, Spink & Co.

Orans, Martin, 1965. *The Santal: A Tribe in Search of a Great Tradition.* Detroit: Wayne University Press.

Padel, Felix. 1995. *The Sacrifice of Human Being: British Rule and the Konds of Orissa.* Delhi: Oxford University Press.

Sachchidananda. 1997. "Emergence and Growth of Tribal Ethnicity in Chotanagpur," in A.M. Shah, B.S. Baviskar and E.A. Ramaswamy (eds.), *op. cit.*

Sarkar, R.M. 1971. "The Santal Insurrection through Ballads", in L.P. Vidyarthi and G. Choubey (eds.). *Bihar in Folklore. Study.* Calcutta: Indian Publication.

—. 1986. *Regional Cults and Rural Traditions.* New Delhi: Inter-India Publications.

—. 1993(a). "Culture and Politics in Tribal Bihar", in M.K. Raha and I.A. Khan (eds.), *Polity, Political Process and Social Control in South Asia.* New Delhi: Gyan Publishing House.

—. 1993(b). "Tribal Unrest in West Bengal", in Biswanath Roy (ed.), *West Bengal Today: A Fresh Look.* New Delhi: Mittal Publications.

Sarkar, S.S. 1938. *The Malers of the Rajmahal Hills.* Calcutta: The Book Company.

Sen, Jyoti. 1972. "The Jharkhand Movement", in K. Suresh Singh (ed.), *The Tribal Situation in India.* Simla: Indian Institute of Advanced Study.

Sen, S.C., Jyoti Sen and Sudhir Panchbhai. 1969. "The Concept of Diku among the Tribes of Chotanagpur", *Man in India,* 49(2).

Singh, K.S. 1977. "From Ethnicity to Regionalism: A Study in Tribal Politics and Movements in Chotanagpur from 1900 to 1975", in S.C. Malik (ed.), *op. cit.*

EIGHT

SOCIETY, POLITICS AND CONFLICT
Some Observations on the Santals of Jamboni Area of Midnapore District, West Bengal

RAJAT KANTI DAS

Introduction

A precondition of the society is the presence of social persons. A social person is an individual and at the same time he or she is representative of a society. So a social person may be viewed as an interplay between individual and society. Based on social persons, the next step is formation of social organization at the community level. This calls for taking a close look at who does what with whom, and how a society is maintained through time. Here it may be profitable to bring in the concept of social institution, which could be defined as a custom in vogue, or a system of social relationships including power relations, or a set of rules and code of conduct enduring through a considerable period of time irrespective of persons enacting those. From this point of view, a society exists through its institutions. If a situation develops where the institutions fail to function in the way they are intended to, it gives an indication that the society in question has been changing in some fundamental ways. In a tribal society, which was once better integrated socially, this change is particularly in evidence in the political field either in the context of new political alignments, or as a new direction to the traditional socio-political organizations in the face of mounting pressure from the modern political institutions represented by the state and political parties, or a combination of both.

The contemporary developments among the Santals of Jamboni area of Midnapore District of West Bengal demands such an approach. For some time Jamboni has been in the news relating to political violence involving national-level political parties, C.P.I. (M), Congress and the Jharkhand Party.

The paper is based on field information collected by Nabendu Bera, M.Sc. in Anthropology from Vidyasagar University, Midnapore during 1996-97.

The latter has been spearheading, the movement for an autonomous Jharkhand State. Jamboni lies in the Jhargram sub-division of Midnapore under the jurisdiction of a single police station. It covers 10 anchals with an estimated number of 316 villages, of which more than 200 are tribal villages dominated by the Santals and the rest are Hindu caste villages and villages with a mixed population. Clearly, there is numerical dominance of the tribals, particularly the Santals, in an area which falls within the region claimed by the Jharkhandis. At the political front also some of the Jharkhandi protagonists have been more active in this area. In a situation of acute political rivalry the Jharkhand movement has got a new dimension here imbibing and in a way reviving the traditional socio-political organizations. In the present study observations are limited to the Santals only.

Growing Importance of the Jharkhand Party

Admittedly, the main problem faced by the Santals of Jamboni area is socio-political in nature. Even some two decades back, when the political parties were yet to establish themselves in a big way by cutting across Santal corporate existence, the traditional socio-political organizations did not function to the full possible extent. *Pir pargana* and *muluk pargana,* the two important territorially-based socio-political organizations of the Santals, were non-functional in this area for quite some time. As a result, the Santal socio-political life was in disarray. The intricately organized Santal life, which was a demonstration of blending and binding experiment of collective existence, gave way to alien life style signifying a reduced value of traditional components of life. Going for economic transactions at the individual level across community line, organizing Western-style birth day parties, paying dowry and marital gifts, reorganizing the funeral ceremony by giving up some of the traditional ritual components, belittling the importance of social symbols like the *gira*—all of these are indicative of a process of erosion of traditional values and belief system. The situation was well utilized by the political parties, whose main interest was to extend their range of influence among the tribals so as to create a sort of tribal vote bank. The weakening of the traditional socio-political base of the Santals may not be the direct outcome of the increasing influence of political parties. It may be more pertinent to speak in terms of national-level politics making inroads into the tribal world. Willingly or unwillingly, the Santals came within the fold of political parties. In other words, they became a part of the modern political system. The devalued image of the traditional set-up was not necessarily a precondition for the acceptance of the new political system, but it certainly gives an impression that the two were somehow interlinked. But ultimately Jharkhand became their central concern, particularly to those who could not meaningfully identify themselves with the new system dominated by persons belonging to other communities. And even to a casual estimate they form the bulk of the population today. Their concern for the loss of identity made them rely heavily on the Jharkhand party, which could catch their imagination by trying to reorganize them along traditional line. A large number of Santals came out in the open to support the cause of Jharkhand, which became a sentimental issue to them. Meanwhile, the C.P.I. (M), which could establish a support base in this region during all these years, changed their line of approach by creating an impression that it was all for encouragement and preservation of the Santal culture and tradition. On June 30, 1995, the party organized the *hulmaha* ceremony as a proof of their genuine interest in Santal culture. Most of the Santals, however, became suspicious of the intention of the party. They thought that the party was not so much interested in reestablishing their socio-political base but in extending its range of influence among them. This brought them into conflict with the party workers. A large number of Santals supporting the cause of Jharkhand started joining the Jharkhand party.

In the so-called Jharkhand movement aimed at safeguarding the interests of the Jharkhandis, a substantial number of Santals were actively involved. Even the Santal women participated in this alongside their male counterparts. The movement got a boost with the performance of *hulmaha,* when all the Santal villages showed a rare display of solidarity by unfurling and raising green flags as a mark of respect to the martyrdom of Santal national heroes, Sidhu and Kanhu. This act of theirs made them the target of attack by the overenthusiastic supporters of a political party, who were concerned about their eroding support base. The Jharkhand party provided the political platform, the organizational base to the Santals engaged in confrontation with their political adversaries. While taking upon itself the role of spearheading the Jharkhand movement, the party could feel the necessity of strengthening the organizational base in line with the traditional pattern of socio-political order.

Traditional Socio-Political Profile

In the Santal society village organization is considered to be an essential component of the socio-political life. The village organization or *panchait,* as it is called, used to take the role of guiding, controlling and directing the interaction pattern necessary for making an enduring social system work through the formation of shared social and political institutions with a certain degree of continuity through time. Usually, *manjhi, jog manjhi, naike, paranaik* and *godet* form the village organization. But in Jamboni, as also is the case in some other areas, all the office bearers do not find a representation in the village organization. For example, in the village organizations of Sonahara, Dhunamari, Nunia, Degaria, the posts of *paranaik* and *naike* had been lying vacant for a long time. In some villages no office bearer other than *manjhi* and *jog manjhi* was found to be actively involved with the activities of the village organization. Clearly, the ritual functions carried out by the village organization have been reduced to a level of virtual insignificance. The main functions of it today center around striving to maintain social relationship at the institutional level and periodically renewing inter-village link within the broad framework of a Santal society. Obviously, the latter has more political overtone. Even otherwise, regularizing an irregular union concerning two villages has greater implications than the immediate purpose of maintaining amicable relationship between villages. A specific example may be cited. Biru Hambrom of Mamurda village had an affair with a Santal girl at Baraghat, Silda, where he had gone to take part in the ritual and celebration associated with the worship of the Goddess Bhairabi. Biru and the offending girl were apprehended by the girl's father and his associates. They were brought to Mamurda, the village to which Biru belonged. The father of the girl formally approached both the *manjhis* of the concerned villages. The *manjhis* of the two villages met and asked the respective *jog manhis* to resolve the matter. The *jog manjhis* of both the villages demanded *handia* (country liquor) in sufficient quantity and Rs. 50 each from both the guardians in the form of fine. The *jog manjhis* then arranged *jomjot,* the function at which such irregular activities committed by individuals could be regularized. After *jomjot* it is left to the individuals to decide whether to marry or remain separate. At that stage, the *manjhis* and *jog manjhis* could not enforce their decision on them. What emerges from the above mentioned case is that though the village organization is singularly responsible for regularizing an irregular union giving it the necessary social sanction, the right to exercise individual choice within the framework of the society is not completely curbed. It suggests that individual perspective is not completely submerged in the social and cultural milieu. Secondly, it is the village organization which gives a Santal village a stamp of individuality in the form of a distinctive socio-political status. This has wider ramifications extending to the whole Santal society. Even in the context of Jharkhand the level of Santal participation seems to be conditioned by the stagewise representation of socio-political formations having village organization at the root.

Besides village organization, Santal socio-political life finds expression at different organizational levels, such as *pursi, pir, muluk, dishom* and *la mahal.* Functional relations within and between these organizations give shape to the socio-political structure of the Santal society. The totality of this structure qualifies the society and contributes to its culture. Politics has become a way of life to an increasing number of Santals today and to an extent this has been forced on them. Moreover, they have come to realize that in the event of society losing its credibility as a boundary-maintenance system, as a political unit they can still carry weight in the contemporary world. It may be worthwhile to bring in the labels of "group" and "grid" proposed by Mary Douglas (1970) to explain the nature of Santal society today. The group dimension takes into account the degree of social cohesion displayed by persons and societies, whereas the degree of shared classifications or knowledge forms the basis of classification according to grid dimension. While it may not be possible to place the Santal society as representing a fixed type following Douglas's scheme, indications are there that an oscillating process between the two dimensions has gripped the Santals of Jamboni. Neither they can be rigidly classified at the societal level, nor can it be proposed that they themselves have given up the tendency to create rigid boundaries with respect to outsiders.

The neighbourhood principle is applied to the formation of *puris* organization. In general, 5 to 10 villages come together to form a *puris*. *Pir* refers to an *anchal* or a region with *pir parganait* as its head. Between 10 to 22 villages could find a place in a *pir*. Besides the *pir parganait,* other office bearers are *jog pir, pir naike, pir paranaik, pir godet.* If a problem relating to intra-village or inter-village relation could not be solved either at the village organization level or at the *pursi* level, it will be referred to the *pir*. The next higher grade is *muluk,* which stands for *mouza.* Anything between 7 to 15 *pirs* form a *muluk.* There may be still larger *muluks* also. The following *muluks* could be identified in Jamboni area: (i) Silda *muluk,* (ii) Motop *muluk,* (iii) Bhat *muluk,* (iv) Zujin *muluk,* (v) Tung *muluk,* (vi) Raipur *muluk,* (vii) Bugri *muluk.* At the *muluk* level, the officials are designated as *muluk parganait, jog muluk, muluk naike, muluk paranait and muluk godet.* Above *muluk* is the grade of *dishom,* which literally means *desh.* But it cannot possibly be equated with the state as is understood in common parlance. Territoriality spread over a region is the basis of a *dishom,* which may consist of 7 to 15 *muluks.* A *dishom* is headed by the *dishom parganait.* Other office bearers are, *jog dishom, dishom naike, dishom paranaik* and *dishom godet.* The *dishom* exercises control over *muluks,* which are accountable to it. The highest grade is *la-mahal,* which refers to the whole Santal society. *La-Mahal* cannot be formed with less than 10 *dishoms.* Theoretically at least, this justifies the existence of a Santal society. All these grades find a representation in *manjhi marua,* the meeting at the highest level where decisions from the perspective of Santal society are taken with a degree of firmness. According to one version, *manjhi marua* will be called to tackle a crisis—like situation that cannot be solved at any other level. Statelevel Santal representatives are required to be present in *manjhi marua.* In actual terms, *manjhi marua* provides the much-needed link between the different grades of Santal socio-political organization.

Social Ambiguities and Political Conflict

All these are ideal constructs. It would be wrong to assume that the Santal society functions in a perfect order maintaining the integrative character of the society, controlling and channelling organizational activities to every sphere and stage of the Santal socio-political base. For more than two decades *muluk* and *pir* organizations were almost functionless in Jamboni area. As some protagonists of the Jharkhand movement claimed, these organizations could be reestablished and given due recognition only through the ongoing movement. According to them, the Jharkhand movement was not an ordinary political movement. It had social purpose too and that was its source of strength. The society had to be revitalized by following the traditional order because taking advantage of lack of social cohesion individuals indulged in anti-social activities, they argued. The case of Fakir Tudu was cited by them. Fakir Tudu married a Mahato girl and the couple had a son and a daughter. But they were not accepted in the society. Fakir Tudu was asked to arrange *jomjot* where he and his family members could seek social recognition. Being a leader of a political party at the local level. Fakir Tudu defied the order, following which two *manjhi maruas* were held to decide the issue. In the second *manjhi marua* the *muluk parganait* announced the following decisions taken unanimously:

(i) that Fakir Tudu would never be allowed to arrange marriage of his son and daughter in the Santal society;
(ii) that he would not be allowed to perform his mother's funeral ceremony in the customary way and would be prevented from visiting the river Damodar in this connection;
(iii) that if any Santal boy would put vermilion on the forehead of Fakir's daughter, it would be considered an anti-social activity on the part of the boy; and
(iv) that his property would be considered an enemy property.

Coming to know about these decisions, Fakir Tudu arranged his mother's funeral ceremony as an act of defiance. The villagers and even the *pursi* villagers protested against holding the funeral. A conflicting situation developed and the police had to intervene. The situation deteriorated to such an extent that the police had to open fire, in which one Shyamal Soren (25) was killed. For the death of Shyamal, the Santal society held Fakir responsible and his defiance was considered to be an act directed against the interest of the society.

The case of Purnima Soren of Kamarbandhi village also highlights the process of Santal social control. Purnima, a student of class IX of Kamarbandhi

High School, attracted the attention of Sanjoy, a Santal boy student of that school. Sanjoy fell for her, but did not get any response from Purnima, who was already socially married. Once, when Purnima was on her way to the school, Sanjoy threw vermilion on Purnima's forehead. This was considered an immoral act on the part of Sanjoy. The *manjhi* of Kamarbandhi convened a special meeting of *panchait,* in which the fathers of Purnima and Sanjoy, and the husband of Purnima were also present. *Jog manjhi* was asked to decide the case. In the meeting Sanjoy questioned the right of Purnima's husband and demanded Purnima to be recognized as his wife. But Purnima refused to accept Sanjoy as her husband and preferred to remain the wife of her socially married husband. *Jog manjhi* decided Sanjoy to be guilty and demanded a sum of Rs. 3500 as fine from his father to be paid at a specially-convened *jomjot* function. *Jog manjhi* communicated his decision to the *pir parganait* and *jog pir,* who also approved of it. Sanjoy however, refused to accept the decision and sought police help for protection in the ensuing conflict. He wanted the police to sort out the problem. But he did not get any response from the police, which only confirms the observation that in social matters even the state-appointed guardians of law do not like to intervene. This also proves that tradition still counts, particularly when it comes to the question of displaying group solidarity as a manifestation of social identity. And this may be considered to be the take-off point for launching a large scale movement for the establishment of political rights.

Of a series of incidents in Jamboni area, a particular one may be described to explain how the tribal tradition was utilized by the political activists for their own cause. In July 1995, the first-ever *manjhi marua* was arranged at Goido village. Before doing that, the *manjhi* of Goido sent the message through *gira* to villages falling under *Anchal* No. 1 to 10. *Gira,* symbolically represented by a root or the bark of a sal tree, stands for news or message regarding marriage, funeral, outbreak of epidemics, conflict, organization-level meetings or any other matter of social significance. Unexpectedly, five villages Bhatur, Chutia, Balidinha under *Anchal* No. 9 rejected the *gira* thereby indicating that they were not going to attend the proposed *manjhi marua.* It was alleged that they did it at the instigation of a political party. They even went up to the extent of burning down the *gira.* Because they were active supporters of a political party, they did not want the first ever *manjhi marua* covering all the villages under *Anchal* No. 1 to 10 to be successfully held at Goido, the people of which did not subscribe to their political ideology. On the next March, the *manjhi* of Balidiha, one of the five villages who had earlier rejected the *gira* announcing their absence from the grand conference, arranged the performance of *Baha Bonga* coinciding the appearance of season's fruits and flowers and offering them first to the *bonga* (god). At this all other Santal villages excepting those five villages got extremely annoyed. They sought an explanation from the *manjhi* of Balidiha as to why he had not participated in the conference held at Goido. They maintained that Balidiha and four other villages, who also behaved in the same way, had no right to arrange the performance of *Baha Bonga.* By refusing to accept the *gira* they had insulted the whole Santal community. Ultimately, they did not allow the ritual to be performed at Balidiha. Tension mounted and at the request of the *manjhis* of the targeted villages a police force was deployed. But the police also could not control the situation and sought the help of a popular political leader to bring the situation under control. The political leader brought all the *manjhis,* excepting those representing splinter group of five villages, under his control. He took the role of mediating between the *manjhis* representing the majority group over whom he could establish control and the *manjhis* of the specific group of five villages, who were led by a political leader of a different Party. The latter questioned the significance and utility of Santal beliefs and customary practices to which the leader of the other group charged him with conspiring with the police to cause harm to the Santals. The leader of the minority group was subsequently made the target for deliberately belittling the importance of Santal culture and traditions. The situation became tense and the police had to intervene. A temporary compromise solution was worked out by the leaders of the two groups of villages. Of late, the national-level political parties, their agents and supporters have concentrated more on Santal culture to see that no solid boundary could be built by the tribals around their customs and traditions and that could only ensure promotion of their own political interests through a process of modernization inducing the tribals to learn the relevant political game. Nobody could deny that they have not succeeded in their attempt so far. But little they could realize that learning the political game may not always go to their advantage. The Santals have now turned the tables on them. Together with learning the rules of the political game, the Santals have developed a local and regional political strategy of challenging power by overcommunicating amongst themselves their point of view and by putting up their own front after drawing on the strength of their socio-political root.

There is, however, another side of it. Their evaluation of prestige and power in the contemporary situation appears to have lost direction giving rise to conflicting tendencies in their society. When Lakshmiram Mandi, the *manjhi* of Sonahara village, sent the *gira* to Champa Murmu, the *manjhi* of Satparti village, relating to a cultural function to commemorate Sidhu, Kanju and Birsha Munda, there was no indication that much trouble was lying ahead. Champa Murmu duly attended the cultural function. Trouble started when Lakshmiram arranged for the sacrifices of a goat in honour of the Santal national heroes. Champa Murmu objected to it on the ground that as

Sidhu, Kanhu and Birsa Munda were not *bongas,* they could not be raised to that status. They were not entitled to animal sacrifice. Lakshmiram was, however, in favour of raising the status of three freedom fighters to that of the *bonga.* So he would not change his decision and ultimately the goat was sacrificed. Champa Murmu immediately left the place of celebration and returned to his village without participating further in that function. The very next day Champa approached the *dishom parganait* and narrated the whole incident. After hearing him, the *dishom parganait* gave the verdict upholding Champa Murmu's stand. It was resolved that sacrificing animal blood in honour of a freedom fighter was against the social norm. Champa personally went to Lakshmiram and informed him about the decision of the *dishom parganait.* Such cases of dissension are on the increase.

Disturbing Trend

Now Jamboni is literally boiling. It cannot be denied that imposition of party politics and, together with it, political rivalry, political victimization have alienated a large section of the Santals. If any thing, it has strengthened the cause of Jharkhandis. The Jharkhand People's Party has made its presence increasingly felt, which is a proof enough to support the contention that the Santals have come within its fold in a bigger number. Even some members of caste Hindus and smaller tribal groups lend a moral support to it. This may be more out of compulsion to, or fear from the party activists. But these days applying pressure tactics by a political party has become the recognized, if not accepted, way of operating at the political level. A situation of conflict has developed and it has pervaded almost all aspects of life. True, in this situation the Jharkhand People's Party has been able to catch the imagination of a greater number of Santal people, but in this exercise the real beneficiaries will be the political activists. They have been successful in politicizing the issue, which, however, involves the risk of increasing the number of disenchanted people holding no genuine love towards their customs and traditions, instead trying to utilize them more like a cultural broker. Their political interests lie more with the modern political institutions and consequently, their primary concern is to induct more of their representatives into the modern political sphere, which was once alien to them. This change in focus may partly be related with the changing nature of land relations as tenurial rights based on kinship have been eroded in recent times.

REFERENCES

Douglas, Mary. 1970. *Natural Symbols.* London: Barrie and Rockliff.

Eriksen, Thomas Hylland. 1995. *Small Places, Large Issues: An Introduction to Social and Cultural Anthropology,* London: Pluto Press.

NINE

HISTORICAL PERSPECTIVE OF THE TRIBAL SUB-MOVEMENTS IN FREEDOM MOVEMENT
With Special Reference to Andhra Pradesh

S. KRISHNA REDDY, K. RATHNAIAH and
M.P. NARASIMHA RAJU

By and large, the tribal people have remained isolated and backward. Their participation in national politics is not very significant. They are almost the last of the Indian communities to be politicized. But research into the freedom movement in different parts of the country, which has been recently undertaken in terms of the social composition of regional movements, has revealed a rich pattern of the involvement of local communities in regional politics. Evidence suggests that like other communities, tribals participated intensely in local politics, but with a difference. There was an attempt on the part of the tribal community to seek integration into the regional and national systems and also to preserve its own identity.

A careful review of literature reveals that there exists a very limited number of studies on tribal movements in India. Further most of the existing studies are fragmentary by nature and thereby do not appreciably add to our understanding on the problem at hand. However, here mention may be made of Singh (1982), Jayaprakash Rao (1985), Krishna Rao (1985), Sivarama Krishna Rao and Bobbili (1985) and Doshi (1990) who have done some useful research in this regard.

In the present paper an attempt has been made to analyze the historical process of integration of the tribal people during the pre-Independence period, their assimilation with regional movements and their search for identity. The tribal movements in Andhra Pradesh are entirely different from those elsewhere in the country because of the different socio-economic and political set-up.

The role of tribals in regional politics was deeper than is generally known, it was also more diverse, as it centered around specific issues concerning land and forest. Its manifestation was often violent, despite valiant attempt made by the Koyas, Konda Doras and Jatapus to remain non-violent. Further, there was the process of sanskritization. All these led to achieve solidarity among the tribals at the regional level. The process of integration, however, did not extend to the national level. Tribal problem never forwarded in the resolutions passed by the Congress sessions until the early 1940's.

Unfortunately, in spite of the great sacrifice made by the tribal people during the Gandhian phase of freedom movement, most of their socio-economic and other problems remain unsolved even after about 50 years of independence. The land they lost has not yet been recovered and their natural rights on forest and on others are not yet fully preserved. Without proper appraisal of their inspiring role, the history of India's freedom movement will be incomplete.

It was not always the politics of non-violent movement and social reform that interested the tribal people. In Rampa-Rekapally the tribal people were capable of mobilizing through their traditional institutions of chiefs, clan and village assembly. Tribal assembly held the key. All elements of the tribal corporate life were carried into their movements. Dacoities, loot and murder were the modes of the rebels' strategy which were ruthlessly enforced. Spontaneity and speed of the tribal movements have often been commented upon, but the elements of planning and organization behind them also deserve to be highlighted.

The results of the uprising were also not uniform. In British India they achieved a non-regulation administrative system for tribals and special agrarian laws to protect the tribal land, but little was done in the princely states.

Between the land and forest, the latter thus emerged as the focal point of tribal unrest, with increasing restriction placed on shifting cultivation (podu). Probably the first uprising resulting from this process, occurred in 1879-80, known as Rampa and Rekapally Rebellion, after the place of its occurrence, Rampa, a small hilly sleepy village in the Chodavaram division of Godavari District of Andhra Pradesh. The two tribes who led the uprisings were Koyas and Jatapus. A guerrilla warfare was waged by Alluri Seetharama Raju (1898-1923) who was a Kshatriya ruler. He had acquired the reputation of a *sanyasi*, astrologer and magician—a versatile personality which attracted the rural folk who sought to overthrow the British Raj and set himself up as the *raja*. Influenced by the non-cooperation movement, he preached temperance and the wearing of Khadi which did not go down well with hill people.

In Rekapally, one of the main grievances of the tribals, which was focussed upon during the civil disobedience movement, was the restriction placed on their traditional forest natural rights as they depend on the forest, on its roots and fruits, during days of famine and distress since times immemorial. In disgust of this, they violated the forest laws and cut down and even burnt plantations of timber trees.

Restrictions had been imposed on forest and the customary tax of four annas, i.e. 25 paise had been trebled by the then Madras government, which also imposed a tax on the felling of certain species of reserved trees. This was part of the policy of the reservation of forest. The colonial records attributed the rebellion to the "oppressive acts of the Mansabdar" and the "absence of proper supervision and control on the part of European officers".

In Rampa, another important part of the rebellion was over new toddy rules, a new abkari regulation, preventing the drawing of toddy for domestic purposes and leasing the toddy revenue to renters or lessees who demanded that tribal masters *(muttadars)* should pay fees *(chigurupannu)* for the right to tap toddy. The *muttadars* chief, *mansabdar,* threatened to levy an additional tax *(modlupannu)* at the rate of one-half to two-thirds of the *chigurupannu.* This was the proverbial last straw on the camel's back. The old grievances were once again reviewed; the constables taking advantage of the civil law grabbed their land and extracted fowls from the traders.

The rebellion started in March 1879. Two constables were sacrificed before the chief shrine by the insurgents. In its sweep the Rampa-Rekapally insurrections could be compared with those of Kol and Santhal. The affected area, comprising about 5000 square miles, was wooded hilly country in which the rebels resorted to guerrilla warfare, avoiding direct confrontation with troops. They attacked isolated police stations and looted the villages of those who collaborated with the government. The gravity of rebellion for the authorities could be assessed by the strength of the forces they deployed to quell it. Harassed by guerrillas, and struck down by malaria, the state forces, aided by Hyderabad, succeeded in capturing or killing its leaders and suppressing the rebellion.

While there were factors of agrarian discontent arising from the restrictions on Podu or shifting of cultivations, extraction of forced labour and ill treatment of coolies, the movement was essentially political, designed to achieve independence. Raju with the support of the Doras the upper crust of tribal society, was able to establish a mass base for his movement. He took meticulous care not to antagonize the people and in turn enjoyed their support.

He denounced the British officers and the police station establishment but there were no "incidents" involving the Indians. The agrarian issue, which was relegated to the background, did not manifest itself in the attack on the money-lenders or traders. This was suppressed, but Raju's martyrdom helped to strengthen the freedom movement in Telugu region. The Rampa-Rekapally rebellion resulted in the abolition of the *monsabdari* of Rampa, establishment of direct administration by government and reduction of toddy taxes of Rekapally.

Conclusion

Tribal involvement in regional politics was deeper than is generally known; it was also more diverse, as it centered round specific issues concerning land and forest, its manifestation was often violent, despite the valiant attempts by the tribals of Andhra to remain non-violent. Further, there was the process of sanskritization. All this made for integration into the regional system. The process of integration, however, did not extend to the national level, tribal problems never figured in the resolutions passed at the Congress sessions and few Indian leaders, with the exception of Mahatma Gandhi and Rajendra Prasad, showed any keen awareness of tribal issue until early 1940's. Tribal Isolationism was the backlash of a sense of neglect and fear of losing identity, it was the characteristics response of backward communities at a certain stage of their development.

REFERENCES

Doshi, S.L. 1990. *Tribal Ethnicity, Class and Integration.* Jaipur: Rawat Publishers.

Jayaprakash Rao, P. 1985. "The Struggle for Land. Tribal revolts in Two villages", in K. Murali Manohar *et al.* (eds.), *Political Economy of Tribal Development.* Warangal: Indian Institute of Public Administration.

Krishna Rao, M.V. 1985. "Tribes of Andhra Pradesh: A Peep into their Past," in K. Murali Manohar *et al.* (eds.), *op. cit.*

Singh, K. S. 1982. *Tribal Movements of India.* Vol-I and II. New Delhi: Manohar Publishers.

Sivarama Krishna Rao, C. and A. Bobbili. 1985. "Tribal Movements in Andhra Pradesh: A Short History," in K. Murali Manohar *et al.* (eds.), *op.cit.*

TEN

A CRITICAL ANALYSIS OF A TRIBAL UPRISING IN ORISSA
Case of Kandhamal

DEBENDRANATH JENA

In recent past, Phulabani, literally known as "forest of flowers", a peaceful district, situated in the hilly terrains of central Orissa was burning with intense caste-tribe conflict. Bailey's Phulabani during 1960's which had attracted world attention for its peaceful surroundings, orthodox practices and widespread superstitions turned into a battle ground for *adivasis* and *harijans*. Now the district is renamed as "Kandhamal" as a strategy to appease the sentiment of dominant Kandhas in the area. "Kandha" is the name of the tribe and "Mala" implies hilly terrains. Etymologically "Kandhamal" signifies the mountainous nature of its landscape as well as dominating presence of the Kandhas. The recent conflict between *adivasis* (Kandhas) and *harijans* (Panas) in Phulabani assumed such proportion that it was given coverage on the front page of national dailies for more than a month. It also thrilled the Parliament and the State Legislative Assembly. The conflict was generally considered by most of the people as politically induced and motivated. But history teaches us that no movement can be militantly organized, pervasive and intense by mere political instigation and motivation, unless it is related to some fundamental deep rooted socio-cultural needs and scarcities. Hence such type of conflicts should be analyzed from various socio-cultural angles over and above the obvious political and economic dimensions.

The ugly facade of political rivalry combined with intense class hatred and long standing *jajmani* feuds was instrumental in triggering this conflict which claimed 20 lives besides rendering thousands homeless. In the said conflict, the harijans, traditionally the most oppressed and socially handicapped community in the country, were at the receiving end. It was also significant to note that a particular lower caste group, i.e. Pana was singled out by all other groups as the sole oppressor and that the aboriginal *adivasis* were able to get the support of the caste people, including high caste Brahmins. Because of such uniqueness, this problem demands a deeper diagnosis which can reveal some relevant facts. In this paper we try to focus on the underlying historical as well as social factors which finally lit the dangerous fire in the forest of flowers (Phulabani).

Theoretical Debate

Tribal revolt is neither new nor rare in India. It has a long history. Important studies on tribal revolts have been carried out by various eminent scholars like Orans (1965), Singh (1974), Gough (1974), Oommen (1977), Roy Burman (1977), Singh (1982), Sharma (1986), Rao (1987), Bipin Chandra (1987), Jain (1991), etc. Initially these tribal uprisings used to be directed against economic exploitation, colonial administration and towards upholding of traditional culture. Most feuds were agrarian in nature and were based on land tenure system. Cultural shock, relative deprivation, domination by external forces and identity preservation have been the other important elements in tribal revolts. But, of late, these uprisings have taken up a regional or ethnic colour and become caste-class based. Moreover, such movements are tending to take up a distinctly political character mainly because of the increasing involvement of organized political associations and the growing political aspirations of the local budding tribal leaders.

Though literature on tribal movements in Orissa has been scarce, mention may be made of a few uprisings. The first major uprising in Orissa had been the famous "Kandha meli" of Ghumusar in 1853 to restore the deposed Raj family. The Kandhas took lead in this movement. In 1930, another Kondh insurrection was organized in Boudh against the oppressive and tyranical rule of the king, "bethi" (forced labour) and the increase of land revenue. In 1938 widespread tribal-peasant agitations were launched in various parts of the state like Dhenkanal, Talcher, Nilagiri, Ranapur, Keonjhar, etc. against the misrule of the respective Rajas. During the early 1980's the tribals of Sambalpur organized the "Balco Andolan" to protect thier habitat as well as ecology of Gandharmardan hill from the polluting onslaught of industrialization. The recent Jharkhand movement is staged by the Santals of North Orissa and Bihar demanding a separate state for the tribals. All these movements testify to the tradition of organized rebellion among the tribal masses. Those also show a tendency of the leaders to extract political advantages from these uprisings, which they use as the launch-pad for their political careers.

Methodology

The present study, focuses on the recent crisis in some of the areas of

Phulabani (Kandhamal) district involving the conflict between *adivasis* and *harijans* following the Linepara temple issue. Hence our attention has been focused on the sporadic riots between these two communities beginning from 14th January, 1994 upto August, 1994. Though the problem under our study is specific in nature, its scope in multifaceted. Various aspects of the sample respondents, like their socio-economic condition, inter-personal relations, beliefs, ideology, political participation, socio-cultural reality, etc. have been taken into account to carry out a complete diagnosis of the conflict. Some of the conflict torn areas of the district were selected as our universe. In all, six villages were chosen for the study. They are, namely, Khajuripada, Dalapada, Kiranapada, Nugaon, Linepara and Hatapada. Of the six, the first four villages are within Khajuripara block, while Linepara, from where the conflict originated is under Chakapada block and Hatapada is under the Phulabani N.A.C. On all the 15 blocks in the district, Khajuripada was most severely affected by the conflict. The selection of the respondents was done on the basis of stratified random method. A total number of 200 sample respondents were selected from two different communities (Kandhas and Panas). Table 10.1 shows the distribution of our respondents in terms of their villages. For the purpose of collection of data, a structured interview schedule was used. Besides some second-hand information were also collected from various sources like panchayat offices, block offices, police stations, libraries, etc. Most of the Kandhas and Panas were extremely genial and were eager to

TABLE 10.1 Showing the distribution of Sample Respondents in Terms of the villages.

Name of the Village	Number of Respondents		Total
	Kandhas	Panas	
Khajuripada**	15 (481)	31 (811)	46 (1292)
Dalapada*	16 (645)	13 (371)	32 (1016)
Kiranpada*	17 (545)	11 (305)	28 (850)
Nuagaon**	07 (215)	12 (345)	19 (560)
Linepara*	33 (1105)	15 (408)	48 (1513)
Hatapada**	09 (294)	18 (515)	27 (809)
Total	100 (3285)	100 (2755)	200 (6040)

Note: Figures in the parenthesis indicate the total population of Kandhas/Panas in the village.

* Villages dominated by Kandhas, ** Villages dominated by Panas

share their experience with us.

Phulabani: An Overview

Phulabani, the present district of Kandhamal, has had a varied and chequered history. Its district headquarters is located in Phulabani town. It was only on 16th June, 1994 that it officially and formally got its latest name "Kandhamala". The population of the district is 9.8 lakhs of which 51.1 per cent are females. Thus, the females outnumber the males. Ninety-five per cent of population live in rural areas and in southern hill areas. Majority of the population (82%) is engaged in agriculture (Census, 1991). Since the people use the primitive agricultural techniques, the harvest is not good. Hence most of the people depend on forest products to earn their livelihood. The percentage of literacy in Kandhamala is only 28.69.

Tribals are the original aboriginal Dravidian inhabitants of Phulabani. They constitute 51.51 per cent of the total population of the district of which 36 per cent are Kandhas. Scheduled Castes constitute 18.21 per cent of which 10 per cent are Panas (Census, 1991). The Panas have migrated to this place from the plains of Nayagarh, Cuttack and other nearby areas and settled in the Kandha dominated hill area, the reasons for which are obscure. It is found that the Kandhas are more a homogeneous and close knit group than that of the Panas. The Panas have experienced more life-cycle changes than the Kandhas and they are also engaged in a variety of occupations while the latter are more tradition bound, superstitious, xenophobic, non-materialistic and satisfied with the *status-quo.* The Panas in general seem to be more resourceful, ambitious and tenacious in adopting to the changing circumstances while the Kandhas are more confined to their ethnic enclave.

Dimension of the Conflict

The prime aim of our study is to identify and analyze the etiological factors that might have gone in brewing the conflict. The various dimensions going into the issues were historical, economic, political and socio-cultural.

Historical Aspect

History is the breeding ground for future wars. Though history cannot be recreated and past blunders cannot be corrected. Atrocity committed in the past is never forgotten and continues to be a ground for future dissension. In our study, the cases of personal grievances against the rival community were reported in plenty. Most of the Kandhas alleged that Panas usually commit theft, deceit, exploitation, molestation of their women, while Panas reported that Kandhas commit hooliganism and insult them in various occasions. Though the alleged petty thefts (goats from the hill sides, fruits from orchards, etc.) by the Panas were not the major ground for conflict but Kandhas considered those to be offensive. Table 10.2 gives a comparative account of alleged offences of both the categories.

TABLE 10.2 : Showing the Nature and Extent of Offences Committed by Rival Communities

Nature of offence	No. of Respondent's Complaining	
	Kandha	Pana
Molestation of women	72	00
Physical assault	13	32
Theft/Deceit	52	00
Hooliganism	15	45
Insult	18	48
Exploitation	45	08

A general complaint of the Kandhas was that Panas continually "eye their wives and young daughters". Very often Panas commit theft/deceit. On the other hand Panas did not report against molestation and theft. In the past, minor conflicts had also occurred during the festive occasions like Nuakhai, Shravana Purnima and Gahma Purnima. During such occasions Kandhas usually drink "salapa", home made liquor and under inebriated state they often abused Panas and Oriyas. In many villages also, the Panas have encroached upon the land of Kandhas. Many Kandhas having legally lost their land to the Panas, have become dejected and continue to trespass those land out of frustration to create disturbances. As a whole, most of the Kandhas were antagonistic towards Panas.

Economic Aspect

In the present study an attempt has been made by the author to scrutinize the economic aspect of Kandha-Pana dissension.

In Dalapara, Kiranpara, Linepara and Nuagaon villages, the Kandhas are major land owners whereas in Khajuripara and Hatapara, Panas are dominant. Most of the respondents from both the categories reported having been exploited by the cheating class *mahajanas* (money-lenders). Usually, a Kandha does not deal directly with the *mahajanas* rather deploy a Pana intermediary to get loan by mortgaging his land and other belongings. Often, the intermediary and the money-lender joining their hands together exploit the poor Kandhas. Hence, Panas are called as "cheats" by the Kandhas. It is surprizing to note that 48 per cent of the Kandhas reported that they sell their land at a very low price during crisis. An old Kandha told that he had sold two acres of land two years ago for two hundred rupees only.

Most of the Kandhas live in high up hills and are well acquainted with the jungle. They are the traditional users of forest and forest products. They go to interior jungles, bring firewoods and heap them at foothills. 52 per cent of the Kandha respondents said that the Panas steal those firewoods. On the other hand many Panas (48 per cent) complained that Kandhas have monopolized the forest and are not allowing them to use it. Much dissension was also observed among Panas and Kandhas with regard to the use of mangoes and its kernel. Over the past few years Panas have been entering into mango orchards to collect green mangoes and its kernel, which is marketed as a local food and exported for oil extraction. It has become a profitable business for Panas. Hence, Kandhas get very much frustrated on this account and warn the Panas not to enter mango orchards. In fact Panas are clever and more shrewd than the native and proud Kandhas who consider trade beneath their dignity and beneath their capacity (Bailey, 1960). Usually the Kandhas engage Pana intermediary for trade and business and Panas do not hesitate to cheat the Kandhas on this count.

Under various poverty alleviation programme of government like Integrated Rural Development Programme (IRDP), Jawahar Rozgar Yojana (JRY) etc., Panas are the most benefited section whereas Kandhas are most deprived ones. Selection of beneficiaries under such programmes creates much dissatisfaction among Kandhas. Because of their political network Panas have succeeded in getting loans easily whereas Kandhas have been cheated in spite of giving bribe to the middle men. Thus, from the above findings it is revealed that Panas are more cunning and oriented towards immediate monetary gains whereas Kandhas are falling behind economically because of their naivety and too much dependence on Pana intermediaries.

Political Aspect

There was uproar that the conflict was politically induced and motivated to a great extent. But our empirical findings did not corroborate the same. We found little political interest among our respondents. Only three per cent of Kandhas and nine per cent of Panas said that they belong to some political party/association and have had direct link with the politicians. With regard to nature and degree of political involvement the response was very confusing. So an attempt has been made to give an approximate picture of the political scenario. Most of the respondents from both the categories viewed their dissatisfaction and hatredness towards politicians. They opined that political leaders are responsible for corruption, price-hike, and exploitation. It was observed that there is hardly any influence of reputed politicians on either of the communities.

In the wake of recent conflict, a socio-cultural organization named Kui Samaja has been working for the unification of Kandhas. Kui is a tribal dialect of Kolarian (Munda) branch of Austro-Asiatic group of languages spoken by most of the Kandhas. Large number of Kandha youths are attracted towards Kui Samaja. Leaders of the Kui Samaja undertook extensive fund raising compaign to support the conflict. A sum of Rs. 5 and 250 grams of rice were collected from each Kandha household to support the cause. To buy arms and ammunitions, some shops of Panas were looted. Food materials and money were provided by the Kui Samaja to the guerrillas at the training camps in the interior forests.

Most of the respondents said that the political leaders have hardly ever visited their place. Only a few local petty leaders visit the village. It is worthy to note here that 62 per cent of the respondents felt that the local leaders try to create misunderstanding between the two communities for their personal economic gain.

Socio-Cultural Aspect

There exist many socio-cultural differences between Kandhas and Panas. There is significant social distance between Kandhas and Panas, especially in ritual matters. Social intercourse between the two communities is hardly marked. Because of strong "ethnocentrism", one community thinks itself to be ritually and socially superior to the other. Interestingly, in village hotels and restaurants, Kandhas and Panas eat on separate tables earmarked for them. Rarely a Pana or a Kandha is found inviting the members of the other rival community on the festive occasions to his family or *basti* (area). Kandhas claim themselves to be Hindus and do not allow the Panas (harijans) to enter into temple.

In our sample areas the members of these two communities have mostly separate pond for their exclusive use. In case where they have a common pond, the two communities normally take bath on the opposite sides. 23 per cent of the respondents reported that both the communities fetch water from the same source while the rest replied that they have separate sources of drinking water. Use of the tube well for drinking water does not create any problem of purity and pollution, but the use of common well is rare. Even when the village has a single well there are specified times for a particular community to draw water from the well. Most of the respondents said that untouchability has vanished but in the covert sphere communal segregation is widely marked. Table 10.3 shows the incidence of various types of social intercourse between the Kandhas and the Panas.

TABLE 10.3 : Showing Degree of Social Distance between Kandhas and Panas

	Nature of Social Intercourse	No. of Respondents Allowing such with Rival Community		Total (Percentage)
		Kandha	Pana	
1.	Use of same source of drinking water	18	28	46 (23)
2.	Take Bath at the same place	15	22	37 (18.5)
3.	Inviting to visit home	04	18	22 (11)
4.	Inviting to festive occasions and marriage ceremonies	32	44	76 (38)
5.	Inter-dining	00	00	00
6.	Allowing temple entry	00	62	62 (31)

A critical appraisal of the above four broad dimensions of conflict indicate that the economic deprivation of the Kandhas and socio-cultural marginalization of the Panas played major role in the genesis and propagation of the communal antagonism in which historical and political factors acted as the catalysts.

The Final Eruption

Backed with their economic and political advantages, the Harijans, especially the Panas, continually harass the Kandhas. Most of the politicians and government officials of the district are *harijans*. Thus, *harijans* always take upperhand because of such advantageous situation. Harijans also try to affirm their self conferred superior status by forcibly entering into the temple close to them. On the day of *Makar Sankranti,* i.e. 14th January, 1994, in a pre-planned manner, Digambar Nayak, a Harijan, dreaming to be the Nayak of the area forcibly entered into the Barada Balunkeswar Shiva Temple of Linepara crossing the "Laxaman Line" for the untouchables, in spite of opposition from the Kandhas. After the unsuccessful and uncompromised village meeting, Mr. Nayak with the help of his followers beaten a number of Kandhas with iron rods, who had opposed the temple entry earlier. This incident added the highly inflammable fuel to the latent fire burning in the hearts of the Kandhas. Fighting ensued. Event followed event and in one bitter squabble at Linepara, a Pana leader was killed. On 19th January, 1994 some Panas stopped Kandhas from harvesting tamarind from their own field. When Kandhas, protested they put them behind the bars. A massive rally of

15,000 Kandhas was organized by the leaders of Kui Samaj which provoked the Kandhas. Such an organized effort and police inaction opened up the most sanguine chapter in the history of Orissa.

Injuries, Loss and Agony

The Kandhas used dangerous sharp cutting weapons, handmade guns, revolver, bows and arrows to attack the Panas. They had a young guerrilla wing who got their arm training in dense forest of Tikabali-Kuchilagarh camp. The Kandhas usually attacked the entire village in large group. It testified the greater organized structure of Kandhas. The Panas used only sharp cutting weapons and *lathis.* They had neither modern arms and ammunitions nor specialized training for combating. But they were very cautious in attacking and preferred to corner their victims in small group and killing on the sly.

Within a short span of time, the conflict spreaded over 500 villages in 40 panchayats of the district, mostly in Khajuripada, Phiringia, Chakapada, Phulabani Sadar, Tikabali and Tumudibandh blocks. Though the conflict started from Linepara panchayat of Chakapada block yet the Khajuripada block was most severely affected in terms of the magnitude of destruction–both physical and economical. The violent conflict in all took 20 valuable lives from both the communities (nine Kandhas and eleven Panas). Two (both Kandhas) of them were killed in police firing. It is startling to note that out of the first ten killed, seven were Panas and three were Kandhas. It indicates that the violence was first initiated by Kandhas while retaliation by the Panas came subsequently. As dangerous weapons, arms and ammunitions were used in the said violence, the nature of physical injuries were also severe. As reported, 180 people were hospitalized and many others including innocent ones also sustained minor injuries. However, not a single woman received any serious injury. Normally Kandhas did not attack women and children. It is beyond their ethics. Panas do not have such a war ethic. It was proved when they killed an innocent Kandha school boy.

Both the communities incurred a heavy financial loss in the course of conflict. Besides, it also affected the general population as a whole. The normal life was severely affected for more than a month. As conflict continued, most of the Panas left their villages and moved to nearby Pana dominated areas and other districts leaving their women and children behind. This led to the loss of their occupation. For a number of days they moved here and there without food. Acres and acres of jack fruit farms could not be harvested. Ploughing and sowing could not be done in the area because of the tense situation. It thus severely affected the economic condition of both the Kandhas and the Panas. Vast tracks of agricultural land of Kandhas remained untilled because of the non-availability of Panas labour. Kandhas are less skilled and most of them lack the knowledge of trading or business transaction of their own vegetable and fruit. Even they are not skilled to pluck the fruits and vegetables. Kandhas, usually procure, sell and dispose of their agricultural products through Pana intermediaries. For days together the situation remained like that causing heavy financial loss to Kandhas.

Because of the continued violence, the old, traditional and long standing jajmani type relationship between the two rival communities collapsed. Many shops and godowns were looted, hundreds of houses gutted down and thousands of trees were cut down by the militant groups. Thus, the general economy of the area deteriorated to a great extent.

The horrors of the conflict also psychologically wounded the morale of the people. The mental horizon of most of the people was clouded with fear psychosis, mental agony and psychological distress. This was because of the unpredictability of rival group's next attempt. Everybody, at any moment, was apprehending the worst situation. The presence of police and paramilitary forces also created a panic situation in the area. People restricted their movements with the fear of being interrogated or detained by the police. Some of the Panas even left with their families for jungle hide-out. The homeless and fled away Panas staying at the shelter camps were in constant fear of unexpected attack by the militant Kandhas.

The above diagnosis of the conflict amply demonstrates that the Phulabani conflict was the product of opposite pulls exerted on the Kandha-Pana social fabric by a double contingency of deprivation. The first is the economic deprivation of Kandhas and the second is the socio-cultural marginalization of Panas which brought about mutuality of dissension, dissatisfaction and antagonism. Various past misdeeds alongwith political undercurrent of local leaders compounded and aggravated the basic antagonism. Because of such complex nature of the conflict it is not easy to fit it into any standard classification. However, it seems to be a combination of fourth and fifth type of Gough's (1974) classification of tribal uprising.

REFERENCES

Bailey, F.G. 1957. *Caste and the Economic Frontier: A Village in Highland Orissa.* Manchester: Manchester University Press.

—. 1960. *Tribe, Caste and Nation: A Study of Political Change and Political Activity in Highland Orissa,* Manchester: Manchester University Press.

Census of India. 1991. Series (16) Orissa–Part-I, Director of Census Operation, Orissa, Bhubaneshwar.

Chandra Bipin. 1987. *India's Struggle for Independence,* New Delhi: Viking Publications.

Gough, K.E. 1974. "Indian Peasant Uprising", *Economic and Political Weekly, II.*

Jain, P.C. 1991. *Social Movement Among Tribals,* Jaipur: Rawat Publishers.

Oommen, T.K. 1977. "Sociological Issues in the Analysis of Social Movements in Independent

India", *Sociological Bulletin,* 26(11).

Orans, Martin. 1965. *The Santals: A Tribe in Search of a Great Tradition,* Detroit: Wayne State University Press.

Rao, M.S.A. 1987. *Social Movement and Social Transformation.* New Delhi: Monohar Publishers.

Roy Burman, B.K. 1979. "Challenges and Responses in Tribal India", in M.S.A. Rao (ed.), *Social Movement in India,* New Delhi: Monohar Publishers.

Sharma, K.L. 1984. *Caste, Class and Social Movements,* Jaipur: Rawat Publishers.

Singh, K.S. (ed.). 1982. *Tribal Movements in India.* New Delhi: Monohar Publishers.

Singh, Rajendra. 1974. "Agrarian Social Structure and Peasant Unrest," *Sociological Bulletin,* 13(1).

ELEVEN

BIRSA MUNDA
An Apostle of Social Justice

SABITA TRIPATHY and
ABHAYA NARAYANA NAYAK

The tribal people have always kept a self and separate identity, language and cultural distinctiveness and a distinguish fabric of ethnic paradigm in the society as a whole. They have stroven in all sorts of ordeal and adverse socio-political milieu to retain their identity and freedom in the Kaleidoscopic and dynamic administrative arena. To retain their socio-political identity the aborginal people have raised their voice against the exploitative forces. The English word "movement" has been derived from the old French verb *movier*, which means to move, stir or impel. The Oxford Dictionary defines "movement" as "a series of actions and endeavours of a body of persons for a special object." Herbert Blemer's definition of a social movement as "collective enterprises to establish a new order of life" is considered as a classic definition. Social movement is also regarded as a "group behaviour directed in a concerned way at bringing about social change," "a group venture extending beyond a local community for a single event and involving a systematic effort to inaugurate changes in thought, behaviour and social relationships," or "a collectivity which acts with some continuity to promote or resist change in a society or group of which it is a part." (Bharadwaj, 1977: 142).

In India, the man of forest who among innumerable hazards tried to bring social justice for his exploited community people in the days of Maharani Victoria Raj was Birsa Munda. He was a Munda by birth and he took the leadership of the rebellion *(ulgulan)* of Munda tribalmen during 1895-1900. It was however, a complex of revivalism, political action and a search for utopia (Ray Burman, 1974: 47). It was a resistance and religious movement at the same time (Singh, 1996). The colonial economic and administrative policies, and the outrage of landlords upon the Mundas brought them together to lanch a powerful revolution against the Britishers. The germination of the movement occurred due to the conversion of Mundas from *adivasi* religion to Christianity. Birsa appeared at the scene as a socio-cultural reformist to prevent the interference of *diku* (outsiders) Nayak, 1996:5-6). His reforms and reorganization among the Mundas in the subsequent period made the movement more meaningful. The development of the Jagirdari system among the Mundas resulted in economic and social degradation and this in turn produced acute individual stress which subsequently led to "cultural distortion" in which the elements of culture "were not harmoniously related but were mutually inconsistent and interfering" (Jay, 1961). Thus the tribal people went through a period when cultivation of land was no longer useful to keep them fed (became the products of Labour and were expropriated locally by *jagirdars* and *thikadars,* the alien landlords) and, therefore, during the period of revitalization they took the initiative to attack the landlords and their supporters, and even threatened them with destruction. In order to deprive the landlords of the produce. "Birsa asked his followers to give up cultivation and gather at Chalkad" (Sinha, 1967: 172). Birsa's reformative operation in the first stage and an open rebellion against the Britishers in the second stage to establish Munda Raj gave a tangible and transparent picture of ethnic collectiveness. By using the principle of fission and fusion of ethnicity, an ethnic reorganization was made by Birsa to face the exploitation of the minority *(dikus)* against the majority. Like the epoch making work of the late President, Abraham Lincoln, Birsa dedicated his life to abolish the system of tenant farmers from the forest region. He directed all his efforts to raise social consciousness against this system of servitude but he had his own limitations as a forest dweller. The financial and physical resources he commanded were very little as against the opposition of the non-tribal men and the white rulers.

A Sylvan Child

The forest of Chhotanagpur became the field of his belligerent activities. Birsa moved day and night from one part of the forest to another on foot on a missionary zeal to organize the people against socio-economic exploitation. The main reason of his transformation from a spiritual leader, *guru* to that of a revolutionary leader was the conspiracy of the British government. A man born in forest to resurrect the lives of his kinsmen was forced to become a belligerent leader. On the 15th November 1875 Birsa was born in a share-cropper Christian household at Chalakhada, a village lying in the forest region between Ranchi and Singhbhum. Among the five children Birsa was the fourth son of his parents. He led the life of a typical tribal boy tending flocks of sheep, cow and goat. Poverty compelled his parents to send Birsa, then a five years old boy, to his maternal uncle's house. His aunt engaged him as a cowherd boy. While the cattle grazed in the field, he used to get himself absorbed in writing the alphabets on the ground dreaming of a better future. He loved to play on flute and at times meditated so deeply on it that his cattle went astray and destroyed crops. At some occasions he was thrashed black and blue by the concerned field owners. He had to pay high price for his absent-mindedness and was not spared to receive corporal punishment even by his maternal aunt. In all such circumstances Birsa never opened his lips as a word of protest. When he could no longer bear the torture, he left the village and came to his brother's house at Kundigaon.

School of Scandal

His brother got him admitted into a German mission school. Life at the school campus was not a bed of roses for him. He had to put up there in an uncongenial atmosphere. The teachers pooh-poohed his tribal culture and looked down upon him with disdain whenever he defended his culture. As a young man he could hardly accustom himself to the surrounding, particularly the antipathy of the teachers and the priest towards the tribal society. He left the school and got himself admitted into a mission school of Chaibasha. The change of school served no better purpose in his life; it was a change from frying pan to fire. His deep interest in study enabled him to swallow all sorts of humiliation and scorn in his new school. Most agonising of all was the discussion and satire of the people on his Munda culture. From a tender age Birsa showed immense respect for his own custom and culture. Any criticism on Munda tribe was sufficient enough to aflame his spirit. As a reciprocal measure he counter-attacked the priests and Christianity in the school. It was a battle of wits. Birsa reaped the consequence—he was driven out of the German mission school, thus putting an abrupt end to his schooling.

Influence of Hindu Scriptures and Spiritual Transformation

Birsa had unwavering faith in Hindu religion. Through service he met once a *sanyasi,* Swami Ananda Pandey, who taught him the gospel of Hindu *sastra,* the story of the great epics, the *Ramayan* and the *Mahabharat.* The ideal characters of these two Hindu epics inspired Birsa's mind and heart and moulded his thoughts. It brought an inner change in his emotional and intellectual life.

Birsa's life was surrounded with a few legends. In the early monsoon of the year 1895, while Birsa was in a jungle with a friend, there was a thunderstorm, and lightning struck him and he was transfigured. Birsa said that at that movement he had received a divine revelation which related to the deliverance of his people. This news spreaded like wild fire. Soon after this he was attributed with having healing powers and crowds of suffering humanity began to see his blessings. He began holding *Harikirtan* and giving religious discourses. He asked people to worship only one God, i.e. "Singbonga", abstain from violence and from eating animal flesh. All living beings, according to him, were children of Singbonga. He also forbade the drinking of wine and other intoxicants including rice-bear. He asked his followers to use the sacred thread and stressed purity of heart at the time of worship. This religion was known on the Birsa *dharam* (religion) and was a mixture of Hinduism and Christianity. He was called *Bhagwan* (God) as well as *Dharti Aba* or the father of the world by his followers (Sachchidananda, 1979: 235).

Dissemination of Light of Knowledge

Birsa made all efforts to spread the light of knowledge among his tribesmen so that there could be some effective changes in people's life. Under the cloud of ignorance the tribesmen still clung to blind belief and superstitions. They were not prepared to accept rational ideas and new knowledge. Birsa's reformative zeal was directed against the cutworn customs and superstitions and he sought to dispel social evils, taboos and blind beliefs from the society. He taught people to accept the monistic theory of God and not to believe in the diabolic power of witch or ghost. Like Mahatma Gandhi he preached service to humanity as service to God. His humanistic teaching encompassed all men as equal and everyone embodied the spark of the divine. He pronounced service as an alternative path to worship. His theological teachings and monistic theory were directed to improve people's socio-religious life. As in most reformative movements here too we find the feature of "prophetic revelation and legitimacy" (Sinha, 1967:172).

The Enchanter

Like some of the great *saints* and *sufees* of India, Birsa's musical talent enchanted the heart of his followers, old and young alike. He was an excellent flute player like Lord Krishna and in his youth he used to attract people with his musical instrument (bowl consisting of the dried skin of gourd). Once upon a time Birsa's music reverberated the forest region of Chhotanagpur. Maidens thronged around him vying with each other to win his heart. Forest lass: Salya, Gunja, Tara and others were his *gopis*, his fiances who could never bear Birsa's absence. He was the most sought after playboy of the forest land. Suprizingly enough Birsa never accepted anyone as his wife. Wedlock was never in his fate. He was born to amuse, preach, fight and die as a martyr for the right of the forest dwellers.

Reformative Zeal

Birsa wanted to change people's behaviour and attitude in the right direction. He made an intensive drive against the use of narcotic drugs which was one of the chief evils in his society. Day by day Birsa's popularity increased and people showed diminishing interest in religious conversion. Christian Mundas renewed their faith in their ancestral religion. There was a shimmering movement for reorganization of a Munda state and strengthen Munda culture under the leadership of Birsa. The exploitation of the landlords and the discontentment of the Mundas inspired them to organize themselves against the *dikus*.

From socio-religious problems Birsa turned his attention to the political right of his tribesmen. He made the Mundas conscious against the socio-economic exploitation by the non-Mundas, the rich and the landlords. The Mundas were then maltreated as hired labourers and forced to work with low wages. The consciousness of the Mundas was focussed on the various machinery of social and economic exploitation employed by the whitemen as well as the non-tribals. They were so neglected that no one showed any concern for the welfare of these indigenous people. The Mundas had to wrest their political and social rights from others. To the ignorant and illiterate Mundas, Birsa's words rang as the gospel of truth with *mantric* power.

Drawn to Political Whirlpool

The British government took an altogether different view of the increasing popularity of Birsa. He was warned not to speak in an assembly of people. As it is difficult to put an embankment on a flooded river, the government's restrictions fell to restrain people's enthusiasm for Birsa's teaching. Birsa claimed to have taught a new doctrine to his people to resurrect them in the old Hindu religion which would free them from ignorance, social evil, and exploitation. He made fervent appeal to the British government not to misconstrue his sincere efforts to bring social justice to his people. Birsa's socio-cultural and spiritual movement took a different turn in 1894 as a protest against injustice of the government. The government collected land revenue in the drought ridden areas of Chhotanagpur under severe oppressive measures. Unable to bear the inhuman treatment the tribal people were panic stricken and rushed to Birsa's village. Day by day the presence of the crowd in Birsa's village became alarming even though without taking recourse to any violent method. Birsa only consoled the people and advised them to pray God. The British police apprehended a mass agitation and took stringent measures to arrest Birsa. The head constable of Khunti police station, Mr. Yushuf Khan made surreptitious attempts to arrest Birsa. The simple, naive, and loyal followers of Birsa could hardly tolerate the presence of the police in their village. They were infuriated that the police was engaged in an act of sacrilege in accusing their living God and every attempt was afoot to arrest him. The head constable of the police party Yushuf Khan had to face the stroke of their axe for which Birsa later on paid a heavy price. He was held responsible for the murder of Yusuf Khan and was remanded to police custody at Ranchi.

The Prophet of Peace Turns a Belligerent Warrior

Birsa's two years of imprisonment did not abate people's enthusiasm for his movement. After his release from police custody, Birsa movement gathered new momentum and it took suddenly an unexpected turn. The spiritual *guru* took up arms against the injustice of the British government. He led a vagrant life organizing people against the injustice meted out to them. The impregnable forest of Chhotanagpur was his hideout where he adopted guerrilla tactics. He moved ambushed from one part of the forest to another on foot day and night, at times without food and rest. Birsa's guerrilla fight unnerved the British police. The district administration called for the army to tackle the critical situation arising out of Birsa's insurgency. The military force surrounded the Chhotanagpur forest and carried out combing operation. The British expedition may be compared to that of hunting a wild animal in the jungle. Birsa's reformative zeal turned into military vigour. The sylvan cowherd boy became the defensive supreme of the tribal revolutionaries. The followers of Birsa were harassed and maltreated. So they led a life of uneasiness and suffering. The British police imposed a reign of terror. All sorts of instruments of torture were inflicted on the poor to reveal Birsa's hideout. So much of people's faith Birsa commanded that a cash award of a lucrative amount never could tempt the poor men's heart who in those days hardly got a handful rice once even in a month. A simple forest dweller never betrays his loyalty which is the distinguishing trait of the character of tribal people. The tribals dislike, even oppose to the Aryan's who resort to deception, treachery and double dealing.

In February 1898 the representatives of various Munda regions assembled at Dumburi to discuss the oppressive measures of the British police and the newly framed repressive government rules. For the first time violence was used to fight against the enemies. Birsa's messianic role even in the struggle for freedom was never questioned or disbelieved by his followers. The establishment of a Munda state, the forest land of the tribals, was declared as their cardinal goal based on the principle of ancestral right of the forest dwellers. The last uprising of the Munda tribe took place in the evening of 24th December 1899. Police stations were attacked with bow and arrows, ransacked and set on fire. The British police was unequal to the overwhelming force of Brisa's followers. The government was forced to deploy military force. Bow and arrows of the Mundas were unable to withstand the bullets and gunpowder of the British force. The barefooted Mundas moved with lightning speed in the hilly regions over mountainous rocks without any regular supply of food. The British force was well equipped with transport facilities. In the biting cold waves of January a Munda revolutionary had to remain content with a small piece of loin cloth. The British succeeded in hatching a plot to capture Birsa along with his 482 followers old and young. About 98 Mundas were convicted, death sentence was pronounced on three

Freedom to Martyrdom

The trial scene of the revolutionaries was most pathetic. Birsa and his compatriots neither employed any defence counsel nor opened their lips. They were charged with false allegations. Spontaneously Barrister Jacob took up the case of the revolutionaries. Without any trial Birsa had to accept solitary confinement in Ranchi prison from February 1900 onwards. Prior to that he had to move in the Chotanagpur jungle for few months without food and clothes to evade the surveillance of British force. The Superintendent of Ranchi Prison very much wished Birsa's death. For ages to come people would worship Birsa as God incarnate in the jungle land. The condition of Birsa's health eventhough became critical from 30th May 1900, he was not treated properly. At last (on the morning of 9th June) his frail physique gave in, he vomitted blood and soon lost his consciousness. The Superintendent of Ranchi Jail failed to prepare a convincing death report of Birsa from morning till evening. At last the doctor found out a way to convince the government about Birsa's death. He wrote that Birsa died of cholera even though he did not touch water for several weeks. The police was so much afraid of Birsa that the fetters on his body were removed after his death only. In his most critical moment he was never released from fetters in his solitary cell. His dead body was neither handed over to his relatives nor to the public who revered him as their living God. The reason seems to be very much clear the government did not venture to face public discontentment. The fated one to perform his last rituals were sweepers of the jail who set fire to his dead body in a night at a lonely place on the bank of river. The jail sweeper who lit the funeral pyre of Birsa Munda was one of his admirers. To him it was not an official work, but a piece of sacred work, an auspicious assignment.

The Undying Spirit of Freedom

Eventhough the British government established a pyrrhic victory, the eternal flame of Birsa's spirit would enkindle millions of heart to raise voice against social exploitation. Birsa's life will be remembered as one of the pioneers like Nelson Mandella and Mahatma Gandhi who raised their voice for the exploited and oppressed class and caste, not only for his revolutionary activities but for his social commitments. He ranks high among the religious poets. His religious teaching moulded the simple lives of the *vanavasies,* the settlers of the forest. He freed the mind of his people from the fear of ghost and necromancy, urged them to surrender themselves to the ever encompassing love of the Divine. He taught his followers to remain neat and clean, pure in mind and heart and sing the devotional songs. The followers of Birsa led austere life on vegetarian diet. Birsa's devotional songs embodied profound love for God and a sympathetic attitude towards fellow beings. The songs ushered in a renaissance in Munda culture. The basic tenets of Birsa's principles were based a social justice for the forest dwellers, and his humanistic teaching drew innumerable followers towards him.

REFERENCES

Bharadwaj, G. 1977. "Socio-Political Movements Among the Tribes of India", in S.C. Dube (ed), *Tribal Heritage of India.* New Delhi: Vikas Publishing House.

Devi, M. 1980. *Aranyara Adikar,* (tr. A. Ray) Cuttack: Grantha Prakashana.

Jay, E. 1961. *Revitalization Movement in Tribal India in Aspect of Religion in Indian Society,* Meerut.

Mirdha, H. 1991. *Saheed Birsa Munda Geeban Sameeskha.* Sambalpur: Nikhila Odissa Adivasi Sanshkrutika Sansada.

Mishra, R. 1980. *Birsa Munda,* Cuttack: Janashakti Pustakalya.

Nayak, A.N. 1996. "Birsa Munda Movement: A Case of Tribal Identity Formation", Paper presented in the National Seminar on *Tribal identity Formation and Development,* organized by Institute of Social Research and Applied Anthropology, Bidisa (W.B.)

Roy Burman, B.K. 1974. "Ethnicity in Chhotanagpur with Particular Reference to the Tribal Communities", paper prepared for a UNESCO expert committe meeting on *Race Relations in Asia and Oceania.*

Sachchidananda. 1979. *The Changing Munda,* New Delhi. Concept Publishing Company.

Singh, K.S. 1966. *The Dust Storm and the Haging Mist—A Study of Birsa Munda and his Movement in Chhotanagpur* (1974-1901). Calcutta: Firma K.L. Mukhopadhyay.

Sinha, S.P. 1967. "Portrait of a Munda Leader: Birsa Bhagwan (1895-1900)", in L.P. Vidyarthi (ed.), *Leadership in India.* New Delhi: Asia Publishing House.

TWELVE

GOND REVIVALISM AND REINTEGRATION

B.M. MUKHERJEE and F. MOLLICK

The Gond are the largest tribal group in our country. They are an important ethnic group who inhabit the central region of India known as Gondwana. According to 1981 census Gonds, the largest tribal group in Madhya Pradesh had a total population of 53,49,883. They constituted 44.6 per cent of the total Scheduled Tribe population in the state. This paper seeks to analyze the religio-cultural revivalist movement amongst the Gond inhabiting in Bilaspur district of Madhya Pradesh. Bilaspur district acquires the fourth position in the state with a total Gond population of 3,47,028, Bastar district being first with a total Gond population of 10,50,632. They comprised 50.2 per cent of the total Scheduled Tribe Population in Bilaspur district.

A revivalist movement is a process of reinterpretation of cultural and religious values and rejection of religion and culture of the other groups so that people can adjust to the new situation. Many authors have attempted to study the religious/revivalistic/reformist/development movements. (Ekka, 1972; Bhadra, 1977; Desai, 1977; Troise, 1979; Ekka, 1982; Pant, 1990; Paul, 1991). Mahapatra (1968) states that "social movement occurs when a fairly large number of people, or an otherwise identifiable segment of the population, deliberately band together for collective action in order to alter, reconstitute, reinterpret, restore, protect, supplant or create some portions of their culture or social order, or to better their life-chances by redistributing the power of control in a society." Oommen (1990) opines that "social movement is an effort to redefine or recapture the past, to restructure the present and reorient the future".

Data were collected from the different blocks of Bilaspur district with the help of an interview guide. The factors which influenced the selection of site was the availability of relevant data. Observations, content analysis, informal interview and group discussion were employed for data collection. The major sources of the information were various records like pamphlet, literary writings, written decisions of the different meetings. Different opinions, views and activities are published through pamphlets and written documents. The group meeting technique has an advantage in the sense that if a member of the group do not remember or explain a particular situation or fact, then other members of the group help him to remember or explain that fact or situation. Therefore we used this technique quite off and on to collect detailed information on the nature and causes of the movement, ideology and pattern of the different organizations and associations. For informal interview we identified some key informants keeping in view the objectives of the study.

Tribal movements appear among the numerically strong, usually the settled agriculturists and the economically well off tribes (Oommen, 1990;82). Solidarity movements will be weak or absent under following circumstances: small number and low-economic level which is inadequate for striking power, absence of educated elite to provide leadership *(ibid).* Against the baekdrop the researchers selected Gond tribe for their study. They were perhaps the largest and most significant organized group which had once come to rule over regions of Chandagarh, Garhkatanga, Mandlagarh, Kheragarh, Bhoramdeogarh, Devgarh, etc. The Gonds were an independent, self ruling people. They played a significant role in Indian history between 15th and 18th century. The Gonds, who form the greater portion of the population of Gondwana, have been conjectured to be the aborigines of Hindusthan (Thomson, 1860). In an analysis of revitalization movement it is important to give special consideration to the historical background and the contact of the people of that group with the people of other cultures. Earlier studies and literatures provided us with a knowledge of the historical background of the group. The social contacts of the Gonds with the Hindu society have influenced their rituals and practices and changed their socio-cultural life. Now they have become the part of Hindu society. The entire Gond population professed faith in Hinduism. In Bilaspur, earlier in 1931 census 1,23,950 Gonds were returned as professing faith in Hinduism and 48,410 in tribal religions. Under the influence of Hindus, their pantheon includes *Bhagwan* (Mohadeo). They have also adopted the social and moral codes of their neighbours (Shrivastav, 1978).

The basic aim of the movement among the Gonds of Chanda in 1946 was to unite as many as forty-one categories of tribal groups comprising the Gond, Bhil, Pardhans, Kolam, Baiga, Khond; and a few others groups who followed the indigenous religious beliefs and practices and worshipped various Devs as the Gonda. According to Gond Raja, Gondi or Koitor *dharma* is different from Hindu *dharma* (Thusu, 1982). Rajmohini Devi's movement in the Surguja district of M.P. occurred in 1951. She told the people to give up drinking of liquor, to earadicate social and communal evils, to propagate Hinduism and Gandhian ideology, not to sell the mahua in the market. Mahua dev movement started in this century in the village Ratanpur of Bilaspur district and gradually spreaded to other regions of Chhattisgarh. The aim of that movement was to give up drinking liquor and eating meat, to eliminate the belief in and practices of *bhoot* and *pret,* to eradicate the social evils. "In this movement the traditional gods and goddesses of the group were also kept in view and new beliefs and practices were introduced in the background of the old ones" (Shrivastav, 1978: 103).

The present movement originated because of dissatisfaction of the Gond with their social and economic conditions. This movement has been launched against irrational beliefs and practices, social evils prevailing in their society. For the preservation of their religious and cultural identity they have formed different social and political organizations, viz. Gondwana Maha Sangh, Gondwana Maha Sabha, Gondwana Mahila Mandal, Gondwana Krishak Sangharsh Samiti, Gondwana Mukti Morcha and Gondwana Mukti Sena. This organizational network aims at uniting all the Gonds under the name of Gondwana and creating a society free from exploitation. Some other major objectives of the network are to establish a Gondwana Bank for their economic development, to work for advancement of education and women, to retain their religious and cultural identity and to propagate their religion and culture.

Kangla Majhi demanded the formation of a Gondwana state and more employment opportunities for the tribals. He founded the Bharatiya Gondwana Sangh in August, 1959 (Singh, 1982: 183). The national level set-up of Gondwana Maha Sangh has its head office at Nagpur. It has remarkable control over the Gond society all over India. Bilaspur and Nagpur are highly influenced by the activities of Gondwana Maha Sangh. The Maha Sangh has its activities in some other districts too, but not as intense as that in Bilaspur. The prime objective of Bilaspur district Gondwana Association (Sangh), which came into being in the year 1952, was social reforms, but it remained ineffective for a long time. A conference was organized on 27th March, 1993 and a social organization Gondwana Mahasabha, was formed. Mostly the educated Gonds formed the Mahasabha to make Gondwana society free from exploitation. The objectives of the Mahasabha are: creation of a Gond society free from exploitation, building of awareness among the members of the society, prohibition on drinking and overspending, development of culture, art and religion and its conservation, formation of service organizations for free service of the mass. The duties of the Mahasabha are to follow the social rules and orders, to unite the Gond society to eliminate the customs which are against the dignity of women and to protect the Gondwana culture. The work of the Mahasabha can be divided into four categories, i.e. executive *(karya palika),* judiciary *(nyay palika),* finance and organization. The main office bearers of the Mahasabha are president, vice-president, secretary, joint secretary, treasurer and other executive members. Next to Mahasabha is circle and Gram Sabha. Representatives of each circle are the official members of the Mahasabha. The officials should be the life members of the association, teetotaller, educated and of good character, between 21-50 years ago. These are minimum requirements for the officials. Elected members of each circle are empowered to elect one person as president. President is empowerd to select the vice-president and the other office bearers. The president is empowered to run the society, but not empowered to formulate or amend any law relating to the society. In case of an objection raised by a person over any judgement of circle President, then he or she may appeal to the president by paying the appeal fees. On this the president can call on a meeting of Judiciary for giving the decision. In any dispute, groupism, controversy arising in the circle, the president is empowered to dissolve circle body. At that time the executive body controls all the activities of the circle for six months and after that a new body will be elected. The president has to arrange the meeting of the executive body in every six months with a prior intimation of seven days. Meeting is headed by vice-president in absence of president. Insult of the president is regarded as the insult to the entire community. In such a situation the offender will be penalized and fined Rs. 500. The president, vice-president and members of the Mahasabha can be ousted by the majority of the circle members. If any member remains absent from the meeting consecutively for 3 times he or she can be ousted without any warning.

Secretary is the head of the executive body of the Mahasabha. Members of the executive body visit each circle for organizing general meeting and forming circle as per the consensus of people. The main function of this body is to propagate their religion and culture for their own development. Judiciary body of the Mahasabha has five members. This body is only empowered to make and amend any law relating to the society. If the president thinks that a rule is not good for society, then he places it before the judiciary body. Then the judiciary amends it and presents before the Mahasabha for its approval. Five members from the Mahasabha form the finance body headed by the treasurer. Financial year is from 1st April to 31 March. The function of this body is to prepare financial planning of the Mahasabha and its annual budget. The sources of the income are membership fees, donation, marriage registration fees (Rs. 25), etc. President or person nominated by the president has to audit the annual income and expenditure. Three-fourth part of income is kept in the accounts of circle and one-fourth in the accounts of Mahasabha. Treasurer keeps not more than Rs. 100 and deposit extra money to the joint account of the Mahasabha. Organizational body of the Mahasabha is constituted by five members of the Mahasabha, headed by secretary and co-ordinated by co-secretary. The main function of this body is to visit the whole area of the Gondwana, keep the organization strength intact, keep contact with members, make campaigns for membership, develop social awareness and collect annual membership (Rs. 15).

Between 10 and 20 number of villages forms a circle. The number is not specified. All wrong doings of the society are controlled by the circle according to the direction of the Mahasabha. All the members of the circle sit at a particular spot and take decision to solve the disputes among members. The officials of the circle are president, vice-president, secretary, asst. secretary and treasurer. The councillor *(panch)* of the village is the active member of the circle. The circle has four branches, namely, the executive body (Circle Karya Palika), Judiciary body (Circle Nyay Palika), the finance body and the organizational body. The functions of the executive body are to make registration of marriageable girls and boys to maintain unity among them, eradicate jealousy among them and motivate them for higher education, protect the religion and culture in every village of the circle, construct shrines for the Gond deity (Burha Deo), propagate the Gond religion through mass-media and construct Gondwana shop in every villages. A special jury of five members is formed for the judiciary body. Normal disputes can be dealt by the jury of the circle. The main objectives of the branch of Judiciary body is to solve internal disputes within circle, settle disputes relating to divorce and premarriage ceremony *(sagai).* It does not have the power to make rule and amend it. If a person has committed a crime, then the power to ostracize him from the society or to forgive him does not rest with the circle. Only judiciary body of the Mahasabha has the power to decide such cases. Circle finance body and circle organizational body work according to the direction and order of the finance body and organizational body of the Mahasabha. Any application to circle society must be accompanied with a fee of Rs. 25. Next to the circle is the Gramsabha which has some powers too within its jurisdiction in the matters of solving local problems. The members of Mahasabha, circle and Gramsabha are elected for a three years term.

Now Mahasabha claims that Gonds are the aborgines of this area. After coming to India the Aryans captured their land, made them slave and superimposed their cultural practices on them. That is why their people say that they are Hindus. The Mahasabha raises many questions pertaining to their identity like, if they are Hindus, then why do they worship dual Gods? Why is their God not being worshipped by the Hindus? Why are their festivals not being observed by the Hindus? It indicates that they are not Hindus but they are made out to be Hindus.

Some of the lengthy and expensive traditional rituals have been reviewed by the Mahasabha and necessary modifications have been made in order to make those less time consuming and expensive. In those days a woman was allowed to remarry upto six times. But now this has been modified as it is thought to be an evil practice. The widow has the right to remarry under the name *churi marriage.* She is allowed to remarry twice. Widows are allowed to marry only with the widowers. Sometimes the wife may leave her husband

and would marry another person who may be a widower or unmarried person. Marriage of a married man with another woman while his wife is alive, is disapproved by the Mahasabha. In such cases, the concerned person will be penalized by the Mahasabha. In earlier times girls of 15-16 years used to marry men of 40-45 years of age. There were problems arising out of such relationships. Now Mahasabha has banned such marriages. People over 40 years of age are not allowed to marry in the society. If he does marry, under difficult situation, he can do so with the widows only but not with unmarried woman. Mahasabha has formulated a set of rules to bring reformation in the marriage practices. Registration of bride and bride-groom is essential during betrothal period *(sagai)* by paying registration fee of Rs. 25. Child marriage is strictly prohibited and if detected is punishable. Age of the girl and the boy should be 18 years and 21 years respectively at the time of marriage. Boy's or girl's party, whoever breaks the *sagai,* will be fined with Rs. 500. If both of them (husband and wife) consented to break their relation, they give Rs. 3000 as fine to the society. For one way breaking of relation, the concerned party will have to pay Rs. 5000 as fine. The collected money is distributed in the following order: the aggrieved party would get 60 per cent of the total money; 40 per cent of the total money is deposited equally in the account of the Mahasabha and the circle. In case of elopement, the boy's and the girl's party have to pay Rs. 5000 and Rs. 2000 respectively as fine. All these directives of the Mahasabha have to be followed. This helps maintain law and order situation in their society.

In olden days the punishment for both economic and social offences was lighter; it was one of the reasons for higher degree of involvement of people in criminal activities. But at present the directives of the Mahasabha have been able to bring down the anti social activities considerably. For instance, if a person marries more than three times, he or she is exterminated from the society or forced to pay large amount of money as fine to the society. If the excommunicated person wants to regain his or her membership in the community, then he or she has to pay Rs. 2100 with the special permission of the Nyay Palika of Mahasabha.

Owing to the influence of Hinduism they were cremating the dead body. Mahasabha has now stopped this practice and encouraged the traditional practice of burying. Hindu culture stipulates taking the ashes to the holy water of the Ganges, but they do not observe this tradition. There is no sacred thread ceremony in their tradition and culture. However, in the past the adult males used to wear sacred thread and change the same after attending a death ritual. During those days Brahmin used to perform a number of rituals in their society. Now all rites performed by the Brahmin and the wearing of sacred thread by adult males have been banned by the Mahasabha and most people have stopped such practices. Now the Mahasabha tries to minimize the influence of Hinduism upon their culture. Further it takes interest in their ethnic revitalization. When a person attempts to get himself converted to another religion he or she is excommunicated.

They think that a person who leaves his culture and switches over to a new sets of religious beliefs and practices would be considered dead. So when someone is excommunicated by the community, he or she has to be declared dead. He or she has to perform *mritak sanskar* (death rites) and arrange a *mritak bhoj* (funeral feast). All converted persons are referred as *hurra hurra,* i.e. a name of an animal which digs out the dead bodies and eat it up. In view of the above facts, the Gondwana Mahasabha, Gondwana Mohila Mandal, Gondwana Gantantra Party, Gondwana Mukti Sena have been playing active role in bringing revivalism among the members of the society. The prime objective of this movement is to accept some of the selected aspects of the culture and religious values and bring in necessary modifications in others. However, it outrightly rejects the culture and religion of Hindu society. The movement has been designed to restructure their society. This movement is also directed against irrational beliefs, values and social evils prevailing in their own society.

REFERENCES

Bhadra, Ranajit K. 1977. "Revitalization Movements among the Gonds of Madhya Pradesh", *Eastern Anthropologist,* 30(2).

Desai, I.P. 1977. "The Vedachni Movement", in I.P. Desai and Banwarilal Chaudhary (eds.), *History of Rural Development in Modern India.* Vol. 2. Delhi: Impex India.

Ekka, Philip. 1972. "Revivalist Movements among the Tribals of Chhotanagpur", in K.S. Singh (ed.) *Tribal Situation in India.* Simla: Indian Institute of Advanced Study.

Ekka, William. 1982. "Reform Movement of Rajmohini Devi," in K. S. Singh (ed.), *Tribal Movement in India.* Vol. 2, Delhi: Monohar.

Guess, Edward, 1984. "The Span Magazine", in B.H. Mehta (ed.) *Gonds of the Central Indian Highlands,* Vol. 1, New Delhi: Concept Publishing Company.

Mahapatra, L.K. 1968. "Social Movements among Tribes of Eastern India". *Sociologus,* 18.

Oommen, T.K. 1990. *Protest and Change: Studies in Social Movements.* New Delhi: Sage Publication.

Pant, Mandakini. 1990. "Khasi Revivalist Movement", *The Eastern Anthropologists,* 43(1).

Paul, Madan C. 1991. "Reform Movement among the Bora-Kachari", *Eastern Anthropologists,* 44(1).

Shrivastav, P.N. 1978. *Madhya Pradesh District Gazetteers-Bilaspur.* Indore: Modern Printery Limited.

Singh, K.S. 1982. "The Gond Movements", in K. S. Singh (ed.) *Tribal Movements in India.* Vol. 2. Delhi: Monohar.

Thomson, Edward. 1984. "A Gazetteer of the East India Co.", in B.H. Mehta (eds.), *Gonds of the Central Indian Highlands.* Vol. 1. New Delhi: Concept Publishing Company.

Thusu, N.K. 1982. "A Movement among the Gonds of Chanda", in K.S. Singh (ed). *Tribal Movement in India.* Vol. 2. Delhi: Monohar.

Troise, Joseph. 1979. "Social Movements among the Santals", in M.S.A. Rao (ed.), *Social Movement in India.* Vol. 2. Delhi: Monohar.

SECTION III

COMMUNITY LIFE

THIRTEEN

THE SUKUMA OF TANZANIA
A Traditional Social System Enabling Adaptation to Modernity

R. E. S. TANNER

Introduction

Any description of a tribal society or discussion about it by its own member, starts from the assumption that they are "different", and that in the process of development or change, they have lost or are in the process of losing all that made them distinct, so that in terms of what they were there is little left; a mournful catalogue of what used to be so vibrant.

This is perhaps an extreme statement and would refer to the western impact on South Pacific island cultures, New Guinea mountain and coastal societies and the Bushmen and other hunter-gatherer cultures. These tribal societies are usually small and tied to a way of life in a particular environment and a pattern of social behaviour in which there is no in-built elasticity allowing change while leaving a specific and acceptable tribal culture intact.

East Africa contains many tribal groups which have experienced radical change to their traditional patterns of life. The Kikuyu of Kenya have suffered from the expansion of land given to European settlers; the pastoral Maasai have suffered from the preference of successive governments for agriculturalists so that the area of their grazing lands have been progressively reduced.

Other tribal groups have traditional institutionalized structures which cannot be combined with economic changes and the sovereignty of colonial and then national governments. Examples of this would be the age-grade system of the Maasai and the Warusha, the paramount chiefs of the Buganda and Bunyoro and the feudal land-owning system of the Haya and Hangaza. None of these could survive the pressures of local political and economic modernity and the influences of globalization.

In such tribal cultures what may have been their specific way of life has either disappeared or has become so modified that it must now have very little resemblance to what may or may not have been their practices in pre-colonial non-literature centuries. For these areas we have only the sketchiest of archaeological data and some written records from visiting sea-borne foreigners.

In studying cultures other than one's own and indeed any culture outside the urban-industrial world, there is a tendency to concentrate on differences rather than similarities. Indeed it is difficult to do otherwise when everything facing these researchers is expected to be new to them.

The case to be discussed here is that of the Sukuma of north-western Tanzania who appear to have weathered the trials of colonialism and the contemporary pressures of an invasive modern national society with much of their culture intact.

Those who have studied the Sukuma never started by saying to themselves that there is much in their society which is understandable because that it is how modern people behave. They have concentrated on abstracting traditionalism and the exciting topics of magic, witchcraft and their so-called secret societies.

Thus there seems to be a theoretical possibility that the rather bland face of Sukuma culture which has passed through a number of quite radical historical and political changes without much obvious tension and social disturbance, may have been able to do this at least in part because of existing features in their society.

The Sukuma

The Sukuma occupy at least 35,000 square miles of the cultivation steppe to the south of Lake Victoria and number at least five million, a quarter of the total population of Tanzania in which it is the biggest tribe. They are a Bântu people speaking their own tonal language with complicated verb forms as well as the noun classes common to all Bantu languages.

Although they are now sedentary subsistence farmers, they own large numbers of cattle through the ownership of which status is shown. They live in widely dispersed homesteads well separated from their neighbours. Historically they have only lived in villages for protection from cattle raids in pre-colonial times and during the compulsory villagization period which started in 1976. They are not a migratory people but annually a significant number move away from their perceived difficulties to seek better locations for their farms and livestock with more congenial neighbours. Traditionally they were divided into a number of chiefdoms whose rulers carried out religious rituals to ensure the welfare of their people and who otherwise acted on the advice of their elders.

They have a patrilineal system of kinship through which only a few married sons live with their fathers when it was to their material advantage to do so. Marriages and children are legitimized by the payment of cattle to the bride's family.

Despite over a century of evangelization no more than 12 per cent are Christians (mainly Roman Catholics) and only a few thousand Moslems even though Arabs have been in the area even longer. This absence of religious change is particularly surprizing when other tribes have high percentage of Christians or Moslems, even though much quasi-traditional religion is practised parallel to their monotheistic affirmations.

It is not suggested that the Sukuma culture was so collectively insignificant that it could not stand in the way of change but that traditionally and indeed today, their culture contained and still contains a number of wide ranging similarities to contemporary urban-industrial social systems.

Let us now examine the various aspects of the Sukuma social system which has changed without noticeable tension or has enabled change to take place.

Sukuma Subjective Sense of Identity

Nationalism and tribalism can be an obstacle to change when the identity of those people is clear to both themselves and outsiders; they look and dress differently to their neighbours and where they live is geographically distinct.

The Sukuma area is bounded on the north by Lake Victoria and to the east by the open plains occupied by the martial Maasai, but to the south and west there is no boundary and in those areas whether individuals call themselves Sukuma or not is a matter of personal and political convenience.

They are not physically distinct and have not altered their appearance in any way by hair styles, scarification or tattooing which marks them out as Sukuma. Their clothing is much the same as most other Tanzanians, a mixture of western styles with coastal wrap around cloth. Even for the recreation of their cultural identity, they do not produce tribally distinct styles of clothing.

Their tribal identity appears to have been demarcated by outsiders as the "northerners" who lived to the north of the central caravan route crossing Tanzania in the 19th century. Pockets of population under independent headmen who depended on their ritual successes in retaining and augmenting their numbers, which gradually filled up until it became an occupied area from which expansion had to be outwards principally to the west.

So it seems that they were never collectively Sukuma until the colonial administrative requirements perhaps made them aware of this. Their culture had no single supreme traditional authority and no culture-wide rigid institutions. The main theme of their lives as Sukuma seems to have been as individuals, living as separate families, in loosely conjoined neighbourhoods and in chiefdoms of varying sizes which had little or nothing to do with each other.

The Geographical Movement of Sukuma

The Sukuma, except for chiefly families, do not appear to be attached to particular places; they come from different areas and indeed it would be hard for them to be more precise when so much of Sukuma is featureless. They do not mark their graves and since their houses are mud and wattle, there is little to denote occupation a year after a family has moved away.

As many as a quarter of adults may move in any year because until land became scarce and valuable, there was nothing to hold them in a particular area if they did not get on with their neighbours or felt that it had a bad reputation for adequate harvests. Livestock can move easily enough and there is usually not more personal property than can be carried. The poorer ones may only move into an adjacent area while the more innovative and ambitious, the pathfinders, may go to open up new homesteads in the forest areas to the west.

There may be a core of people with land and substantial houses who do not move, but even that is not a real restraint against movement, since land can be rented out and the valuable parts of the houses moved to the new locality, but the majority do move quite often because they have no particular reasons to stay put. While development in Europe and Asia has usually meant that peasants move to the cities, here some work seasonally in the towns while keeping their farms worked over weekends or by leaving their women to retain ownership and provide food.

The result of all this movement is that blood kin and in-laws are widely distributed, although they may be within walking distance. There are no neighbourhoods dominated by a particular family. A man can settle and go to wherever he finds himself acceptable and the ambience attractive. Traditional ideas that land belongs to the chief are no more than archaic memories which have not stood in the way of these adjustments to modernity.

Kinship and the Sukuma

At the back of most studies of tribal communities is the spider's web of kinship but this may not be true for the Sukuma. If kinship was all that important then we would find related families living close to each other and extended families being more or less in the same area, but this is not so.

Marriage is exogamous with regard to clan membership which has nc other surviving use other than to provide food taboos. At least initially a man is supposed to live with his father-in-law, but with the decline of pre-nuptial agreements and the increase in concubinage with marriages being negotiated much later to establish the right of the genitor to the bridewealth of his daughters, this is now rare indeed.

The fact that the Sukuma live in dispersed homesteads as near to their farms as possible, means that kin closeness has not been a major concern this century. Even after compulsory villagization had been cancelled, at least 70 per cent have returned to their distant homesteads.

Their kinship system is partrilineal and the customary distribution of property is clear, but much depends on possession and being there at the time that it is distributed. To establish the right to cattle which are out on loan requires the claimant to be resident and to dispossess an actual farmer would require local support. Non-literate establishment of property rights is very much a matter for negotiation rather than confrontation.

In both European and Sukuma societies there are many relatives who are off the map as far as active social relationships are concerned, and of course the rising popularity of concubinage means that many are not well-in with their respective families. For the Sukuma to seek them out for regular contact, would seem to them not to be a rational use of their resources. Of course if they live near, there would be a sense of obligation, independent of reciprocity.

There has been a gradual development of individuality and "isolated" nuclear families, living with whoever and wherever they choose which has led them to see kinship as just one of the elements in their personal social network which they may choose to develop and utilize.

Social Networks

Certainly the Sukuma see their kin and their affines as important and it is to them that they would appeal over serious difficulties, but there must always be the proviso that they live near at hand and are willing to help. The ideas that kin will always help each other is based on the rationale of reciprocity and that they would be able to help. Above all to be able to pressure a family into helping an indigent relative is much easier when the protagonists live less than three hours walk away.

Since most Sukuma do not live where they were born, nor close to their relatives, they spend much of their social time in creating potentially helpful networks. Although they do not live near to other houses, they of course have neighbours whom they help when necessary on the basis of anticipated reciprocity house building, preparation of fields and harvesting.

The dry season involves considerable beer drinking in which the drinkers come mostly from the same neighbourhood and this provides drinkers there with the opportunity to create other elements in their individual networks of reciprocal relationships.

Sukuma society contains large numbers of social groups which have mixed social and economic functions. Some are semi-permanent such as the dance societies which are rival groups, other are professional but the majority are created for specific purposes where a group of people earn money by working in other people's fields.

The creation of these networks is essential in a subsistence society in which there is no national welfare system and a government which can only step in to offset disaster if it is both widespread and involves many thousands. One is tempted to suggest that these wide-ranging social groups owe their presence and constant recreation to the comparative absence of effective kin support.

The looseness of the Sukuma social system allows any individual to invest in social relationships in much the same way as it is done in the urban-industrial world for a wide variety of reasons and where kin are not all that ready or available to provide help. There is a careful working out of the costs and benefits in these utilitarian relationships.

In the Sukuma pattern of living the network of useful relationships is geographically spread out, but not so spread out as to be difficult to maintain. If most active social relationships in Europe are within a few miles even allowing for cars much the same would apply in Usukuma for walking.

Rites of Passage

The Sukuma passage through life is not marked out by a series of obligatory rituals and if anything it could be said that they have a social system which is noticeably free of rituals expressing collective life, even the rituals of the chiefs performed for the well-being of the whole community were not public communal affairs. It is not a social system marked by public ceremonies.

The traditional ceremonies to mark the baby's entry into life and to being a Sukuma involving a ritual involving sheep's milk, is now no more than the semi-private rituals of any family rather than something correlating to the functions of christening. There are no puberty ceremonies for either girls or boys and no circumcision as well as no age grades in which groups of young men work their way up the social ladder by stages. Puberty is recognized by domestic rearrangements in which the girls will no longer sleep in their parents' houses.

The traditional marriage had no ritual focus and other than saying that a couple was more or less married than they were previously, it was more a feast in which the couple had no particular significance. Since the majority now cohabit, there could be no appropriate ceremonies anyway.

Parents would certainly like the public display involved in their children's marriages, but it is not just a ceremony culminating in sexual intercourse, but the culmination of negotiations between elders representing the two families; not the families themselves. The one wants more cattle and money and the other to provide less and none of this needs ceremony; if anything the two families avoid each other until there are children making them blood-related.

The disposal of their dead involves some ceremony but not much since it has to be carried out as soon as possible in a hot climate and thus those that attend are as much likely to be neighbours rather than relatives. The main reason that burial is taken seriously is the division of the property. In the absence of any written wishes, most relatives would make an effort to be there as otherwise there would be none who would feel any obligation to act on their behalf.

Overall this seems to parallel contemporary Europe where puberty is ignored, marriage except for high status ones, involves food rather than ceremony and of course concubinage comes to be tolerated rather than celebrated. The only ceremonies which continue would appear to be funerals.

Status Seeking

There are a number of common factors in Sukuma society which are equally common in urban-industrial societies. The most important is that social status is achieved rather than ascribed and has always been so and the result of education, industry and politics. None has a right to rank because of their birth and even their traditional chiefs were chosen by procedures which often meant that the chosen man would not even know that he was being considered. Indeed their traditional preference for matrilateral choices clashed with their patrilineal kinship structure.

Overall ascription played little part in their society since children might become traditional healers or subordinate chiefs but there was very little that was ascriptive about it, just that certain families may have had just such an aptitude from socialization which is common enough in urban-industrial societies.

So the acquisition of status in Usukuma has never been the result of some uniform and regular ascriptive structure; of course the old are given a measure of respect, but status is largely earned. Apart from the few who have charismatic elements in thier personalities, if they want status they have to work for it; thus it is a combination of personality and economic success with the use of beer and meat, a "potlatch" method of at least gaining a measure of status, which is common enough in urban-industrial societies.

A distinctive feature of the Sukuma social system are these non-kin based societies which have a wide range of functions of which one is the provision of opportunities for gaining status. Individuals can join for a personal need relating to loneliness, the cure for an illness as well as because of an aptitude. But all such societies have a large number of titled office-holders mimicing political office holders and it is to these roles that people aspire. They have been described as non-sectarian churches since individuals could belong to several at once. They formed strong, disciplined fraternities involved in mutual assistance and the protection and perpetuation of professional and technical secrets and obligations (Cory, 1938, 1951, 1953).

With a decline in law and order and the inability of the police to cover the rural areas, the Sukuma recreated the youngmen's association under the name of "sungusungu" (Bukurura, 1995), vigilante groups in each administrative area. These again had offices with titles after the old political structure of chiefs.

So in every part of Usukuma there were these associations available for interested men and women to join and gain status by a mixture of presence, propinquity and persistence. These seem to resemble membership and success in a wide range of voluntary groupings in non-African societies; prominence in professional associations, work in voluntary charitable societies such as the Masons and Rotary, all of which have similar structure with large number of named positions.

Religious Affairs

The Sukuma religious ideas do not make any distinction between magic and religion possible since there is just the belief that there is a spirit world in the first instance occupied by their ancestors and lately by non-ancestral spirits which can all influence the lives of the living. Moreover, they spend as they have always done, a great deal of time and effort in promoting their own good and preventing bad possibilities.

Since they never had any regular programme of religious activities other than the "constitutional" obligations of their chiefs nor have they had any religious institutions and personnel overarching generations, it is easy to see how they failed to see much to attract them in Christianity. (Tanner, 1967, 1995; Tanner and Wijsen, 1993).

Their own traditional religion operated through self-made healers and for the last century they have been available everywhere. The diagnostic sessions are carried out in their own natal language and in which all the data considered in situational rather than abstract so that the solutions are understandable.

The fact that their healers have always been paid by results resulted in. The whole system being self-adjusting and as families became less coherent, their religious ideas moved from the ancestral spirits to spirits that had no such connections and to a focus on individualism and the tensions of modern life explicable in terms of the animosities of witchcraft.

It was also self-adjusting to communal needs and the system provided for rain-making and to cope with the fears engendered by the spread of AIDS.

There are parallels here to the practices and beliefs of the western world. It is not that the Sukuma are secularized any more than the average European is with his beliefs in luck and some sort of unspecified God. The religion of both types of society are activated by misfortune and amulets and charms are common enough.

It would seem that the Sukuma have traditionally shown the main features of the "popular" religious practices of the western world which have only recently been recognized as the mainstay of religious practices there. So if what is happening in Europe and north America today in religion is the result of urbanism and industrialization, then the Sukuma system of beliefs and practice were already in common use before these influences had any effect in Usukuma.

The parallels here are to the proliferation of "fringe" cults and medicine in western urban societies but also to the growth in prayer groups (McGuire, 1987). The Sukuma groups are similarly low key and are not to any great extent institutionalized.

This is not so much a numerical parallel but a functional one in which the Sukuma through their religious system could be seen as adapting better to the strains of urban-industrial living than westerners. Their religious system of spirits acting on individual Sukuma is automatically adaptable to an infinite number of situations and in an infinite number of ways without the institutional constraints provided by moralizing religious institutions.

The Sukuma Language and Social Change

Any language has its semiotic as well as linguistic usages and of course small languages disappear as their users convert to the larger languages. However the enormous numbers of Sukuma speakers has meant that it is their natal language and outside matters involving the government, institutionalized religion and education, it is the tongue in which they conduct their daily affairs even in the main towns and more importantly in their emotional lives; their songs whether for amusement, as a stimulus to communal effort and for political protests. It is hard to even imagine the social lives of women being carried out in the national lingua franca Swahili.

For any Sukuma thier own language is a valuable and adjustable resource in which they can conduct their own lives independently of the outside invasive world. It is the language of their quasi-traditional religious practices. They can switch to it in political meetings when they do not wish outsiders, the new invasive civil servants and politicians, to hear.

More importantly since it is largely unwritten except for the *Bible* and cultural materials coming out of the Tribal Centre at Bujora, it is adaptive with new words and phrases coming into use without any clashes between their language stabilized in literacy and its popular uses. It is an institutionally unsupervized language and its continuing complexity is thus entirely in the mouths of its contemporary speakers.

Their language provides for their cultural survival and supports the "us" and "them" nature of their social and political lives in a new nation state which dislikes tribal differentiations as much as languages elsewhere sustain cultures and cushion change.

Conclusion

It is not the intention of this paper to suggest that the Sukuma consciously or unconsciously have adapted to modernity in any significantly unusual way. All along they have adapted in many different ways to what they have experienced from the social, political and economic changes which have invaded their lives.

What is unusual, if not unique, is that the root metaphors and much of their social behaviour which no doubt evolved in the centuries before outside influences became a feature of their lives, were ones which fitted into many of the cultural requirements of the urban-industrial world where such patterns of behaviour developed for entirely different reasons.

This has meant that the Sukuma have absorbed many of the radical changes which have destroyed much of other cultures, simply because their way of life and thinking was already more or less on the same lines as those in contemporary western urban-industrial societies.

Amongst the Sukuma themselves there does not seem to be any popular lament for a way of life that has gone for ever because the experience of change has run parallel to both the conscious and unconscious continuous recreation of their own tribal identity.

By not joining either Christianity or Islam, their religious practices have just changed to meet their needs and whatever has emerged is stated to be what they have always done. Their vigilante groups are also seen to be what they have always done.

Of course people adapt and use the psychological strategies of saying to themselves that this is what they have always done, but the lines on which the Sukuma changed were the very ones which were to be of use in this modern world.

Since ascription did not feature in their traditional system, the achievements gained by examination, accumulating cattle or trading is not a problem which clashes with anything in their culture. Since they have no puberty ceremonies, becoming adult under modern conditions did not break with anything from the past; of course the old and young complain about each other but it was ever thus. They have always moved, so moving more for economic than social reasons is not a major change since they can still attribute the reasons for moving to bad luck, witchcraft or whatever just as they have always done since Christianity and Islamic ideas on causation may not yet have entered their thinking.

All in all we can see that the Sukuma have entered "modern" society insofar as it involves them with considerable advantages and it is this that has eased the tensions which have affected less fortunate societies with rigid institutions and practices which cannot be combined with individualism and minor capitalistic practices.

Sukuma society has system rather than structure and has an absence of institutions with characteristics which would have bound them together to the past and obstructed change. The Sukuma moved with the times because there was nothing there to prevent it; no age grades, no necessary rites of passage, no caste or class incorporations. Social and geographical mobility was built into their system. A religious system which turned on individual difficulties and creative innovations of self-employed quasi-traditional healers in their thousands. Their political system had the sovereignty of their chiefs based on popular consent and the carrying out of rituals supporting the welfare of their people. All in all the Sukuma had the social building blocks already available for the necessary changes before the changes were forced on them.

REFERENCES

Bukurura, S.H. 1995. "Partners and Competitors in the Fight against Crime; the Case of Sungusungu", in P.G. Foster and S. Maghimbi (eds.), *The Tanzanian Peasantry: Further Studies*, Aldershot: Avebury.

Cory, H. 1938. Sukuma Secret Societies. Mss. Dar-es-Salaam: Dar-es-Salaam University Library

—. 1951. *The Ntemi, Traditional Rites of a Sukuma Chief.* London: Macmillan.

—. 1953. *Sukuma Law and Custom.* Oxford: Oxford University Press.

McGuire, R.B. 1988. *Ritual Healing in Suburban America.* New Brunswick: Rutgers University Publishers.

Tanner, R.E.S. 1967. *Transition in African Belief.* New York: Maryknoll.

—. 1995. "The Impact of Christianity and Islam on Two East African Societies," in E. Jones and V. Reynolds (eds.), *Survival and Religion.* Chichester: John Wiley.

Tanner. R.E.S. and F. Wijsen 1993. "Christianity in Usukuma. A Working Misunderstanding," *Neue Zeitschrift fur Missionswissenschaft,* 439(3): 177-193.

FOURTEEN

THE RELUCTANCE OF THE SUKUMA TO CONVERT TO CHRISTIANITY AND ISLAM

An Analysis of Possible Factors

R.E.S. TANNER

Introduction

The Sukuma, a five million strong Bantu tribe in north-western Tanzania have been exposed to Christianity and Islam for more than a hundred years and yet only some 12 per cent belong to a Christian Church and an even smaller percentage are Moslems. Other tribes with the same record of contact have five times that number of Christians.

Earlier quasi-statistical studies of the reasons for the Sukuma becoming, remaining and lapsing from Christianity (Tanner,1968, 1969b, 1969c) showed a strong theme of materialistic reasons. But other tribal societies such as the Haya, Angoni and Chagga have had similar exposure to the pros and cons of Christianity without the same results. One can presuppose that these societies originally had the same proportion of dedicated and successful missionaries as well as failures.

Therefore it seems interesting to ask whether there is not much more to this rejection of conversion by the Sukuma than quasi-material reasoning which are seemingly only part of the answer and at best probably only surface explanations.

The question is more easily asked in the context of Roman Catholicism and Islam which presented themselves to the Sukuma in the style of uniform rituals, the Mass and the Moslem prayer rites. There can be few Sukuma who have not known about the existence of these rituals and indeed most will have seen a priest celebrating Mass since each mission has outpost churches which are visited regularly by itinerant priests.

The question of conversion and non-conversion of those practising quasi-traditional religion and those who practise the major faiths can of course be examined in purely functional terms. This reduces the practice of the major faiths to no more than the expression of temporary needs of an essentially non-religious nature; in fact it trivializes faith and the faithful and is perhaps no more than rationalist reductionism to which many objects on theological as much as personal grounds. This is what has been going on in sociological analyses of religious practices for many decades; the faithless explaining away faith.

It is unwise to apply these somewhat outdated theories to the thought processes as much as the religious practices of the Sukuma since it may be a form of disguised racialism. Since the Sukuma remain largely a non-literate culture whereas the major external religions are the literate productions of a much more totally literate culture, it tends to be assumed without any evidence that they are not capable of and do not indeed have profound and valuable religious insights, ignoring in the process the extent of intellectual capacity among the peoples concerned.

Therefore their religious practices have been evaluated at the lowest common denominator in a scale of religiousness as responses to immediate needs; a sort of religious scratching of an irritant in response to short-term requirements.

Even in the absence of written records or archaeological data about the Sukuma culture, let us at least theorize that it has existed in some form or other for as long as western culture has existed. Furthermore we have to assume that this largely unknown cultural paradigm is still in existence parallel to that of the imported western religious culture with its equally long and only partially recorded existence.

If functional explanations are acceptable for one system of beliefs and practices then they have to be applied to the other and by so doing demeaning the great faiths and those of the Sukuma as well; trivialize one and the other is trivialized as well.

This analysis attempts to see the religious practices of the Sukuma in terms of very long-term evolving social and ecological processes in which their exposure to the new faiths must have been very short-term indeed in comparison to the millennial processes which have produced the particular qualities of Sukuma religious thought and practice.

The Residual Longevity of Sukuma Religious Thinking

Any assumptions about the Sukuma's religious ideas and practices must be looked at in the same analytical framework as those of western societies. Much of their religious activity is due to short-term interests but that their conceptions of what are those interests are shaped by much longer-term social processes and so is the horizon over which they pursue them. In turn their actions in pursuit of more or less short-term interests interweave within their long-term paradigm in a way that involves many unforeseen and unintended consequences. These produce long-term processes which are largely blind and unplanned but never the less have a discernable structure (Mennell, 1989: 93). While this study refers to long-term economic practices, it would seem applicable to any analysis of Sukuma ideas and practices.

We can assume therefore that there is a connection between any long-term structural development of Sukuma society and parallel changes in this people's character and religious personality. However it would seem that any major changes which have occurred in Sukuma society are probably recent and indeed markedly post-colonial.

It seems likely that external contacts and colonial sovereignty had very little effect on how the Sukuma as individuals and local communities actually behaved. How could it be otherwise when the Sukuma were so numerous and so well dispersed and the colonial and/or macro-economic systems to which they were exposed so understaffed and distant from markets? So in comparison to villagized communities and societies near to major centres of trade these changes may have had little influence on the processes of Sukuma thought, although it will have had some influence on certain elements such as the functions of chiefs, which were undergoing radical changes anyway.

It could be hypothesized that the Sukuma are an excellent example in support of the theory that "the peasants will always win" since they can absorb enormous amounts of external cultural interference without making any serious changes in how they think and act. Certainly major changes may come about as a result of overpopulation, impoverishment of their environment and ideological politics, but it is far too early to suggest that they have had any effect on their religious thinking and from this thinking comes the usefulness of their current religious practices.

The Limited Expansion of Social Horizons

One of the most marked aspects of social development is the expansion of social horizons, the extension of the range of those with whom individuals feel a sense of identity without knowing who they are and without having interpersonal relations with them. For some this expansion is correlated to nationalism, economic cooperation and indeed supratribal religions such as Christianity and Islam.

The Sukuma experienced this growth of identity with the entry of colonial suzereignty. Prior to that time it is likely that there were no finite divisions between one tribe and another; they were separated by emptiness or elided into one another. Boundaries as such were an irrelevance since each social group expanded or contracted principally because of its demographic status.

Colonialism came in with maps and bureaucratic orderliness and with this the Sukuma tribal identity was created and the expansion of their social horizons occurred before they themselves had any use for it. But having been created, their large numbers and wide areas of territory provided them with functionally useful and satisfying concepts.

But within this concept of tribal identity, it is inaccurate and a gross simplification to talk of the Sukuma as if they had a single social system. Apart from the name and a non-literate language, there are wide variations in their social, political and economic practices. It may not be pluralistic in the sense that a modern developed state is pluralistic but there was and is no firmly entrenched institutionalized unitary culture.

Perhaps a smaller tribal group would not have been able to retain their identity quite so well in changing times. It has not been that they were isolated in an area, which did not attract specific colonial exploitation because no tribal society has ever been isolated in any strict sense; ideas come and go even if artifacts do not.

Thus a further reason for their reluctance to convert outwards as an accompaniment to widening social horizons may have been that the Sukuma on the one hand were culturally self-reliant; their way of life until recently was not so markedly different to what it may have been in more distant historical times. On the other hand their culture was supported by such large numbers that it was able to continue adapting without any marked difficulties in the use of their traditional religious perceptions and practices, which might otherwise have encouraged conversion to Christianity and Islam because of its failure to provide for their needs. In this sense they had no need to convert.

It seems certain anyway that any reluctance to convert is not the result of any sort of non-exposure to new ideas and practices but that it lies within the structures and functions of a persistent and viable culture. However there may well be other factors such as the bipolar nature of their subsistence anxieties and the continued contingency availability of quasi-traditional religious practices.

The Penetration of Christian Ideas and Practices

Since the Roman Catholics have been in Usukuma for a century it is often assumed that the penetration of these Christian ideas and practices must have been high. This seems unlikely as Usukuma covers an enormous area and the missions were few and far between. For even the most dedicated and active of priests, the proportion of priest to people cannot have been less than one per 100,000 people.

Even where the focus has been much more local and continuous, there has been a similar lack of success although the potential for penetration of Christian ideas must have been high (Lumsden and Wilson, 1981: 30). Bukumbi mission which was visited by H.M. Stanley on his last African expedition in 1884 and has had a continuous priestly occupation since then, has only 10 per cent of the local population following Roman Catholicism.

This could be called a conspicuous missionary failure but not one, which can be attributed to the personal failings of these priests alone. Prior to the present era the missionaries had few leaves in Europe, were required to reach a high standard of speaking kiSukuma before being given leave to practice as full priests and in many cases lived there for many years without transfers to other stations. In some cases these men thought deeply about the problems involved in getting the Sukuma converted to Christianity and wrote extensively about their findings. Such men were as close to the Sukuma and their understandings as it would be possible for a non-Sukuma to get. Similarly it does not seem that Roman Catholic practices and requirements placed severe limitations on any Sukuma who might otherwise feel the need to convert. Some Protestant Churches prohibiting smoking, drinking and dancing over which the Roman Catholic Church had no canonical objections, were even less successful.

Thus it would seem that the failure to get a higher proportion of the Sukuma converted to Christianity cannot be attributed to the strictness of the rules laid down by the Christian Churches or to having few people on the ground actively proselytizing as the failure at Bukumbi with more priests to people than anywhere else in Usukuma except possibly in Mwanza town, the provincial capital where their attentions were shared with any number of people from other tribes and cultures. The fault or unattractiveness of Christianity must lie in other factors.

The Absence of a Religious Structure in Usukuma

Anthropological analysis of pre-industrial religious rituals tend to suggest that they follow relatively closely to a schemata, a framework which exists independently of any outsider's analysis. This conclusion comes in part from the fact that anthropologists in their fieldwork see very few rituals and informants for one reason or another, may suggest that what they do see is repeated and uniform.

This is an inevitable conclusion when these are non-literate societies in which the exact repetition of a ceremony is a virtual impossibility. How could there be any exactitude when circumstances and personnel change and no written rubrics exist. Sukuma propitiation ceremonies, each one of which could have been called typical in the absence of comparisons, were and are in fact each atypical.

Hypotheses about the religious practices of the Sukuma have been based on a limited number of academic studies created from a small amount of data which suggested that the Sukuma have a much more formal religious structure than they have in reality. The author saw perhaps no more than a dozen religious ceremonies in over three years fieldwork in Usukuma between 1951 and 1967 although he was concentrating specifically on their religious ideas and practices.

There is in addition the collective wisdom of Christian local and foreign priests and pastors who are almost by definition in opposition to what they see as magical practices and who were and are unlikely to have ever seen such ceremonies because their presence at them would be seen as condoning them.

Furthermore much of the data collected by these dedicated Christians related to what they saw as magical practices and thus the religious ideas of the Sukuma which produced these practices were probably not considered worthy of examination on some level of equality to those of the Christian missionaries who sort only to displace them.

Christian theologians, priest and pastors have an instinctive as well as moral dislike of anything that relates to magic against which they have worked and argued in vain for centuries with very little effect in Europe, much less in Usukuma.

Since the differences between magic and religion are often presented as a dichotomy, it is the magical side which has always been stressed; the weird and the wonderful to non-Sukuma eyes receive a prominence that is perhaps not justified. The religious thinking of the Sukuma has been consistently neglected because it is in effect invisible but nevertheless at the back of all that they do and think.

Furthermore missionaries just as much as the earlier colonial administrators looked for institutions in Usukuma which might parallel the religious institutions in their own countries. For them there must be a religious structure to account for what the Sukuma practiced in their "pagan" rituals as without such institutions they could not conceive of rituals being performed at all.

The reasons for suggesting that there is no institutional structure to Sukuma religion are clear. Firstly in their religious practices there are no regularities which could come together to form a system. Certainly there is a paradigm of ideas within which rituals take place but they do not occur at fixed times and places. The personnel involved, the traditional or modernized quasi-traditional healers are perhaps more idiosyncratic than conformist since there is no "priesthood" to which entry is confirmed by set procedures.

The reasons for persons becoming diviners and healers, apart from any economic incentives, are the pressure on the individual psyche from a previously unknown ancestor spirit among a vast pool of potentially active spirits to take up an uncertain career as a relief. What they take up is not a vocation in terms of conformity to a set pattern of known ideas but a development of religious individuality within a loose paradigm of ideas.

Religious ceremonies are not calendrical and are carried out when personally evaluated pressures require amelioration through the use of diviners who are self-serving in their training and performance and who are evaluated by public opinion.

There is no structure which could be described as even semi-permanent and no centralizing tendencies except when for a time public opinion supports the skills of particular diviners. Nor does any such person assume any local institutional superiority of other local diviners except possibly in terms of rivalry and jealousy.

There are no centralizing shrines or places of particular religious significance around which cults have developed. The so-called "secret" societies such as the Buchwezi have no predetermined and regular structure of activities. Whether they function and when is much the same as for individuals and families; factors of prestige, stress, money and food supplies are all involved.

It is suggested therefore that the Sukuma have never had a religious structure in the sense that is understood by westerners and that therefore institutionalized religion is and remains essentially alien to their religious paradigm.

The Unattractiveness of Institutionalized Religion

Christianity in its contemporary availability is not the itinerant and elusive religion of its original apostolate. It no sooner arrives in an area than it builds a base from which it attempts to expand. In the missionary sense it constructs an institution before it has any followers to fill the institution.

This works well enough in societies which have numerous other institutions with buildings. Almost every social group outside the family creates a physical base for its activities as soon as it has enough popular support to justify this effort and expense.

In Usukuma there are no cultural parallels to any pattern of formal institutionalization. The Christian pattern of going about religion has no Sukuma parallels at all to which priests and pastors could point and say this is for Christianity and you already have broadly similar institutions for economics, politics, social activities and for traditional religion.

While the Sukuma are not a cattle people such as the Masai who have no centralizing institutions at all, they are perhaps unusual in not having a centralizing political structure which was in the past constantly ceremonially visible and thus a constant reminder of the institution of chieftainship. The houses of the now deposed chiefs were not noticeably different and their tombs were no part of an area ancestral cult.

The pattern of religious activity mirrors the Sukuma social environment of dispersed compounds. Those who develop a religious vocation either individually or by attaching themselves to an established practitioner will develop or follow idiosyncratic forms of worship.

There would be little to gain and much to lose by copying the successful procedures of others and certainly not by developing an area wide form of worship, a liturgy. New practices come from original ideas; some springing from an existing cultural paradigm which is sufficiently diverse to produce new practices from existing sources, hill or valley, wet or dry, patrilineal or matrilineal. Others may spring out of the mental air as cultural mutations (Tanner, 1997).

Then onto this cultural scene comes a religion which occupies permanent sites and to which people are expected to come rather than going to them or at least being split into the small functional religious units to which they are culturally used. In addition the Sukuma are often mystified why these Christian administrators of religion want a legal title to the land on which they build their churches and houses which is alien to their ideas of ownership.

Admittedly the ritual paraphernalia of the Buchwezi are individually owned but ownership in any legal sense is more "we" than "I" and is probably based on affinal and agnatic links. Ownership outside such links is a relatively modern factor of urbanization and a growing cash economy.

Thus there are two factors which are contrary to Sukuma culture, the static nature of the Christian presence and the architectural nature of this faith. There is an interesting point to consider as the relationship with their spirits requires the spirits to be brought to where the petitioners are living or petitioning, so why should they want to go to churches and move the spirits to a location in which they do not want to be active.

Firstly the static nature of Christianity has increased with the years of the Christian presence in Usukuma. The earliest Christian missionaries had to walk everywhere and walking is always an almost endless process of making contacts; there is a bilateral process of curiosity. Present day Christians are probably the descendants of those who were converted from these original highly personal contacts. Then came in order the bicycle, motor cycle and car and with each came a lessening of these personal contacts and an increasing centralization of Christian ritual functions.

Secondly as soon as they arrived, the missionaries started to build churches; a place in which they could feel at home and they copied the church designs of the countries from which they came.

These buildings proclaimed difference rather than acculturation. It is an interesting point that the guest houses attached to the bungalows of British administrators were often round, the traditional shape of Sukuma houses. It was only recently through the enthusiasm of Fr Clement at Bujora that a round church was constructed at the same time as the Sukuma themselves were abandoning the round for rectangular houses.

Noone seemed to have noticed not so much the unsuitability of these church designs for the Sukuma climate but that Sukuma religious activities were always carried out in the open. This meant of course that such ceremonies would usually have taken place in the dry season when there was little obligatory agricultural work to be done.

The conclusion must surely be that the Sukuma have "inherited" or at least operate a set of religious practices which have never been anything approaching an institutional system with all that implies. Presumably one might also conclude that this institutionalless system has functioned very well and to have not so much survived as to have adapted itself so well to modern pressures as to have been incorporated in what Christian theologians call "popular" religion which in the Sukuma context is their religion with Christianity as a peripheral specialized cult.

The Christian Churches in both social and religious terms confront the Sukuma with a whole series of institutionalising factors for which they had no cultural parallels; a fixed locality for the cult, a fixed priesthood and fixed rituals.

Perhaps only the original converts could see a immediate social advantage and material gain but these would appear to be diminishing assets under post-colonial conditions. The standard of Sukuma living is higher, their expectations greater and the amount of money available to missionaries much less, apart from the contemporary western theological tendency to diminish ritualism which for the Sukuma remains the basis of all their religious practices.

The Failure to be Attracted to Monotheism

The Sukuma traditionally had weak corporate institutions. The chief was perhaps the area headman write large who were themselves no more than enlarged hamlet heads. Power was more personal than institutional and each chiefdom did not have specific religious cults other than those which might have related from time to time to the ruling lineage (Cory, 1951). Clans did not have any corporate religious rituals.

Thus the spirit world of the Sukuma was a mirror of their political and social organization. A vague Supreme Being who did not have any very specific powers and a multitude of ancestral spirits related to families rather than lineages combined with a more limited number of non-ancestral spirits. Thus Sukuma religious beliefs appear to be dualistic; the Supreme Being with some vague responsibility for the world in general—a very impersonal force and the ancestors in enormous numbers as a personal force.

If their religious ideas and practices have in the past mirrored their social system and its environment, why then has it failed to keep up-to-date in religious change that has occurred elsewhere. The colonial political structure was monolineal with the Governor at the top of the pyramid and the Monarch was figuratively widely known with his or her picture on every office and court wall and on every postage stamp from 1927, but this was only for less than forty years.

In such a short time it is not surprising that it had little effect on their religious paradigm, perhaps because the colonial government structure was not in practice as authoritarian and centralized as it may have sounded because of shortages of personnel and money. The only effect of this monolineal political structure was that some titles in their competitive dance societies were "king" and "queen".

The post-independence political structure is certainly more authoritarian than their colonial predecessors in such matters as the villagization campaign but beyond this the structure of authority was far from monolineal with different socio-political powers being used by different people in different structures at different times for different purposes (Tanner, 1969a). Thus the combination of economic, political, social and environmental certainties would seem to suggest that the Sukuma would indeed see no particular advantages in a monotheistic religion.

Even in this there is nothing straightforward since only Islam could be described as monotheistic in theory while dualistic in function—Allah and the Prophet. While Christianity in all its prayers remains tritheistic although similarly it would appear to be functionally dualistic—Christ and the Virgin Mary. So the dualism of these so-called monotheistic faiths does not appear to mirror the dualism of the Sukuma religious paradigm. A vague amorphous impersonal power on the one hand and an innumerable and largely unknown body of ancestors on the other.

The Context of Sukuma Religious Ideas

What factors may have constrained the development of their religious ideas in particular ways? Firstly the environment has encouraged if not required them to live widely separated from their neighbours. Even if they had decided to live in villages with secondary houses near to their fields, the water supply and soils would have made it rational to spread out.

If the spirits were connected to human beings, then to cope with the Sukuma or the Sukuma to cope with them, they would have to be spread out spirits. The shrines that exist are based on households and are unsubstantial. No more than an hour's work to erect them and they are not moved to a new position when the household moves.

Perhaps as people who were once more pastoral than agricultural, the spirits are as mobile as the Sukuma once were. Thus the spirits are not here or there but have to be brought into contact with humans at particular times when they are wanted rather than that the Sukuma go to them.

Thus the possibility of any ritual uniformity in the Sukuma religious paradigm is negligible. What is being suggested here is that this religious paradigm contained elements within it that clashed with that of Roman Catholicism at a socio-psychological level before any question can have arisen as to clashes over particular moral issues such as monogamy and the existence of witchcraft and spirits apart from the ever present possibility of "rice" Christians who converted for materialistic reasons. That these are subliminal and strong ideas at that, would explain at least in part why so few Sukuma have Christian affiliations today.

More importantly for the analyst to suggest that the Sukuma do or do not convert for relatively trivial and material reasons is to demean their cultural ability to think and conduct their lives in ways which are not subservient to western patterns of thought which depend essentially on literacy and a highly literate elite.

Now this argument contrasting the rigidity of Christian rituals with the contextual variability of traditional rituals, should account for the rejection of Christianity and a move towards Islam which allows much popular ritual activity and has no supervisory establishment. Certainly conversion to Islam is easy with none of the catechetical requirements which apply to joining Christianity.

What is significant is the uniformity of Islamic ritual with similar wording and physical movements repeated on every occasion. Perhaps it is just too easy for the Sukuma to have seen anything attractive in its practices. At least for the Roman Catholic Mass there are variations implicit in the fact that it is celebrated by an individual priest who must have provided an idiosyncratic performance in the eyes of observant Sukuma. Even the pre-Vatican II Latin Mass had considerable variations in comparison to Islamic corporate and individual prayer ritual.

The Sukuma religious system has no uniformity at all except in the very broadest of terms. Any observation of its practices shows that what happens is markedly idiosyncratic even inspirational. The uniformity of performed rituals in Christianity based on reference books for rituals and teaching; seems to be its most striking characteristic associated more with literacy than with the practices of a personal or familial religion which is the basis of Sukuma religious practice.

So here we have two foreign ritual schemata with the important characteristic of rigidity, and calendrical inappropriateness which the Sukuma seem to have found unsuited to their particular psychosocial needs. So either there is some form of bilateral distaste or the performance of rituals has nothing to do with this issue.

If non-literate religions such as that of the Sukuma have no fixed nor indeed any order of service then their religious performances must be contextual in two ways. Firstly in relation to the agricultural cycle neither Christianity nor Islam pays any obvious attention to this since its major feasts relate to historical events in the northern hemisphere or relate to the lunar calendar.

While the Christian order of services does correspond to the life-cycle, it is possible that its stresses do not correspond to what the Sukuma see and experience as their essential religious needs. Christianity in Africa has always stressed marriage and baptism. For the Sukuma whether a couple are married or not depends on the woman's fertility and the passage of time and not on a particular ceremony, indeed Sukuma marriage ceremonies do not focus on the couple who are too low down on the social scale of importance to have much attention paid to them. Death for whatever reason is the most popular religious event, and its celebration has not received any Christian liturgical priority (Tanner, 1996).

This elides into the second important theme in non-literate religions, the importance of dealing with personal misfortune. While personal anxieties can be incorporated in to Christian ceremonies, these ceremonies are not performed primarily for their alleviation. So the prime reasons for the performance of Christian rituals can rarely be for the personal ones which initiate traditional and quasi-traditional ceremonies.

In fact it can be harshly concluded that the way that Christian ceremonies do not appear on the surface to have any relationship at all to the prime concerns of the Sukuma over death, disease and misfortune may make them think that there is no point at all in joining a faith which is so clearly disinterested in what they are worried about now just as much as in the recent past.

The Importance of Religious Contingency Availability

Subsistence societies cannot have any forward planning except in the loosest terms, and since Sukuma society has no centralized institutions, it is not surprising that their religious practices are not only decentralized but also sporadic and contingent rather than regular and planned.

In this sense the Christian Churches are singularly static and liturgically unresponsive to what is going on in their parishes and communities. Christian Churches in the United States which are perhaps much more competitive and consumer oriented have prayers before football matches and examinations.

The only religious ceremonies in Usukuma which are likely to attract large numbers of people are rain-making ones but only if the drought is widespread and not just local. A rain-making ceremony witnessed in Nassa in 1954 had about a thousand people but even that ceremony which must have been well publicized in advance was a contingent and not a regular performance.

Thus the religion of the Sukuma which has served them well from historical times up to the present has one supremely important characteristic—it is a contingency religion. It comes into operation upon the appearance of contingencies and it disappears when contingencies do not require it to operate. Thus the Sukuma religion is not so much present as absent.

There is little doubt that in so far as it is observable, religion is peripheral to the main thrust of their lives; it has to be looked for as their religious practices do not catch the eye or hit the ear. In this they are probably no different to most Tanzanian societies except perhaps the irrigating Ssonjo (Gray, 1963). They are not a particularly religious people.

So in order to change from what is a widespread but largely inactive relationship with the spirit world, they would be exchanging something that works for something that may only hypothetically work. It is not a question of conversion acting on some sort of a spiritual vacuum.

The factor of availability is of prime importance, the do-it-yourself element which allows a considerable amount of personal initiative and secondly when this is seen to be ineffective or inappropriate, the next stage up is locally and conveniently available. In a sense all religions are individualistic but contemporary Sukuma religious practices are more so; whatever they do is unlikely to be similar to what anyone else is doing. Also there are likely to be many more alternative religious specialists available to do it than would be the case with Christianity and Islam.

An Adapting and Adaptable Religious Elite

The sophistication of western theological thought rather than practice must at least in part be due to the increasing complexity of those societies and to the concentration of certain thinking patterns in an elite and then to a much more limited extent into the society as a whole.

This has happened in western society and has left religious thinking and practice in a dichotomous state between official/theological religion and popular religion, which operates both within and without the ritual boundaries of the former.

In Usukuma the expansion of tribal rather than cultural horizons did not lead to the emergence of any new religious elite but rather to the survival and expansion in numbers of those with quasi-traditional religious vocations. Those with these religious vocations form no permanent elite as their practising came and went without any centralizing theme as the continuation of any individual's vocation depends on popular support.

Since these religious vocations came about from many different types of socio-religious behaviour (Hatfield, 1968) which correlated with their dispersed pattern of living, it allowed practitioners to expand in numbers as well and in their utility for the Sukuma. The absence of villages aided the utilitarian survival of Sukuma religion since these religious practitioners were where they were wanted, while Christian and Islamic elites were definitely not.

Another reason for its adaptability is that Sukuma religious practitioners do not start practising as a result of any initiation ceremony but as a result of a calling and which if it comes directly from the ancestors may involve no training at all. The truth of this calling will have been proved or disproved by the subsequent success of their activities.

The Christian priest or pastor is initiated into his priesthood at an impressive ceremony which has no Sukuma parallels. The calling to the priesthood which the Sukuma may concede as having occurred for religious reasons, may not be vindicated by any observed effects attributable to their spiritual powers. Since they may not have much contingency work, they are more likely to be seen as administrators of canon law, which again has no Sukuma parallels since it appears to be non-negotiable about which some priests are described as "fierce".

So the Christian priest or pastor from his ordination is not seen as being given specific spiritual powers except in the institutional sense of being able to perform a range of approved rituals through which he is connected with God (Gardner, 1993).

The nature of existing clerical life does not have this automatic potential for verification by their parishioner practitioners. Their relationship with God is shown in an interior spirituality which does not show quickly or directly in their priestly functions. These Sukuma men and women have their spiritual contacts verified immediately in the successes of what they prescribe for those who consult them.

The Inappropriateness of Simple Socialization Explanations

It is usually accepted that the young are socialized into their cultures directly or indirectly and that they would pick up their religious ideas in much the same way as they would pick up their secular ideas and practices. This theory seems to rely very much on the positive rather than subliminal transfer of ideas.

The religious processes of the Sukuma can be examined at two levels (Elias, 1982). The individual level through learning the adult standards of behaviour and feeling prevalent in that culture which are linguistic and behavioural rather than structural and institutional, a much more dispersed process than what is usually understood by socialization. Through this form of socialization Sukuma thought processes are much more tenaciously held than they would be if they were more closely connected to social structures and related behaviour.

Secondly by the structures of a society which with the Sukuma has enabled a certain pattern of religion to appear but which does not structure it. These enabling patterns remain unchanged except in terms of millennia. There does not appear to have been any major changes in their religious thinking and practices over the last fifty years.

Such religious ideas are often regarded as critical elements in the thinking patterns of non-industrial societies as if it was something distinctively different to western thought to which it must be theologically inferior.

We have to accept that in the Sukuma culture and more particularly in their religious practices, there is very little that could be positively transferred in a way that could be recognized as socialisation. It is not only that few Sukuma may see quasi-traditional ceremonies except on rare occasions but that some Sukuma may not have seen them at all if they belong to Christian families, and yet these ideas persist.

The Sukuma religious professionals have no institutionalized status which could prolong particular patterns of religious behaviour. Thus their roles are not contingent on the quasi-professional opinions of people with whom they are occupationally or institutionally connected. Each one is on his or her own and indeed most of their activities are part-time.

Thus the structured processes in Sukuma society which are shown in language and its uses remain unchanged over millennia. An example of this would be magical conceptions of causality which apparently remain undiminished in western societies despite the long-term efforts of the Christian Churches to eliminate it from their religious practices and the rationalism with which they conduct their business and scientific affairs. The Sukuma are perhaps just as rationalistic as westerners and indeed on what other basis could they conduct their subsistence affairs, just as similarly they have a wide ranging religious conception of causation largely because it works, not that it is illogical and therefore primitive.

It is not a question that some intelligences are sub-optimal but of a system that can work almost entirely independent of anything more than the minimum of religious socializations. The Sukuma religious paradigm is so amorphous of any specific doctrines that there would be few within an average range of intelligences within a community, possibly even for the higher grade mentally handicapped, who would not get some utility from its premises and practices.

The Sukuma Way of Thinking

Within Sukuma religious thinking, the question of belief is scarcely necessary or indeed used. The accepted existence of spirits acting on them rather than for them or on their behalf is so universal that the question of whether they believe or not is not asked and indeed not worth asking. Thus spirit causation is a fact and does not involve belief. Since it is a fact, then the evidence is there for all to see and experience.

This conflicts with the Christian Churches which lay down certain dogmas which are necessary to believe in order to retain membership and creditability within a Church; dogmas moreover of which individuals can have had limited personal experience in their everyday lives. There can be no permitted theological picking and choosing and even less permitted skeptical cross-checking which are basic features of Sukuma modern quasi-traditional religious practice.

Christian beliefs are finite—a "yes" or "no" situation rather than "may be" and this conflicts with the negotiable ways in which the Sukuma utilize their religious ideas.

The pattern of thinking which we may find among the Sukuma illustrated in their religious practices is not the essentially abstract asocial patterns which western thinkers have tended to view as the only viable pattern into which all thought must eventually fall. Such a pattern for the Sukuma would be to isolate them from their social ways. They would regard such a pattern of cold logic has having very little usefulness beyond the arithmetical calculations of the school-room.

In tests on rural Liberians (Scribner, 1981) it was found that the results of administering a test of syllogisms on a sample designated as "traditional" had a somewhat better than the chance solution rate.

This may well be so but should a Sukuma be involved in such tests, the same results would surely apply for the same reasons. That the educated at whatever level of education would recognize the questions as a test that was not related to any reality other than the school environment in which such types of abstract thinking is normal.

Since the Sukuma have few social or religious situations in which they are not dealing and thinking in terms of people or spirits with whom they are connected, they think in ways that relate facts to social environments. Since they have always done so, any occasions for using asocial and abstract thinking are bound to be infrequent.

The presentation of Christianity to the Sukuma has never been in terms of events which have happened in their past and indeed how could it be. The details which are given are outside their experience of facts and people being connected in a potentially negotiable way which would undercut the rightness of Christian dogma. Thus they may never have seen much point in considering them as facts worthy of serious attention independent of any narrower advantages to be gained by conversion.

The Double Tensions of Pastoralism and Agriculture

Socialization as an explanation for all behaviour for which there are no explicit pattern of deliberate teaching is too glib an answer for the religious concepts and practices of the Sukuma.

How could the growing Sukuma become socialized to a whole range of religious ideas of which their families have no direct knowledge and indeed they may never seen a propitiation ceremony. It would seem that their socialization process has to explain how the Sukuma have maintained a wide range of religious ideas by no more than hearing odds and ends of conversation.

Agricultural and pastoral ideas and practices are picked up by a constant exposure to them and reinforced by their own gradual involvement in fieldwork. This is understandable and commonsense.

But the presence in Usukuma of wide ranging ideas about evil spirits, ancestor influences and witchcraft which are just as pervasive as agricultural and pastoral ideas requires a different explanation.

Some of these ideas may have developed or evolved from experiences or they have heard of them in such striking circumstances so that they are remembered. But why remember them at all in such a culturally specific way rather than just attributing them to statistical accident. After all good and bad luck is almost universally accepted as an explanation in western societies.

Now socialization for growing crops and keeping livestock is a pragmatic business in which certain actions have certain consequences that have occurred so often that further explanations are not necessary. The lessons learned through this form of socialization have a continual usefulness; it is reinforced every time that these farmers sit down to a meal.

Why should they then remember ideas and practices, which seemingly clash with this pragmatism covering their everyday lives as subsistence farmers? Moreover the variability of their religious ideas is constrained by their environment; it cannot have been a free ranging choice of alternatives.

Their experience of the environment is capricious. While meteorologists can talk of seasons, the rainfall is not and historically never has been regular. It appears capricious and so spirit forces would appear to them to have the same characteristics. Christianity would not appear to allow for this capriciousness; it is a religion held together by theological logic and asocial and abstract logic does not fit in with their experiences.

Any subsistence economy has persistent problems (Goudsblom, 1989: 7) over non-human dangers, floods, drought and disease, as well as dangers from human relationships, jealousy, greed and lastly dangers from human mismanagement. Over the centuries the Sukuma as any other peoples, have developed ways of coping. Each of these groups of difficulties has their religious specialists available for consultation and help over causation and prevention. There are of course no Christian specialists dealing with rain, jealousy and mismanagement.

Now cattle-keepers like the Masai have these dangers in relation to their livestock and agriculturalists like the Haya and the Angoni have problems related to their crops. In the former case these problems have apparently been solved adequately enough within their own culture without any noticeable conversions to other faiths. In the latter cases there has been substantial conversion to Christianity and the widespread retention nevertheless of quasi-traditional religious practices running parallel to Christianity.

The Sukuma are different as their survival has depended on agriculture but their personal status in both the contemporary world and as ancestors depends upon cattle. Thus their anxieties and problems are much more schematically widespread and detailed than in a more economically monolithic subsistence agricultural culture.

As their interest in livestock is as much socio-religious as economic, it is used as a medium for ensuring the longevity of the family through marriage alliances, social advancement through circles of indebtedness from the loaning out of cattle surplus to their personal requirements as well as their use as animals dedicated to the spirits. Livestock are an integral part of the status aspirations of most Sukuma.

Thus the traditional religious system of the Sukuma and the paradigm within which it operated and still operates, is based on two sets of tensions, the pastoral and the agricultural. Any alternative religious system would not only have to be based on this polarity but would have to be better at coping with this polarity than the quasi-traditional system which has proved to be highly adaptive.

Despite the stereotypical image of Christ as the Good Shepherd, the particular religious problems which are seen by the Sukuma and indeed other pastoral peoples as related to livestock, have no part in any Christian liturgy. As far as the Christian Churches are concerned livestock problems do not exist and yet their significance for the Sukuma is equivalent to the wedding ring for westerners since their passage from one family to another legitimizes offspring and ensures their survival as ancestors.

Certainly Christian prayers and blessings are available but they are tacked onto what are seen as more important religious ceremonies. Even these are not likely to be widely available or offered by priests and pastors as they become immobilized in the parish office and churches from which they officiate.

It is understandable that contemporary Christianity should see itself in urban terms and that people's problems are concentrated there since western culture is largely urban if not industrialized. Numerically the Sukuma are likely to remain subsistence farmers and their problems for which they have religious needs are bipolar and relate both to agriculture and pastoralism.

The Pastoral Block on Conversion

In some situations such as cattle herders, they may not so much fail to be converted to Christianity but cannot be converted pragmatically. Pastoralists have a culture and social institutions, which are closely integrated into seasonal rainfall and grazing; they are here today and gone tomorrow. So their religious beliefs and practices are integrated to the transhumance of men and their livestock. Their religion travels with them and if it has any foeii other than this it is in seasonal get-togethers.

In such a situation Islam is preferable to Christianity. It has no buildings necessary for worship, its primary rituals can be performed anywhere and it has no officiating priesthood. Thus middle-eastern pastoral peoples practice Islam, while those of eastern Africa largely retain their traditional religious practices. For all practical purposes in Usukuma, Christianity is a static and villagised religion whose earlier itinerant aspects faded with the urbanization of western society.

Clearly the Sukuma are not primarily pastoralists as their cattle move more than the people themselves to take advantage of seasonal grazing within parishes. It is possible that cattle keepers are not emigrants into new areas to the west and south. Firstly they already have status from and through their cattle which gives them grazing rights and secondly tsetse in the new areas would make it a questionable undertaking.

So while the livestock owners are static perhaps environmentally as well as in their patterns of religious practice, the movers into new areas are more likely to be converted to Christianity provided that facilities and proselytizing were available.

Linguistic Issues in Conversion

The Sukuma language is both complicated and sophisticated. Possibly as a result of it being unwritten, its sophistication may be very much a part of ordinary discourse than Swahili which has a literary tradition distinctly separate from its every-day usage.

Since it is a tonal language, this may give particular difficulties to missionary speakers of romance languages in which inference is a combination of both vocabulary and pronunciation. It may be that the Sukuma are more attuned to the sophisticated tonalities of a limited vocabulary, in which much of the interpretation is left to the mind of the listener. This contrasts with meanings spelt out in the form of a catechism approach with which the Christian message is conveyed in the simplest possible way.

So those hearing the Christian message may be expecting the same sophistication as they would expect with a religious message in their own culture when what in fact is being conveyed linguistically is some relatively clear cut message.

Thus the missionaries may have found it hard to learn the Sukuma language to a sufficiently high standard to mirror the ambiguities which the Sukuma may have been acculturated to in their religious activities.

All in all it may be that the Sukuma have evaluated Christianity against the sophisticated uses of their own language in a religious situation. Indeed that the Christian message has been put to them in far too straightforward a way so that they may have believed it to be too simple for their level of religious sophistication. Alternatively that it is just as sophisticated and that the priests and pastors know the true meanings but are hiding them from the Sukuma in order to maintain their social superiority in much the same way that the Fang believed to have been the case with their foreign missionaries (Fernandez, 1966).

The language used in Roman Catholic ceremonies is not incomprehensible enough to be classed as glossolalia nor semantically involved enough to correspond to the ambiguities of their own traditional religious practitioners. Christian sermons aim for clarity and simplicity.

Apart from this being the approved way for the Christian message to be put over, it is probably also the result of two other factors. Missionary priests may not have reached the stage of being fully bilingual and therefore "force majeure" they would not have been able to match the Sukuma use of brevity combined with ambiguity.

Secondly there has always been the aim of simplicity in the Christian message, a parallel simplicity may have been the preconception imputed to recipients such as the Sukuma because none knew any better and it was assumed that they were less intellectually developed and less capable therefore of absorbing any complex message.

There are also more specific difficulties which make it difficult to take into ideological practice one of the basic Christian premises. "Nantogilwe Mungu"–I love God and Mungu anitogilwe–God loves me, are both using passive verb forms. So there is in the Sukuma religious vocabulary a passiveness in relation to God in which there is not the interdependency which seems to be an essential element in Christian practice as well as thought.

The utterances of Sukuma diviners are obscure and have to be interpreted by the listeners so therefore the obscurity of the Latin mass may have been a particular attraction for the early converts; it held as much mystery as their own rituals. Diviners talk to themselves in their rituals paralleling the pre-Vatican II priest saying Mass with his back to the congregation and question those who consult them under ritualized conditions as in the confessional. The interrelationships of priests and pastors with those who consult them are deritualized and may even occur in the parish office so that such situations do not allow for ambiguity.

Conclusions

It is hard to conclude which pragmatic factors influence the Sukuma in their choices of practical religion. Certainly most retain to large extent quasi-traditional ideas and to a lesser extent the associated practices depending on the pressures which they and their families experience under conditions of widespread change.

It seems unlikely that the paradigm of religious thinking within which they operate has changed much this century. Their existing system of thinking about religion is based on their history as pastoral and agricultural farmers with its different as well as combined communal anxieties.

This background has made their traditional religion highly adaptive and contingent on what happens to them as individuals and family heads, particularly as they have no centralizing religious institutions or possibly needs for any such centralization. Socially static rituals and static institutions run by immobilized priests and pastors have a very muted appeal. It must be considered that these differences are so substantive that talk about acculturation by the Christian Churches may well be fruitless.

Perhaps then the key to conversion does not lie in the area of theological flexibility and ritual adjustment, a behavioural mobility of which the main Christian Churches are seemingly incapable, but institutional availability and the opportunities which lie in just that are partial explanations of this failure.

Quasi-traditional healers and diviners live in every rural and urban neighbourhood and they are always ready to deal with the people who come to them. Priest and pastors have become institutionally immobilized and their rituals are not primarily related to the personal problems of the parishioners. In order to sell a product there have to be sales staff and plenty of the products on offer. Personal needs come before products. The existing rituals have not been taken to the people as it has often been seen as para-liturgical and thus somewhat suspect activity for Christians.

If religion is the profession of priests and pastors then they should concentrate on just that and not try and be developmental assistants and social workers. Even under modern conditions quasi-traditional practitioners keep to their professional roles and do not attempt to parallel other roles for which they may not have any aptitude.

The assumption of universalism makes for difficulties but that issue can be safely ignored if the rituals of Christianity can be taken to the Sukuma in ways that parallel their traditional ways of seeking spiritual help. It has to be applied to the Sukuma on their terms rather than expecting the Sukuma to change in order to fit in to Christianity on external ones. In such situation all that would result from widespread conversions is the working of two parallel religious systems which only meet in the minds of those with both these religious needs.

Overall there has been a general failure to understand the sophistication of Sukuma thought and practice which is mirrored in their language and a reluctance to recognize the efficiency of their modernized traditional system to cope with their problems.

REFERENCES

Cory, H. 1951. The Ntemi. Traditional Rites of a Sukuma Chief. London: Macmillan.

Elias, N. 1982. The Civilising Process. Vol 2. State Formation and Civilisation. Oxford: Blackwell.

Fernandez, J.W. 1966. "Unbelievable Subtle Words; representation and integration in the sermons of an African reformative cult", *History of Religions*, 6(1).

—. 1980. "Edification by Puzzlement", in I. Karp and C.S. Bird (eds.), *Explorations in African Systems of Thought*. Bloomington: Indiana U-niversity.

Gardner, D.S. 1983. "Performativity and Ritual. The Mianmin Case", *Man* (ns), 18: 346-360.

Goudsblom, J. 1989. "Ecological Regimes and the Rise of Organised Religion", in J. Goudsblom *et al.* (eds.), *Human History and Social Process*. Exeter University.

Gray, R.F. 1963. *The Sonjo*. Oxford University Press.

Hatfield, C.R. 1968. The Nfumu in Tradition and Change. A Study of the Position of Religious Practitioners among the Sukuma of Tanzania, East Africa. Unpublished PhD mss. Catholic University of America.

Lumsden, C.J. and E.O. Wilson. 1981. *Genes, Mind and Culture*. Harvard.

Mennell, S.1989. "Short-term Interests and Long-term Processes: The Case of Civilisation and Decivilisation", in J. Goudsblom *et al.* (eds.), *Human History and Social Process*. Exeter University.

Scribner, S.1981. "Modes of Thinking and Ways of Speaking: Culture and Logic Reconsidered", in R.O. Freedle (ed.), *Discourse Production and Comprehension*. New Jersey: Ablex.Hillsdale.

Tanner, R.E.S.1968. "Reasons for Rejecting Christianity", *African Ecclesiastical Review*, October.

—. 1969a. *Transition in African Beliefs*. Maryknoll: New York.

—. 1969b. "Reasons for Entering the Christian Community", *African Ecclesiastical Review*, April.

—. 1969c. "The Christian Who does not Practice in Usukuma", *African Ecclesiastical Review*, July.

—. 1996. "Should there be a Change in the Focus of Christian Concern? The Possibility of a New Direction in Eastern Africa", *African Christian Studies*, 12(3): 48-53.

—. 1997. "Cognitive Development, Socialization and Cognitive Mutation. A Critique and Elaboration of Boyer's Naturalness of Religion. A Case Study of the Sukuma of Tanzania", *Journal of Social Sciences*, 1(2): 91-8.

FIFTEEN

JATAPU TRIBE OF ANDHRA PRADESH
An Ethnographic Profile

B. V. BABU, Y.S. KUSUMA and J.M. NAIDU

Jatapu is an agricultural tribe mainly found in the Eastern ghats of Vizianagaram and Srikakulam districts of Andhra Pradesh. Locally they are also referred to as Jata and Jatapu Dora. According to Census of India (1981), there were 86,672 Jatapu people in Andhra Pradesh. They had a dialect of their own in the past, but at present, they speak Telugu, the regional language of Andhra Pradesh. Thurston (1975) referred to Jatapu from Madras Census Report (1901) and defined them as a civilized section of Khond, who speak Khond on the hills and Telugu in the plains. But the contemporary Jatapu people of Srikakulam district do not accept themselves to be a section of Khond. They claim themselves to be a separate endogamous tribe with distinct socio-cultural patterns. However, they do not remember their origin or history. The Jatapu tribe enjoys superior status to the neighbouring Savara tribe. They do not have commensal relations with Savara and Thoti living along with them in a few villages. In this paper, an attempt has been made to present an ethnographic profile of Jatapu tribe. Data were collected, using various ethnographic field work techniques, from tribal areas of Srikakulam district, Andhra Pradesh.

Social Organization

The Jatapu is an endogamous group which do not possess any sub-tribes. However, there exists several exogamous patrilineages within the tribe which are totemic by nature. Sons inherit the surname permanently while daughters retain the parental lineage till their marriage. After marriage, a girl acquires her husband's surname. Some of the common surnames of family names are *Addaku* (a leaf used to make meal plates), *Gedela* (she buffalo), *Kadraki* (wild goat), *Kadrika* (a species of fowl), *Kondagorre* (wild sheep), *Mandangi* (bull or cow), *Thoyyika* (wild fowl), *Banigi, Biddika, Emarika, Himarika,*

Jilakarra, Korangi, Kumbirika, Meenaka, Mutaka, Nimmaka, Ootaka, Oyyika, Palaka, Pathika, Puvvala, Thadangi, Valiki, Vullaka, etc. Exogamy is strictly observed at surname level similar to several Hindu castes.

Dress Pattern and Ornaments

Usually, Jatapu men of older generations wear a loin cloth around the waist while the young people wear *lungi* and *banian.* Older women wear *sari* without blouse while young girls wear blouses too. Women wear ornaments made of brass on nostrils, nasal septum and ear lobes and glass bangles on hands. Occasionally gold and silver ornaments are also used along with black beads as necklets. Usually dress and ornaments are purchased in weekly markets. Tattoo marks are found on the body of some people particularly on arms of women. They use oil for hair care. Women tie their hair on the backside of the head, while men get their head hair dressed periodically. Unlike Hindu caste women, majority of tribal women do not wear *bindi* (red dot) on the forehead except some young girls of recent generation.

Occupation

The primary occupation is agriculture, although several families also depend on casual labour and collection of minor forest produce. Adult men cut the bushes on the adjoining hill slopes to make podu fields, till the land, sow the seeds and harvest the crop. Women–folk help men in clearing the bushes, weeding and harvest in the fields, collecting fuel wood and minor forest produce in addition to regular domestic work such as cooking and cleaning of utensils, house, cattle shed, etc. Old people look after toddler and young children at home. Cattle grazing is assigned to young boys above ten years of age while young girls help the mother in cooking and cleaning. During summer season, young children also collect minor forest produce. Usually, paddy is cultivated in wet lands and millet such as jowar, maize, ragi, bajra, etc. in dry lands. Few people cultivate turmeric and fruit gardens such as pineapple, banana, etc. are raised under various tribal welfare schmes. Integrated Tribal Development Agency (ITDA) provides agricultural loans, high yielding hybrid seeds, fertilizers and technical help. The collected minor forest produces include firewood, hill brooms, tamarind, marking nuts and seasonal fruits like custard apple, mango, etc. The Jatapus domesticate cows, oxen, buffaloes, sheep, goat, chick, etc. along with pet animals like dog.

Village and Settlement Pattern

The settlements are situated at the foothills or on hill slopes, nearer to a stream. The hamlets or villages are relatively small with about 10 to 25 households which are again heterogeneous. Few families of Savara tribe and one or two families of artisan castes are found to live with Jatapus in each village. Usually, Savara settlements are located mostly on hill slopes cultivating dry lands while Jatapu reside at the foothills farming a relatively higher proportion of available wet agricultural land. Villages consist of one or two lanes with houses on either side. Few families together construct house as an elongated single shed erected on centre poles with roof sloping on either side which is divided into compartments; each partitioned further into two to three rooms including a front verandah. These houses are thatched with straw and partitioned by mud walls, without windows and ventilation. Several houses have mud plastered false roof for protection against cold in winter and fire accidents, and a shelf between thatched roof and false roof to store grains and other produce. In heterogeneous villages, the houses are hierarchically arranged; lower ranked caste people will usually be at one end while Savara tribe form a separate colony. Common cattle shed with partitions for each household is a common feature at the backside.

Food Habits

The Jatapus are non-vegetarians without beef. The breakfast, usually after returning from fields in the morning, includes conjee and the left over rice of previous night's dinner. The lunch consists of gruel made of millet. The supper consists of rice along with *dhal* (made of pulses) or vegetable curry and thin soup of tamarind. The vegetables include brinjal, tomato, drumstick, green plantain, okra, gourds, leafy vegetables, etc. During summer the people collect wild tubers for cooking as well as several wild fruits for consumption. Women cook food by using onion, garlic, chillies and other spices. Jatapu are fond of pork. They eat fruits such as banana, jack, guava, mango, etc. In the past, people were not used to milk the cow and consume milk and other dairy products. Now, few families use milk for tea, coffee, etc. Majority of men and a few women drink sago palm extract, home made rice beer and other alcoholic drinks. Many people including women smoke and chew tobacoo.

Family and Kinship

Jatapu is a patriarchal society with a number of patrilineal lineages. Simple nuclear families are more common, while a few joint families (include dependent older parents) are seen. The average family size is about five people. Patrilocal residence is the norm, but young couples stay with boy's parents for a couple of years and later establish a separate family. Unmarried children live with their parents. Older parents are cared by their sons. Father is the head of the family who control expenditure and procure the family needs for subsistence. Mother looks after domestic and household duties. Decisions regarding family matters is taken by father, in consultation with mother and elderly children. The kinship is descriptive type. They use specific terms to refer to their kin members. All the kin terms are in local Telugu language.

Avoidance between father-in-law and daughter-in-law and between older brother and his younger brother's wife is observed. Joking relations with consanguinal cross cousins, wife's younger sister, elder brother's wife and between grand parents and grand children are observed.

Customs and Traditions

Jatapu is a strict endogamous group with clear exogamous surnames. Cross cousin marriages such as marrying mother's daughter, father's sister's daughter and second cross cousins are prevalent. Though marrying niece is prohibited, a few cases of uncle-niece marriages, a practice acquired due to culture contact with plain people, are observed. Child marriage is accepted but relatively rare. Usually, girls marry after attaining puberty while boys marry at about twenty years of age. Monogamy is common, but polygyny is also observed. Marriages are fixed through negotiation and mutual consent. Marriage by elopement is frequently reported. Marriage by exchange or service are very rare. The young boys and girls are at liberty to choose their spouses. Village exogamy is more frequent than village endogamy. The weekly market place is a common meeting point for prospective couples. Formal bride price in kind and cash is observed while in case of elopement the bride price is not paid.

Divorce, due to barrenness, adultery, ill-health and maladjustment, is permitted with the consent of village council and the compensation in that case is paid by the guilt. In case a married woman is eloped by a man, then he will be fined by the council. A compensation extracted from the new husband will be repaid to the former husband. Children are the liability of father. Widow, widower and divorce remarriages are accepted. Junior levirate and senior sororate are noticed. The marriage symbols for women are toe rings and a gold or brass marriage badge *(thali)* in the neck.

Religion and Rituals

Jatapu have their own religion although their beliefs and practices indicate the influence of Hindu religion. They are polytheists and worship numerous gods and goddesses including deities of animistic nature. Of late, they are also aware of various Hindu deities such as Krishna, Rama, Lakshmi, Appanna, Jagannadh, etc. including some Hindu epics. A few of them also visit the Hindu shrines. Their religion centres around supernaturalism and they believe that the supernatural powers control the entire universe. They worship both animate and inanimate things, and they believe in *soul* (animism) and spirits, i.e. souls of dead people. They offer food and clothes to their dead ancestors during death ceremonies and specific festivals.

The regularly worshipped village deity is *Jankara.* A chick is sacrificed during every festival and a pig or an ox is sacrificed on special occasions. Usually they worship *Jankara* and other goddesses with *guggilam* (incense resin of shorea robusta), turmeric and cooked rice. The deity *Sandamma* is offered with twigs of neem and horse-radish tree, and occasionally a pig or chick is sacrificed for the good health of domestic animals and the people. A chick or goat is sacrificed on a Tuesday to the deity *Mutyalamma,* also referred to as *Nukalamma* or *Ammoru* once in 3-5 years as fixed by *disari* (person who fixes auspicious dates for various ceremonies and rituals). The deity *Eswaramma* is worshipped during *sivarathri* by sacrificing a goat or chick for the welfare of the people. The deity *Nukathadammа* is worshipped during *Dasarah* (October) festival. Ganga, the goddess of water, is also worshipped. Each settlement normally has a *Jankara* within the village, and *Gudimelu, Esaramma, Sandamma* and *Nukalamma* on the outskirts. In addition, the regional deities such as *Peda Sunnayamma, China Sunnavamma, Kota Durgamma* are also worshipped. They also believe in some deities of animistic nature referred to as *Kondalodhalu* such as *Engalodha, Burikilodha, Yetalodha,* etc. In a heterogeneous village with Savara and Jatapu populations, separate places of worship for each tribe is noticed.

The Jatapu perceive the existence of two souls, namely *paramatma* (embedded in god) and *jeevatma* (lives in body) which have no particular shape. At the time of death *jeevatama* or soul of man leaves the body and heart stops beating. They believe that when the soul is hurt the body becomes sick. Jatapu decipher the event of death as *jeevatma* attaining *paramatma.* The people believe that *jeevatma* of a crooked person does not reach *paramatma* but hangs aimlessly. If death rites and pollution are not observed properly, they believe that the soul of the dead person may remain in this world without reaching *paramatma* and haunt the people as a ghost or spirit.

Jatapu observe numerous rituals and celebrate festivals *(panduga)* throughout twelve lunar months of the year. The Sankranthi festivals falls in January, during which the people offer food and clothes to their dead ancestors. Puppi festival is celebrated in February by offering a chick to goddess *Jankara* which marks the beginning of collection of hill brooms. In the month of March *(Dolu),* they observe Vippa to initiate the collection of vippa flowers (flowers of a forest tree from which alcohol is brewed). On Vippa festival day the people worship goddess *Jankara* through the priest *(janni)* by sacrificing a chick and goddess *Gudimelu* by sacrificing a goat. In the month of May (vittima) vithanalu panduga (festival of seeds) is celebrated to initiate the agricultural operations. The *janni* conducts the ritual by sacrificing a pig to goddess *Jankara.* He makes a small wooden model of cart and puts it before the goddess. He makes three holes in triangle shape and sows seeds of paddy and other millet in them. Later, all villages visit goddess *Sandamma* in a procession, pulling the model cart along with them. On the following day, Sandamma festival is celebrated. In the month of June (Deshta) Jatapu observe Tenke ritual to break the stone of mango by keeping it in between the horns of a bull before goddess *Jankara.* Then the bull is sacrificed and given to their neighbouring Savara people. The Tenke ritual permits the people to use the pulp of the mango seed for various food preparations. Kondem festival which fall in August-September (Edava) months is celebrated by worshipping *Jankara* with a piglet to initiate the consumption of wild roots and tubers. During the month of November *(kartheeka* or Palaka) Kandi or Bona festival is celebrated by worshipping goddess *Jankara* to initiate the harvest of red gram crop. All these festivals have socio-economic significance since they control the consumption of various agricultural and forest produce. In addition to annual festivals, Jatapu celebrate special festivals to worship goddesses *Esaramma, Godhamma, Nukalamma,* etc. once in 3-5 years.

Life Cycle Ceremonies

Birth

The pre-delivery rituals are not in practice. The woman is taken to her natal house during seventh month of pregnancy for first delivery to be performed by an experienced woman or mother. Later deliveries will be at her mother-in-law's house. If a woman outside the family assists in delivery, she is presented with small cash and clothes on the ninth day after post-delivery pollution period. On the ninth day the mother and child are given a purificatory bath by the woman who has cut the naval chord (placenta) using the symbolic hot water brought by the relatives. An oil lamp is shown to all the attending relatives and a vegetarian feast is hosted. The baby is formally put into cradle on the same day. *Mundan* (head-hair cutting) ceremony for both boys and girls is done within first two months of birth. The head-hairs are cut by barber or an elderly person. The relatives and villagers bring hot water with mugs to give bath to the child as a symbolic expression of solidarity. They are served with a feast. Usually, formal naming of a new born child is done during Sankranthi festival. Normally parents select name in consultation with maternal uncle and paternal aunt. Giving ancestors name to the child is not uncommon.

Menarche

On attaining first menstruation, the girl is kept outside the house in the verandah by erecting a screen. Post-menarchial pollution is observed for nine days. During this period the girl is not allowed to see men. The paternal aunts and other relatives bring special food to the girl during the nine days, but non-vegetarian food is prohibited. On the last day the girl is given a purificatory bath.

Marriage

The formal marriage process is initiated by elders including parents from boy's family through a visit to girl's house with a few measures of rice, vegetables and new clothes as presents to the bride and her parents. The elders discuss the proposal and take the mutual consent of the girl, the boy and their parents. Then, the girl is anointed with turmeric paste brought by the boy's family for the occasion. The bride price, usually few bags of rice, new clothes and a small cash is paid and the *disari* fixes an auspicious day and time for marriage ceremony.

The marriage is celebrated at groom's house. A *pandal* is erected under which a pyol is made. A day before marriage ceremony, the bride along with her party is brought to groom's house in the evening. The next morning *Kallagollu* ceremony (toe-nail cutting) takes place followed by tying of wrist threads *(Kankanam)* to the couple and joining of their hands together at a specified auspicious time by *janni.* The couple then take bath and sit on *pyol* to receive gifts in cash and kind from the friends and all the attending relatives. On the same night young men of the village entertain the couple and relatives by dancing to the tune of playing drums. The date for nuptial ceremony, to be held at groom's residence, is fixed by *disari,* usually a few days after marriage.

Of late, due to various social and economic constraints, dilution in the traditional marriage practices is observed. Marriage by elopement is very common. Usually a boy elopes a girl with her consent and stays at his relative's or friend's house, and return after a few days to his own house.

Death

After the death of an individual the body is kept on the cot in the verandah and the message is sent to all the relatives within and outside the village. The cremation is held only after the arrival of all close relatives, usually the next day by guarding the corpse over night. The women relatives bring little oil and turmeric paste, and anoint the corpse. The corpse is given last bath and dressed with new clothes with a few coins tied to the dress. The corpse, with head directed to east, is carried by men in a procession to the graveyard while a pot of water and fire are carried by the chief mourner. Women are not allowed to witness the cremation. On the way to the grave, the corpse is lowered at a specific place for a while. The men cut the wood and make pyre. The last rite is performed in the graveyard by playing various musical instruments. The body is then laid on the pyre. The chief mourner goes around the pyre three times with a pot of water on his shoulder to which a hole is made after each round. Any of the sons can lit the pyre. If a woman dies, her son will lit the fire even though her husband is alive. While the pyre is burning, the attending relatives and friends utter some words advising the soul of dead person to behave properly and not to quarrel with others in the other world. On the way from the graveyard, men take their bath in a stream. Women also take bath at home.

Jatapu people observe death pollution as fixed by priest for three, five, seven or nine days. On the third day, a little amount of cooked rice and a curry are offered to the dead person's soul at the cremation place by three men of whom one must be the son of the dead. On the day of purification, the male relatives visit the cremation place and offer rice and green gram cooked without salt to the departed soul. While returning they also take bath in a stream. On this day, the family of the deceased host a non-vegetarian feast to the attending relatives and friends who console the bereaved family.

Political Organization

Traditional village council is headed by Naidu and a community council for each tribe is led by the headman. The offices of these councils are hereditary and succession is by the eldest son. Village council looks after the maintenance of social norms and also settles intra-village and inter-tribal disputes while tribal council solves intra-tribal disputes including family disputes. Elected president of the village *(panchayat sarpanch)* also involves himself in the council's decisions. These councils impose fine in the form of cash or kind on the guilty. The sacred specialist *janni,* who performs priesthood for various festivals, ceremonies and rituals, belongs to Jatapu tribe. Another specialist *disari* belonging to Savara tribe fixes auspicious dates for conducting ceremonies and rituals.

Though village councils are important in tribal societies, the constitutionally elected bodies such as *village panchayat* (at village level) and *mandal praja parishad* (at block level) play crucial roles in the developmental activities and tribal welfare schemes. In notified tribal agency areas, all these statutory positions are reserved for people belonging to the Scheduled Tribes.

Property and Economy

Jatapu have a subsistence economy. They own both wet and dry land. The family property includes domestic animals, household furnitures, utensils, ornaments, agricultural implements, etc. The inherited property will be shared among sons only as per male equigeniture norm with a major share to the eldest son. The common property includes fruit bearing trees in and around the village; the yield will be shared by all the families. Each village possesses a piece of land for the village goddess *Jankara* which is cultivated by *janni* as an allowance for priesthood. Agriculture produce is primary source of economy supplemented by minor forest produce. Casual labour for farming is usually exchanged between families. In many cases the payment is in the form of grains to the people of their own tribe while it is cash for others. Exchange of goods on barter basis is observed occasionally.

Education and Health

Most of the older generation Jatapu men and women are illiterates (above 95%). Among the middle aged people about one-tenth are literate. Among youngsters, aged between 10 to 20 years, one-fourth attend schools and can write and read. Relatively higher percentage of Jatapu people are literates than other tribes of Andhra Pradesh.

Although the people are aware of the problem of population explosion, only a few (17% men and 3% women) have adopted birth control methods. The fertility is relatively lower with about 4.2 conceptions, 3.8 live births, 2.4 surviving children and 1.4 post-natal deaths per Jatapu couple. Most of the deaths are infantile and juvenile, occurring due to water borne and other infectious diseases. Also the malnutrition related morbidity is prevalent. It is important to note that most of the births/deliveries take place at home, which are not attended by medical or para-medical personnel.

REFERENCES

Census of India, 1981. Series II, *Andhra Pradesh, Part-I, Provisional Population Totals, Final Populations*. Delhi: Government of India Publications.

Madras Census Report. 1901. Referred by Thurston, 1975.

Thurston, E. 1975. *Castes and Tribes of Southern India*. Vol. IV. Delhi: Cosmo Publications.

SIXTEEN

TOTOS
A Primitive Tribe in Transition

AMAL KUMAR DAS

The general characteristic of the tribal population of India is their exclusive geographical habitat. There are some groups among them who live more or less in isolation in inaccessible difficult terrain and maintain a life-style which remains almost static through centuries. In general their population size is small with low growth rate in comparison to others. Referred to as the "lowest layer" among the Scheduled Tribe communities by the Dhebar Commission, 1961, seventy-four Scheduled Tribe communities have been identified so far by the government on the basis of their (a) low growth rate, (b) pre-agricultural level of technology, and (c) extremely low level of literacy (Working Group Report, 1984: 87).

At the beginning of the Fifth Five Year Plan, in drawing up the strategy for tribal sub-plan, particularly for more backward tribal communities, certain primitive tribal communities were identified for programme implementation. During the Fifth Plan, the number of identified primitive tribes was 52 with a population of about 10 lakhs. During the Sixth Plan period, additional 20 tribal groups were identified raising their total to 72 with a population of about 14 lakhs. In subsequent plan periods two more were added. At present there are 74 communities in the list of primitive tribes with a population nearing seventeen lakhs. They live in 15 tribal sub-plan states and union territories. As the population size of the primitive tribal groups is quite small, the objective is to achieve total development of the entire population as quickly as possible. The funding is provided out of the special central assistance for the purpose.

In West Bengal, three Scheduled Tribes have been identified as primitive tribes. They are Lodha, Birhor and Toto. The Lodha are a "vimukta jati"; the Birhor, a semi-nomadic tribe and the Toto grouped under the Bhutias, a Scheduled Tribe in West Bengal.

The purpose of the paper is to present a glimpse of the Toto life and activities, a little known primitive tribal group of West Bengal.

II

Totopara, the only tract of land where a small tribal group of about one thousand people known as "Toto" is found to live in a cluster, is a small village situated in the Madarihat police station of Alipurduar sub-division of Jalpaiguri district (West Bengal), lying at latitude 89°20' and longitude 26°50'. They live on this cluster of three small hillocks (750' to 1250' above sea level) at the foot of the Himalayas. They belong to Mongoloid racial stock and have a dialect of their own. Due to contacts with others they can speak in Nepali and in broken Hindi and Bengali languages. They have attracted the attention of administrators, researchers and planners since the eighteenth century due to certain characteristics and demographic features.

The settlement of the Totopara village, consists of several roughly defined territories (Panchayat gaon, Mondal gaon, Subagaon, Mitrang gaon, Puja gaon and Dumchigaon) demarcated for the members of the different clans (Dankobei, Dantrobei, Nubebei, Machingbei, Mantrobei, Mankobei, Bongobei Budubei, Baudhbei and Pisochangobei). Each and every area, occupied by respective clan members, bears a separate name of its own. Toto houses exist in clan-wise demarcated areas and are more or less clustered in the middle of the village in an assymetrical fashion covering an area of half a mile in length and one-fourth mile in breadth.

During Sanyal's visit in 1955 and my first visit in 1969 both of us noticed existence of a tribal welfare centre, a primary school, agricultural marketing society, five shops (two grocery owned by Beharis, one cloth shop owned by a Marwari, one tailoring shop owned by a Nepali and a petty jewellery works run by a Nepali) and a dispensary run by Swedish Mission in Totopara.

At present, Totopara has two primary schools, one junior high school with ashram hostel, two *anganwadi* centres, one rural library, six adult education centres run by Toto Kalyan Samiti, one six-bedded primary health centre, one veterinary centre (insemination centre), one commercial bank, one post-office, one agricultural marketing cooperative. The village as well as some Toto house have electric connections at present, supply of drinking water has been improved, tribal welfare centre is provided with quarters and guest house, traditional religious centre (demsha) has been renovated and a club house (poikimsha) has been constructed for the youths, one video-house run by a businessman in a rented house in the marketing centre. In the marketing centre within the village there are shops and eating places and regular *hat* (weekly market) takes place on every Thursday. All these have taken place due to the effort of the government, non-governmental organizations as well as private entrepreneurs.

The nearest railway station from the village is Hasimara, situated at a distance of 16 kms. The Madarihat railway station is situated at a distance of 21 kms. There is a regular bus service during fair weather from Madarihat to Totopara.

III

Totos remained unknown to the outside world till the end of the eighteenth century. Existence of Totos was first came to the notice of Babu Kishen Kanta Bose in 1815 in a village in Lukepur under Falakata Tahsil of Western Duars. He was an employee of Rangpur Collectorate at that time. The Toto population have a record of migration from one place to another. In this connection Sanyal's comments and observations are worth noting. He states:

> "Although the Totos are now found in only a single village there is evidence of other Toto settlements in the western Duars, a tract of country spreading from the river Teesta on the west upto the river Sankosh on the east within the district of Jalpaiguri in West Bengal . . . The whole area of western Duars was under Bhutan till 1865 and probably due to depredation of the Bhutias, due to influence of other cultures and also due to the notorious malaria of western Duars the number began to fall off till there remained no trace of any Toto in the old settlements in the plains of Duars. The small number that survived moved from place to place in search of a shelter. . . some of them are absorbed in Mech family, some went to Nepal and upper Bhutan and were probably incorporated into the people of the place. The few that could save themselves had to seek shelter in the very secluded and healthier portion of a hill surrounded by deep wood where they confined themselves strictly within its limits. This is the Totopara where they are slowly increasing in number" (Sanyal, 1955: 67,69).

Mr. D. Sunder, settlement officer, Jalpaiguri was deputed to survey the western Duars in 1889-1894 and to take a stock of the people, their lands and the crop. The whole of western Duars was then full of howling forests. Yet he had been to the Totos and found them settled in the present day Totopara. He was the first person to publish some notes about Toto language and habits covering about seven pages (Sunder, 1895).

There is a myth that the Totos are a dwindling tribal community. But the demographic profile does not reveal so. According to 1901 census their population was 171. Since then their number has increased manifold as would be visualized from the Table 16.1. At present (1998) they number slightly above one thousand.

TABLE 16.1: Toto Population as per Different Surveys and Studies*

Year	Source	Population		
		Male	Female	Total
1901	Census	72	99	171
1911	Census	125	110	235
1911	Gait and Grierson**	149	110	259
1921	Census	140	131	271
1931	Census	130	204	334
1941	Census	159	162	321
1951	Census	161	160	321
1962	Indian Statistical Institute	206	189	395
1971	Official Register***	332	318	650
1972	C.C. Sanyal**	—	—	584
1976	Anthropological Survey of India	—	—	641
1979	Cultural Research Institute	343	332	675
1985	A. Sarkar**	407	378	785
1986	Official Register***	—	—	825
1991	B. Majumdar**	473	453	926

* Das and Das, 1993: 222; Sarkar 1993: 5-6 and Majumdar, 1993.

** Individual studies of the authors

*** Register of the Social Worker of Totopara

Table 16.1 reveals that the population variation among the Totos was less during the pre-independence era but it gradually increased during the later phase.

Besides the Totos, twenty-four other communities live in Totopara. They belong to thirteen Nepali speaking castes (Tamang, Mangar, Rai, Chhetri, Gurung, Kami, Sanyasi, Brahmin, Damai, Limbu, Ghate, Newar and Sarki); five Hindi speaking groups (Sunri, Sunwar, Marwari, Chamar and Muslim); one Bengali speaking caste (Goala) and five other tribal communities (Garo, Oraon, Mech, Sherpa and Lepcha).

The Totos were the sole inhabitants of Totopara in 1901. But in 1991, they shared only 41.6 per cent of the total population of Totopara (2174). Though once a dominant population in their own locality, they gradually became a minority group with the influx of various other communities into their locality. The changing situation in this respect will be revealed from the Table 16.2:

TABLE 16.2: Population of Totopara in Different Decades

Year	Toto Population	Total Population	P.C. of Totos to Total Population
1901	171	171	100.0
1911	200	235	85.1
1931	328	334	98.2
1951	314	567	55.4
1961	376	1160	32.4
1971	557	1205	46.2
1981	716	1497	47.8
1991	904	2174	41.6

Source: Majumdar, 1993.

The problem the tribe confronts today lies in the demographic imbalance in the locality with the influx of migrant population of different ethnic origins. This has changed the land-man ratio which is ultimately putting pressure on this small agrarian community of the Totos (Das *et al.,* 1993: 222)

The Totos generally prefer simple families (nuclear type), average size generally varying between 4-7 members. There are joint families with vertical and lateral extensions. The extensions of kin-ties are traceable upto the third generation, and for parental generation these are extended upto the first step only. The families are patrilocal and descent is traced through male line. The families are of monogamous type.

IV

About a few generations back orange trade was the main source of livelihood of the Totos. But at present there is no orange at Totopara. Most of the Totos at present earn cash by acting as porters for carrying oranges from gardens of Bhutan to Totopara where from it is exported to outside market.

Now-a-days agriculture may be regarded as their main subsistence activity. Cultivation of *kaoni, marua* (millet) and *bhutta* (maize) are practised by almost all the families. Some have taken to paddy cultivation also and grown *Kalai* or *kala dal* (pulses). Most of the Totos are owner cultivators. Some cultivate as share croppers also. Some earn their livelihood as agricultural and day labourers. Totos recognize two types of land, *leita/dala* or low land where paddy is cultivated and *wuita/danga* or upland which is of inferior type.

Previously, Totos were accustomed to shifting cultivation growing millets and maizes. They have become settled agriculturists about five decades back, but their technological adoption is of rudimentary nature. The Totos have been immensely benefited by learning the techniques of settled agriculture from the Nepalis, but they have been greatly losers too. All the best lands have been taken over by the Nepali settlers during less than two decades. The whole area of Toto mouza was recorded in the name of Toto "Mondal" or chief on behalf of the whole community during the first settlement operation conducted by Sunder in 1889-1994. But it was decided by the state government in 1969 to record the quantity of land on individual Toto names on the basis of the existing quantum of land already in the possession of the Totos. This was done for protecting them from exploitation from encroachment of their land by others (Das, 1969: 14-17).

In 1969, there were 89 Toto families, that increased to 123 in 1979 and to 180 in 1991. This increase has gradually affected to their land holding position which led to fragmentation of land with the division of families. In the case of newly emerged families, neither homestead nor cultivable land was recorded.

Most of the Toto families still live below the poverty line. Hardly one-fifth of the families attain position above the poverty line.

The change in land rights from traditional community ownership (earlier recorded in the name of Toto chief, i.e. Mondal) to individual ownership have both good and bad effects in their socio-economic life and mode of thinking. The Totos now realize the value of the asset. Previously, Toto Mondal used to settle these lands with the Nepalis behind the eyes of the Totos, but now-a-days, the individuals taking the advantage of their ownership settle such matters with outsiders beyond the knowledge of the authority. Some of the Totos are profitably utilizing this asset for their socio-economic betterment.

V

The Totos made some progress so far as "literacy" is concerned. In 1979 there were 47 literates (male-44 and female-3), whereas the said number increased to 94 (male-81, female-13) in 1991. In 1972 when there were only 36 Toto students (boys-35, girl-1) in the primary stage (upto class IV), the said number increased to 67 (boys-58, girls-9) in 1991. Non-Toto students numbered 19 (boys-12, girls-7) in 1972, and the said number in 1991 was 95 (boys-49, girls-46).

In 1980, there were 14 Toto students (boys-11, girls-3) reading in Dhanapati Junior High School. The same number remained almost same in 1991 (boys-12, girl-1); the number of total students being 57 (boys-41 and girls-16).

Modern education has made an impact only in the filial generation. Of the total literates (94) in 1991, 47 had education upto primary level (I-IV), 32 upto junior high school level (V to VIII) and remaining 15 upto class IX, X and S.F. Maximum number of students belonged to Dankobei (15), Dantrobei (34) and Bongobei (9) clans. Majumdar found that growth of population among the Totos during 1979-91 period was 68.6 per cent, whereas the rate of literacy has increased among the Totos from 8.5 per cent in 1979 to only 10.1 per cent in 1991. Chittaranjan Toto was the first among the Totos to pass the Higher Secondary Examination but unfortunately he died before taking admission in the college (Majumdar, 1993).

At present two employees (supervisor and peon) of Uttarbanga Kshatriya Gramin Bank, located in Totopara since 1984, belong to Toto community. A few among the educated Totos are gradually acquiring the qualities of middle class both economically and culturally. Some among the neo-elite group, mostly of educated youths, have already shown the qualities of an entrepreneur. They may profitably be inducted and utilized for the progress and development of their community, thereby inculcating a sense of belongingness for avoiding and falling prey to the evil forces.

VI

The Totos are endogamous group having 13 exogamous clans *(sarkhae)*. Each clan consists of a number of families. In 1901, there were only 36 Toto families which increased to 180 in 1991. About 70 per cent of the families are of nuclear type, the number of members varying between 3 to 6. About 20 per cent of the families are of joint type with vertical and lateral extensions. The remaining 10 per cent are of non-familial and conjugal units.

Of the 13 clans, about 70 per cent of the families belong to 5 dominant clans, namely, Dankobei, Dantrobei, Badubei, Bandhbei and Bongobei. The clan names have been derived from the places of their earlier migration. Some of the clans have also sub-clans (e.g. Dikbei is the sub-clan of Bandhbei, Dantrobei has four sub-clans, etc.).

The Totos follow endogamy strictly, marriage outside the tribe is strictly prohibited. Violation of the rule leads to social boycot and expulsion from the community.

The average age of marriage for the boys is 19 years and girls 16 years. The average marriage duration of the population recorded was 10.7. Dhali during his survey in 1979 found 9 widowers and 14 widows, although widow remarriage is not forbidden. The norm of intra-tribal marriage is strictly adhered to. The feature of selecting mates is influenced by inter-clan choice within thirteen identified clans. This inter-breeding of a small population within a village is restricted to only thirteen clans might have biological consequences affecting the gene pool. It is felt strongly that proper serological research alone will reveal the real drama in the genetical world of the population (Das *et al.*, 1993: 225)

Among the Totos "lineage" also plays an important role. Each lineage has a deity "Chima" who is worshipped by the head of the family. The deity is considered as "Buro-Buri" of other tribal groups. Abode of this ancestral spirit is within the darkest corner of the house. The tie among the lineage members is stronger than that of the clan. Lineage exogamy is strictly followed. Regulation of marriage is more strictly associated with lineage than clan. Any sort of sexual relation within the lineage is strictly prohibited.

Some authors have also mentioned about the existence of loose type of clan-wise moieties or ceremonial divisions among the Totos based on "religious group" and "non-religious group", clans grouped on the basis of "Hui-hwa" or relay porterage system.

VII

The common diseases at present among the Totos are dysentery, fever, cold and cough, ulcer, Toto sore, carries in the teeth, malaria. Previously they suffered from yaws and deficiencies (Vitamin A, D, B complex, iodine and calcium). Though they at present go for modern medical treatment in serious cases, they at the beginning of any ailment depend on their traditional way of treatment through exorcism where herbal plants are used as medicines to get rid of. The Totos have an intimate knowledge of local environment and its various flora having medicinal values. They keep this knowledge secret and well guarded from outsiders. They take the help of the various types of medicinal plants for curing the following diseases:

Skin disease, ulcers and headache, stomach trouble, cold and cough, bleeding from wounds, diarrhoea, eye-inflammation and night blindness, bleeding of gums, fever, small pox, fracture, scorpion bite, swelling, blood pressure, labour pain, fever (Sarkar, 1993: 40-43).

Like Sarkar, Majumdar also observed that the modern medical treatment could not make much headway among the Totos in spite of several steps taken by the government as well as non-governmental organizations. In case of illness the Totos still approach *baidangi,* their traditional medicine man for diagnosis and treatment. A Toto in general is afraid to stay in hospital due to alien environment. At present after the formation of the Toto Kalyan Samiti (Toto Welfare Organization of their own) the situation is gradually changing. The Samiti is making them aware and assisting them in taking to the health centre or town hospitals at Alipurduar or Jalpaiguri.

Their hygienic habits and home environment have not yet changed upto the mark. Their eating habits have changed to a certain extent. The literate section of the Totos have given up taking carrion meat and some other insects. They have developed the habit of taking milk and milk products. Oil and different types of spices are now used while cooking their food (Majumdar, 1993).

VIII

Since the beginning of the plan periods welfare measures were undertaken for the betterment of the life condition of the Totos. At the beginning, voluntary organizations like Bharat Mahajati Mandali, Swedish Mission, etc. undertook programmes for the spread of education and betterment of health and hygiene. However, since the Fifth Five Year Plan period intensive drive for their over-all development in an integrated manner was undertaken, when they were declared as a Primitive Tribal Group of West Bengal. During my first visit to Totopara (prior to their declaration as a Primitive Tribe) in 1969, I found many of the attempts for their betterment had failed due to their psychological make-up. Totos living in isolation for generations developed a defeatist mentality. This added with lack of competitive zeal had given rise to inferiority complex among them. The main task was therefore to create an atmosphere for ensuring growth of "confidence" among them through psychological approach. Since then, the situation has changed to certain extent due to the impact of various developmental programmes.

During the period 1965-66 to 1988-89, about Rupees one crore were spent towards various developmental programmes for the betterment of the Totos and the Totopara. Among different sectors of development agriculture tops the list followed by health and public health engineering, roads and communications general development, dwelling, community hall, demisha, animal husbandry, education, library, etc.

No doubt these programmes have brought changes in Toto life (as noticed by me in 1990s), their attitude and behaviour but there remains still a wide gap between the target and the achievement. This is mainly due to the tradition bound nature of the elderly generations with limited exposures as also due to the failure of the implementing agency to impart effective and meaningful training and knowledge to the younger generation for creating an atmosphere of acceptance of new innovations by the Totos replacing their traditional one.

There was a myth that the Totos were a vanishing tribe. But the reality is that the Totos are in increase from decade to decade. They are no more a closed society and have overcome to certain extent the fear psychosis of a losing race. The pace of change in their life has varied from plan to plan. But from the Fifth Plan onwards the pace of change has increased manifold due to an integrated approach.

IX

It is quite a known fact that in spite of several developmental activities carried out in Totopara amongst the Totos for a number of decades, the result so far achieved is not upto the desired extent. It is high time now for the planners, administrators, and researchers to think why cent per cent success could not be achieved in the case of Totos, a small tribal group living in a somewhat isolated pocket. Different types of inputs (social, economic, political, etc.) which have been given for the last few decades are to be measured for finding out the lacunae and also to sort out the required doses in different spheres to be given for overcoming the deficiency.

For ensuring optimum result within a specified period, a special cell may be set up to keep close watch on entire affairs of the tribe. This cell will suggest corrective measures relating to demographic, economic, social and other environmental spheres and will be manned by experts from concerned fields along with administrators and planners (Das, *et al.* 1993: 226).

Traditional village council of the Totos and statutory Panchayat should function in co-operation rather than in rivalry for achieving maximum success. Side by side, the Toto educated youths, who are an emerging willing force, should be inducted in the development process, for the betterment of their own society and culture. The Toto Kalyan Samiti, who have won the confidence of the Totos on account of their constructive deeds deserves encouragement for acting as a change agent. Research-cum-Action Programmes deserve special attention for a balanced adjustment and healthy development.

REFERENCES

Das, Amal, Kumar. 1969. *The Totos*. Cultural Research Institute, Govt. of West Bengal, Calcutta.

Das, A.K. and S. K. Basu. 1993. "The Totos: A Primitive Tribe of West Bengal", (pp. 221-226) in S.B. Roy and A.K. Ghosh (eds.), *People of India: Bio-cultural Dimension*, New Delhi. Inter-India Publications.

Govt of India. 1984. Report of the Working Group on Development of Scheduled Tribes During Seventh Five-Year Plan. New Delhi: Govt. of India, Press.

Majumdar, Bimalendu. 1993. Cultural and Economic Transformation: A Study of the Totos (unpub. Thesis), Centre for Himalayan Studies, University of North Bengal.

Sanyal, C.C. 1955. "The Totos: A Sub-Himalayan Tribe", *Journal of the Asiatic Society, Science*, XXI (2): 59-126.

Sarkar, Amitabha. 1993. *Toto: Society and Change. A Sub-Himalayan Tribe of West Bengal.* Calcutta: Firma K.L.M.

Sunder, D.H.E. 1985. *Survey and Settlement of the Western-Duars in the District of Jalpaiguri, 1889-95.* Calcutta: B.G. Press.

SEVENTEEN

SAHARIA
A Primitive Tribe of Madhya Pradesh

DEBABRATA MANDAL and SUPARNA SANYAL

Introduction

The Saharia are one of the numerically dominant Scheduled Tribes of Chambal region of Madhya Pradesh. The Saharia territory covers an area of 45,534 sq. kms. They are mainly concentrated at the northern districts of Madhya Pradesh, viz. Shivapuri, Guna, Morena, Gowalior and Vidisha and also in Kota district of Rajasthan. According to 1981 census, the total population of Saharia is 2,61,816 consisting of 1,34,065 males and 1,26,751 females. About 88 per cent of the Saharia are inhabiting in Madhya Pradesh and only 12 per cent in Rajasthan. The population of Saharia have increased by 14.5 per cent in 1981 from 1971.

There exists a few systematic studies giving ethnographic coverage to the life of the Saharia. Here mention may be made of Saxsena (1964), Tod (1971), Naik (1984), Mandal (1994), etc. who have done some useful work in this regard.

Saharia generally speak the language of the region. Locally the language is known as *khariboli,* which is a mixture of Hindi with Rajasthani and *Malwi* accent. Saharia also speak a language of their own which is known as "Sohariya", influenced by Bundelkhandi dialect. The Saharia inhabited area is surrounded by hillocks and forests, which facilitates slash and burn cultivation as well as hunting and gathering for livelihood. The territory is divided into two divisions, one is an elevated plateau and the other is a valley.

According to Venkatachar, the Saharias of today perhaps have migrated from the deserted areas of Western part of India. Due to sudden climatic change, the green vegetation begins to dry up. This has resulted migration of the animals to more favoured region and subsequently the inhabitants like Saharia have also followed them for hunting. The Saharia appeared as aboriginal in 1881 census, animist in 1901, 1911 and 1921 and thereafter as "tribe". They are mostly forest dwellers. Today they do not live alone, many of them have now settled in multi-ethnic villages. In a multi-ethnic village they, of course, live in separate hamlet, not far away from the other groups. In this paper, we have tried to depict the economic structure and society of the Saharia tribe and how they are assimilated under regional changes. Field work was conducted in one acculturated village and an isolated village of Guna district.

Economic Aspect

Ecology plays an important role in shaping the mode of livelihood of a people. The Saharias prefer to live nearer to forest and depend considerably on forest products. The impact of ecology on their economy is indispensable and the environment has significantly influenced on the economy of the Saharias. In the past, the Saharias were nomadic in nature and used to practise shifting cultivation, food gathering and hunting. The present day's Saharias live in the stage of food producing economy. They are mostly settled agriculturists and supplemented by domestication of animals, fishing, hunting and collection of forest products. Moreover, many of them have become wage earners. A trend of occupational mobility from traditional to modern is observed among the Saharias. They have shifted from clan oriented (bond type) food gathering stage to pre-agricultural stage to family based settled agriculture to a dependent economy of wage-earnings. In the village Godhar, out of 72 families, 15 families are cultivators, 33 families are labourers and remaining families are engaged in seven other different kinds of occupations, such as selling of firewoods, service and petty trading, etc. Land is the primary source of their livelihood. About 62 per cent families of Godhar village have possessed dry land. The quality of land is not so good and most of them have insufficient land. 55 per cent families possess land upto half acre and only 22 per cent families have more than one acre of land. Only two families have more than 10 acres of land. Only 20 per cent of the above land come under the category of fertile black soil. Major portion of cultivable land is held by the original clan people of the village.

The Saharias do not like to work as *hali,* i.e. contract labourers, because they get low wage and ill-treatment from the employer. Sometimes due to some unavoidable circumstances such as rites of passage or illness, the poor Saharias work as contract labourers for a specific period. In the past, the men were engaged as bonded labourers in the house of land-owner and the remuneration was very low. Usually men and women are engaged on *rajyana*, i.e. daily wage basis. In the past, Saharia used to get free meals, clothes and nominal payment. But now the practice of bonded labour *(hali)* is no more visible in urban area but it is still focused in the interior areas in modified form. Generally, Saharias are now employed as *samasi,* i.e. for six months only. Besides wage labourer, cooperation labour *(katum kam)* system is also common among the Saharias. Method of cultivation by the Saharias is not much different from that of the neighbouring people. Mainly winter crops are produced by the Saharias. Share-cropping is not popular among the Saharias, because most of the Saharias are poor. They do not have bullock and agricultural implements. Most of the women work as daily wage earners or sell firewood in the market. Usually they get a sum of Rs. 10 to Rs. 15 from a headload of firewood.

Every year a good number of Saharias migrate temporarily to neighbouring wheat producing area at the time of harvesting season. Seasonal migration is a common feature among the Saharias of this region. They harvest on contract basis and get the wage in kind (wheat) instead of cash. This brings them a good collection of wheat grains, which last for three to four months for family consumption. Almost all of them eager to earn cash by selling forest products during the lean season. Sometimes, they are also engaged as labourers in forests and for road construction. Indebtedness is common among the poor Saharias. The factors generally responsible are the indebtedness, the low income, landlessness, lack of education, habit of drinking, frequent remarriage, huge expenditure on rites of passage and in other ceremonies. Such deficit of money are met by borrowing money from money-lenders or by selling property. Nearly 81 per cent of families of Godhar village are in debt and have been unable to return the loan since long.

Social Aspect

The term Saharia means inhabitants of the jungle. The word is derived from the Persian word "sehri" meaning jungle. The position of Saharia tribe in the caste hierarchy does not consider them inferior as untouchable castes. They ally with some Hindu communities and look down upon Scheduled Castes like Chamar, Dhanuk, Bhangi, Methor, etc. whom they consider untouchables. The position of the Saharias in the tribal population may vary from one part to other, depending on their numerical strength and pattern of life. However, the Saharias consider themselves superior to the Bhil, Kharua, etc. but below the status of Bhilala and Mina. They believe that Saharia is a sub-group of Bhil tribe.

The Saharia is an endogamous group, divided into a number of exogamous patrilineal clans called *(got).* Each clan is again sub-divided into a number of exogamous lineages. Most of the clans are totemistic in nature and worship the specific deity object plant, animal, etc. Some clans are territorial in origin. Some clan people have common deities and they believe their common origin. The members of a clan known as *gatia bhai* believe themselves to be the desendents of a common ancestor. Usually a Saharia village is dominated by people of a single clan. The clan is patriarchal. There are about 50 clans recorded among the Saharias.

The totemic objects are respected by the people who abstain from killing and eating these objects. All the clans are in same status except the Chowhan clan. It carries little higher status because it belongs to clan of Rajput. Members of different clans are free to marry one other. It is customary among the Saharias that one cannot marry within its own clan, one's mother, father's mother, mother's mother clan. So a person has to leave at least four clans for marriage. Agnates are strictly prohibited to marry one another.

A smaller unilinear unit is known as lineage, i.e. *(kutum)*. Members are genealogically related. They describe themselves to be a part of one house. A lineage is characterized by active cooperation among members during rites of passage and other socio-economic activities. Among the Saharia, there is a person known as *Rao* or *Jaga* who has to maintain the record of genealogy of these people. The fission in a clan or lineage may be caused due to famine, drought, epidemic and migration. Now-a-days, the Saharia migrate frequently from core region to plain areas to pursuit their livelihood.

Family is a unilaterally related group, consisting of a man, his wife and unmarried children. Sometimes, married brother or son-in-law, their wives with children or married son live together. Nuclear type of family is most common. They practise patrilocal as well as neolocal residence. The authority of a family lies with the eldest male member. He governs the socio-religious and economic cooperation. He is the chief agency of social control. Land and other properties such as ornaments, cash, utensils, etc. are equally divided among the sons during the old age of father.

Marriage is a socially sanctioned relationship between a man and a woman with some objectives, viz., sexual cohabitation, procreation, economic cooperation and common residence. Monogamy is the general rule of the society. Polygyny is rarely practised only by the well-to-do families. Early marriage is common to them and is introduced due to the influence of Hindu society. Usually Saharias follow the marriage by negotiation. Marriage by service is not uncommon. Besides, marriages by elopement and by exchange occur occasionally. Since no bride-price is required for such type of marriages, a nominal fine is to be given to the village council. In marriage by service, the bride-groom has to work under the father-in-law's house for a specific period after marriage. Cross-cousin marriage is unknown to them. At present junior levirate is not practised, however, junior sororate is allowed. Marriage between known lineage is strictly prohibited. Besides bride-price, *(dahej)* i.e. dowry is given to the acculturated bride-grooms. Divorce and remarriage are common phenomena among the Saharia. A Saharia man is at liberty to divorce his wife at any time due to maladjustment. Tribal council known as *panch* ask some *ghagra,* i.e. fine from paramour of woman if he marries her. A part of this money has to be given to her previous husband and the remaining portion is spent for communal feast. Kinship terms are Howaiian in nature. The Saharia inhabited area is now settled by a number of other tribals and non-tribal ethnic groups. Saharias have acculturated in different spheres of their life. The Saharias are now inter-dependent with other ethnic groups in the day-to-day life to adjust themselves with the new environment.

The Saharia village organization is very effective unit in regulating their socio-cultural aspects. The tribal village council is led by village headman, known as *makadom.* The post is hereditory. He plays the role of an arbitrator in matters of social as well as economic dispute. Besides secular duties, he performs some sacred duties also. *Makadom* also acts as a representative to the village panchayat. Besides *makadom,* patel, barhai, prodhan, janker, etc. have their respective duties in the tribal council.

The Saharias worship a number of deities like Bheran, Takur, Bhumij, Naharsing, Ghatoiya, etc. Due to their age-old contact with Hindu society they have adopted the Hindu gods and goddesses. Different altars are used as panthoeons. Now-a-days Saharias actively participate in the Hindu festivals like Dewali, Holi, Rakhi, Dasehara, and the like. Besides their own priest, Brahmin priest *(pandit)* is also called occasionally to perform the Satyanarayana puja.

Observation

The Saharias of Chambal region of Madhya Pradesh were originally semi-nomadic hunters and food gatherers. In course of time, other caste groups have immigrated to this region from the neighbouring areas for livelihood. Ultimately a good number of Saharias have settled in the multi-ethnic villages. The Saharias of acculturated villages have changed their life style to some extent due to their cultural contact with Hindu Society. Traditional way of mechanical solidarity has been replaced to a considerable extent by organic solidarity. As in present day the exposed segment of Saharias is no longer self-sufficient in their economic pursuits. On the contrary they are now very much dependent on a good number of peasants, artisan and service castes.

REFERENCES

Mandal, D.B. 1994. The Saharia of Chambal Region—Social Structure, Economic Transformation and Challenge. Unpublished Ph.D. Thesis, Ranchi University.

Naik, T.B. 1984. "The Saharia", *Bulletin of Tribal Research and Training Institute.* Serial No. 22, Gujarat Vidyapith.

Sexsena, R.P. 1964. *Tribal Economic in Central India.* Firma, K.L. Mukhopadhya; Calcutta.

Tod, J. 1971. *Annals and Antiquities of Rajasthan,* Vol. 1 Delhi: Motilal Banarsidas.

EIGHTEEN

CHANGING WAY OF LIFE OF THE NOMADIC TRIBES OF IRAN

MOHAMMAD TAGHI SHEYKHI

While discussing on the nomadic peoples of Iran, it is important to analyze what the nomadic society is, what their problems are, and how far the tribal issues continue to be influenced by the urban culture and way of life.

Tribal or nomadic people are organized into political, social and cultural groups, with loyalties towards their fellow-tribal people and leaders. Following pastoralism, they have family-based livestock economy. Their demographic structures have also been influenced by their pastoral way of life. They are mostly found in mountains and deserts and thus placing them in a special socio-demographic structure.

Nomadic pastoralism is a specialized form of economy which efficiently uses a particular category of abundant natural resources with few alternative uses. It is found broadly across Iran.

Social organization of the nomads is such that they must adopt rational adaptations to meet their requirements in risky and marginal environments. Most nomadic societies are still organized according to customary forms of social and political organization.

In almost all nomadic societies and pastoral economies there is a substantial emigration which has kept the pastoral population density low. Mobility of the tribal people creates special difficulties in delivering services such as schooling and human animal health. Therefore, new forms of service delivery need to be developed. Successful experiences of other countries may provide possible models.

To define tribe we can say that tribe is a group of persons, families or clans descended from a common ancestor and living under a chief or leader. Nomadic/moving tribes as organized communities are registered in 22 out of the 24 provinces of Iran.

Tribal communities comprised a large part of the country's population in the past. A century ago, about a quarter of the population of Iran was estimated to be of nomadic tribes. With the passage of time, it has decreased to only about 2.3 per cent (Table 18.1). The decline has been due to different social, demographic, economic and cultural reasons which will be discussed in this paper.

TABLE 18.1: Total and Tribal Population of Iran in Different Years

Year	Total Population (000)	Tribal Population (000)	Percentage of Tribal Pop'n Relative to Total Pop'n
1861	7,654	1900	25.0
1963	21,000	2000	10.5
1976	33,700	2400	7.0
1986	4,98,57,384	1152	2.3

Source: Ettela'at, a daily newspaper, August 31, 1992.

Tribal communities in Iran have summer quarters *(yeilaq)* as well as the winter quarters *(qeshlaq)*. They start their summer migration from the first week of April and onwards, and their winter migration from the end of September and onwards.

Historically, they have had vital role in guarding and protecting the country before the modern and motorized army was established about seventy years ago. Currently, the nomadic tribes have a determining position in the Iranian food and protein production. Previously, say about three decades ago and earlier, because of other competitors, their economic position was not so much vital for the country. That was because the rural husbandry system was quite active. Moreover, in the urban areas and the city suburbs cattle raising was quite prevalent. So far as the meat production is concerned, with the passage of time, and while the socio-economic settings in the rural and urban areas have changed, cattle raising has much diminished, and consequently the country's dependency on nomadic tribes has increased.

The tribal communities supply the country with their sheep and goats production for at least one-third of the year. The cultural homogeneity among these tribes has a vital role in their economic productions. In the primary economic functioning, such cultural homogeneity is of great significance. Their single language, that is the communal language, spoken by them in different geographical areas and provinces, functions as a means to an end.

Tribes in Iran in the past were both organized political units and economic units, but today, they are rather more organized economic units than political ones.

Lerner's (1964) theory of modernization is very much relevant to the change in the life-style of the tribal communities in Iran. According to him, the growth of new urban centres in the Third World as similarly progressive, encouraging individualism and weakening "traditionalism", is sociologically a contrary movement against tribal life. He argues that urbanization is a force for increasing the level of "participation" in communities: residents become more "active participants" as they develop new attitudes. Tribesmen too being members of the greater society, become vulnerable—a new openness appears. Moreover, the requirements of non-tribal living encourage specific features of modernity to develop such as literacy. People need to be literate to read timetables, street-signs, and so on, if they are to move freely in the town or travel to work. Therefore, the modernization process is an agent to bring down tribalism.

Modernization too produces new cultural orientations, new social developments and new life-styles and that is where the changeover in tribal life also eventually appears.

As compared with the rural farmers, the tribesmen have lesser means within their reach, not many alternatives, whereas the rural farmers may get new farm equipments, fertilizers and new high yielding seeds to push up their crop production for both their own consumption and for sale. The "Green Revolution" has much been in the favour of the rural settlers rather than the moving tribes.

The condition of insecurity which often prompts people, rural as well as tribal, to migrate to towns, also means that urban growth occurs under highly unfavourable circumstances. That usually and mostly happens due to the welfare and modernization forces in the urban areas.

Anyhow, social change in general has brought about the tribal consciousness, and that has eventually caused detribalization. This process in itself has had the social and economic consequences for the country. Rapid urbanization occurring in Iran is, therefore, due to the processes of tribal-rural migration and tribal-urban migration and settlement.

According to the Human Development Report 1992, published for the UNDP, wide discrepancies exist within many countries. Comparing the one milliard richest with one milliard poorest, that ratio would leap to at least 150 to 1, i.e. the richest one milliard people are 150 times wealthier than the poorest one milliard. Such differences in a narrower sense is more or less true between the urban and tribal people, and that is where detribalization starts from.

Historically and generally, exactly when people began to control herds of herbivorous animals in order to maintain access to steady supplies of meat and perhaps to facilitate the animals reproduction, is not known. But nomadic herding cultures in some semiarid regions unsuitable for cultivation may date as far back as the earliest farming. Like the development of agriculture, that of herding may have been a gradual process, as groups of people following migrating herding represented a radical new departure in the ability of human beings to manipulate their environments and the renewable resources on which they depended. The planting of crops means, first a replacement of the natural flora.

The advantages of the new way of life to the first farmers were quite clear. Food supplies were more dependable and much more abundant, many times more people could be supported by the agricultural production of a given area of land than through hunting and gathering. A settled way of life, as necessitated by farming, was a more secure existence than constant wandering in search of food.

Unplanned and unsuitable land-use have resulted in many adverse problems. The Greek philosophers have described such processes and warned of the consequences of continued deforestation and of over-grazing, specially by goats. The warnings went unheeded. That is why Greece today is nearly a desert, its soils thin and poor, the vast majority of its original forests long vanished.

In case of Iran such overuse and misuse of land, deforestation, over-grazing and the like have occurred, but there are no clear documents on them. Processes of environmental deterioration and degradation of the natural-resource base, which in various forms are known today as "deforestation", evidently have occurred locally numerous times in human history. A human tendency towards over-exploitation of renewable resources by the tribesmen seems to have been established almost as early as agriculture, if not before.

Demographic Circumstances

According to the 1987 Census of Iran, there were about 96 different tribes spreading over 22 provinces, except for the provinces of Yazd and Kurdistan, with a population of 11,52,000. These people with their own particular demographic features have a total fertility rate (TFR) of over 8 children for a woman. While generally the girls marrying at the age between 12 and 15, the females' life expectancy stand at a very low rate. It culminates to a surprizing sex ratio at different age groups, varying between 108 at the time of birth to 150 at the age of 65 and above. That is to say, at the age of 65 and above, there are about 150 males to every 100 females at the same age (Table 18.2). Life hardships, women's sufferings, frequent conceptions and such other factors cause women's high mortality and also maternal mortality. Polygamy is also a feature of tribesmen. They do it more, to find more children (more human power) rather than to enjoy sex.

TABLE 18.2: Total Population by Age and Sex Group 1986

Age groups	Total		Males	Females	Sex Ratio
	Number	Per cent			
All Groups	11,52,099	100.0	5,97,774	5,54,325	108
Less than 1 Year	32,669	2.8	16,693	15,976	105
1—5	2,33,794	20.3	1,16,339	1,17,555	99
6—10	2,03,736	17.7	1,04,409	99,327	105
11—14	1,21,245	10.5	66,389	54,856	121
15—24	1,93,535	16.8	1,01,293	92,242	110
25—64	3,34,216	29.0	1,72,979	1,61,237	107
65+	32,786	2.8	19,682	13,104	150
Unspecified	118	0/0	90	28	*

Source: Documents on Census of the Moving Tribes of Iran, Statistical Center of Iran, 1987.

Fertility Motivation

Among the tribesmen, human action is largely governed by sacred norms. Since both technology and social organization are underdeveloped, members of the society can hardly understand and control the environment. They tend to believe in the existence of some divine forces, more than the urban and rural people. These sacred norms become very powerful pressures for high fertility motivation. In many, if not all, tribal communities, the birth of a child (particularly a son) is an important occasion of celebration, congratulation and thanks giving.

Culturally speaking, all the tribes in Iran are similar in certain cultural features such as son preference. Happiness, love, companionship and fun are included in this category. In reverse, loneliness is very much avoided among them. Economically speaking, much economic benefits is derived from children's help in farmwork, herding and security in oldage, including psychological security. Early marriage is also a tradition among the tribal communities. Although clear and accurate statistics are not within reach, over 60 per cent of tribal girls marry under the age of 15. In a wider sense, and on the basis of an international research, in all, by the age of 15, 18 per cent of girls in Asia, 16 per cent in Africa and 8 per cent in Latin America are married. In some African and Asian countries, as many as 40 to 75 per cent of young women ages 15 to 19 are already married.

Usually and among some tribes as a tradition, girls who are supposed to be the birdes of the other clans, or in the other words, the would-to-be brides are sent to live with the groom's family even before the age of 10, so as to adapt to the norms and traditions of the clan with whom she will eventually interlock and live in the future, when she is a bit more mature.

To turn to the economic circumstances of the tribes of Iran we can add that: the nomadic tribes have rather got good economic position with the least foreign exchange and imported materials/items dependency; but low standard of living, the least social welfare and highly in need of natural pastures have made them feel ambivalent about their occupation. What has made them cling to that way of life and be active is the high price of meat products.

Eventually with the high protein/meat need of the country, it is preferable to make the grounds so, that the nomadic tribes be active, and lead that sort of life. In other words, so far as there are no other alternatives, tribes must cling and continue their traditional lives, and thereby arresting the ongoing process of detribalization.

Tribal Problems

The Iranian tribes mainly have two types of problems: Firstly, those which are also faced by the other people of the country, and secondly, those which are peculiar to the tribal people. As for the latter type of tribal problems, the following are the most important:

Cultural Problems

Due to contact with other cultures, the tribal culture is undergoing a revolutionary change. Due to the availability of the means of communications, their cultural norms are no more intact. The young generation try to imitate the urban way of life. Also the transfer of education which is an inevitable phenomenon has made specially the youth exposed to a "double-standard" in which they eventually choose the non-tribal standard. They migrate to towns and cities, become urban consumers and cling more to the material culture. The influence of the cultural contact has more or less led to new modes of living, the degeneration of tribal life and arts, such as music, folk-lore, and different types of crafts.

Social Problems

Child marriage which has been a part of tribal culture, is now being counted as a social problem due to the change in values in urban regions, modernization forces and the like. Due to contact with the non-tribal society a number of dissolutions of marriages occur among them. Therefore, abolition of child marriage and spread of family planning may be counted as some social problems faced by the tribal communities in Iran.

Economic Problems

The contact with the civilized world has somehow or the other disintegrated the entire economic system of the tribal people. They have forgotten their ancient crafts. Most of them working as day-pay labourers in urban plants, factories etc. The employers everywhere misuse the ignorance of tribal people, extract maximum work from them, and give them the minimum money in return.

Increase of consumerism and the decline of traditional products have changed their habit patterns. It has made the tribal people economically dependent. Such a situation has in many instances caused them to feel poorer and deprived.

Conclusion

I may add that the tribal community as a minority is worth studying sociologically. Although very productive, but under the geographical, economic, social and modernistic factors, the tribal population shrinkage is inevitable. Although many of them are very destitute, it must be so planned and organized to make full use of their carrying capacity in order to support the non-tribal people.

Because of their peculiar conditions, the implementation of some of the national plans and policies are not that easy. Those therefore, must be planned according to their culture and life-style. That is to say, the tribal problems must be handled and solved according to their needs.

REFERENCES

Documents on Census of the Moving Tribes of Iran. 1987. Tehran, Statistical Centre of Iran.

Lerner, D. 1964. *The Passing of Traditional Society*. New York: The Free Press.

NINETEEN

AGING IN THE TRIBAL CONTEXT
A Study of Chenchu

P. VENKATA RAO

Introduction

Following the tradition of aging studies in the west, researchers in India concentrated on the aged mostly coming from the urban middle classes, especially on retired persons. In a review article Fernandes (1982) observed that conditions of aged in India are different from those of their counterparts in the west. It has been pointed that "marginalization of the aged", a concept developed in industrialized countries based on retirement from a full-time job is not applicable in India where 90 per cent of the active population are in the informal sector and lacking in social security (1982: 2). There is general agreement that contrary to the situation in the west where alienation and emotional deprivation are important problems of the aged, economic problems are more important in India. Urbanization, industrialization, occupational mobility and migration are affecting the living conditions of the aged. Even in rural areas where people are supposed to be bound by traditional considerations, the aged no longer enjoy the respectful status. There are very few studies on the aged in tribal areas. Life of the aged among tribals is said to be better than that of rural and urban aged due to the presence of a strong community feeling (Saxena and Narendra Kumar, 1989). The tribal societies are undergoing rapid changes in the recent decades. Opening up of tribal areas through expansion of communication facilities, governmental policies and measure ushering in economic changes, and entry of market economy are transforming the life style of the tribal communities. The present paper focuses on the position of the aged and the changes taking place due to various forces in a tribal village inhabited by Chenchu.[1]

The Chenchu

Chenchu are a primitive tribal group of Andhra Pradesh, known for their pre-agricultural level of technology. Chenchu are found mainly in Kurnool, Mahboobnagar and Prakasam districts of Andhra Pradesh. They have different sub-divisions such as Adavi Chenchu, Bontha Chenchu, Deva Chenchu and Krishna Chenchu. Haimendorf (1943) described Adivi Chenchu as having digging stick culture. Traditionally Chenchus depended on food gathering, i.e collection of roots, tubers, leaves, berries, nuts and honey. Over centuries, the Chenchu area had been invaded by several rulers. Chenchus had a long history of contacts with non-tribals. Under their impact, many Hindu beliefs and practices have been adopted by the Chenchu (Sastry, 1993). Efforts were made by the government of Madras Presidency in 1932 to settle Chenchus on agricultural lands in Kurnool districts. Similar efforts were made by Nizams' government in Telangana district like Mahaboobnagar in 1942. Chenchus were allowed to clear forest for cultivation and were provided with house sites and grazing lands. A Chenchu Reserve was established under the guidance of Haimendorf (1943: 376; 1985: 120). Commercial economy penetrated Chenchu areas in the form of contractors who started purchasing the minor forest produce collected by Chenchus. From food gathering they moved to gathering of commercially important items like gum and started working for the forest department and contractors for wage labour. Thus, Chenchus are drawn into monetized economy through wage labour and sale of minor forest produce. Government of Andhra Pradesh made efforts to introduce settled cultivation amongst Chenchus through rehabilitation programmes (Reddy, 1979). Commercial crops like cotton and chillies were introduced under irrigated conditions. The "Project Tiger", started in 1973 with the financial support of World Wild Life Fund was extended to Andhra Pradesh during 1982-83. This project meant for the protection of Tigers is located in the Chenchu areas, under which many villages have been shifted from the "core area". Since 1978 this Chenchu area witnessed a series of developmental measures after the starting of an Integrated Tribal Development Agency for Chenchus with headquarters at Srisailam. This special project for Chenchus under the centrally sponsored programme meant for Primitive Tribal Groups (PTG) could be established as Government of India recognized the Chenchu as a Primitive Tribal Group. All these changes have affected the Chenchu economy and social organization. Against this backdrop a study of aged among the Chenchu has been attempted.

The Village and the Aged

The present study is based on the author's fieldwork in the Garapenta village located at a distance of 10 kms. from Pullalachervu, a Mandal headquarters town of Prakasam District of Andhra Pradesh.[2] This is said to be the largest Chenchu village in Prakasam district. This village is classified as an advanced pocket by the tribal welfare department of Andhra Pradesh. The village settlement came into existence about 120 years back with the coming of Thati surname group households to this place. They came to this place from Logipalli located at a distance of 30 kms. Their arrival was followed by other surname groups who joined them over a period of time. About three decades later, settled cultivation made its entry under the influence of non-tribals from nearby areas. The Chenchus started clearing patches of forest and started cultivating dry crops. But the food gathering tradition continued along with cultivation. Villagers shared all the resources such as grazing lands, fishing pools, and hunting grounds until the entry of cultivation. After the starting of ITDA at Srisailam for Chenchus, developmental programmes started reaching the village. Plough bullocks and carts were distributed. Twenty-one oil engines were distributed in the village in a span of eight years, but only eleven could be seen in working condition during fieldwork. Only one pucca house is present in the village and all other houses are circular huts. A school was started in this village as far back as 1940 by the forest department. The school was taken over by the tribal welfare department and was converted into an ashram school in 1974. The literacy percentages in the village are 58 per cent for males and 32 per cent for females. Total cultivated land in Garapenta is 570 acres, and on an average each household own about 5.5 acres of land. There are six households which own about 15 acres of land each. Most of the land is suitable only for dry cultivation and is not sufficient to sustain the Chenchu households. Though 92 households claimed that they depend on cultivation, it is supplemented by other activities. The subsidiary economic activities are wage labour (72 households), food gathering (56 households), fishing (26 households), hunting (19 households), and honey collection (3 households). The village is inhabited by 104 households of which 100 belongs to Chenchu tribe. The remaining four households belong to the non-tribal teachers. The population strength of the Chenchus in Garapenta is 612 which included 310 males, and 302 females. Of the total population of 612, those who are above 60 years of age numbered 24 which included 14 males and 10 females.[3] The distribution of the aged under different age groups is as follows. Age group of 60-64: 10 (7 males and 3 females), age group of 65-69: 4 (2 males and 2 females), age group of 70-74: 7 (4 males and 3 females, age group of 75-79: 2 (females), and age group of 80-84: 1 (male member). The twenty-four elderly persons in the village are living under the following residential arrangement. Four of them are living in joint families, ten are widow/widower residing with married or unmarried children, five are staying with spouse, three are widow/widower staying alone, and two are widow/widower staying with daughter or son-in-law.

Participation in Work

Significant contribution is being rendered by the aged Chenchus to the family economic pursuits in this tribal village. An aged individual goes on working as long as he is fit enough. Aged Chenchus collect grass, soap nuts, tamarind, take goats and cattle for grazing, sell items in weekly market, go for fishing, undertake agricultural and other types of labour. They also attend to works like watching crops, weeding, drying various items under sun and guarding them, rope making, basket making, taking care of children, etc. Females help in cooking, grinding, taking food to those working in the forest etc. Aged women spend more time with children. There is no such thing as leisure time activity as individuals continue to do some useful work or other all the time. Those who are confined to home try to do some light work of useful nature. Transition from active work to no work takes place gradually over a period of time as they become weak, with failing eye sight and other age related physical problems. Aged persons withdraw slowly from outside work to household work like taking care of children. The absence of elderly is felt by those families where both husband and wife go out for work. They need aged members nearer to their hut to keep an eye on the small children who are otherwise left for themselves. The elderly also come handy for those who go out of the village for seasonal employment and wage labour as they are dependable to look after land, house, and other assets like livestock. Many Chenchu youth are going to places like Rajhamundry in East Godavari district for seasonal agricultural labour such as sugarcane cutting. Such persons entrust their house, property, etc to the old parents.

Property related Rights and Obligations

In the food gathering era, Chenchu had no preference for sons. In those days women contributed equally to economic activities, and there was no problem in getting daughters married-off. With the entry of wage labour men got more earning opportunities than women. Settled cultivation enhanced the status of males. The impact of contacts with caste Hindus made Chenchu parents to develop the desire for having sons to continue their ancestral line. Sons are needed for taking care of the parents in the old age and for performing their final rites. Childless couples approach a local diviner being termed as *vaidudu* who undertakes divination locally known as *gadde*[4] to find out the reason for their problem. As suggested by the *vaidudu*, a promise will be made to undertake a pilgrimage, or make an offering, or to give to the baby the name of the deity involved, if blessed with a son. If all these steps do not result in the birth of a son, a second wife is taken. The importance of the sons is evident from the two cases of barren women in Garapenta. Their husbands married again for getting sons.

The Chenchus consider it obligatory to take care of children until they are married. It is mentioned that a child owns every thing to parents. All Chenchus in this village have some livestock apart from the dwelling, implements, and household possessions. After all the sons and daughters are married, father shares the land equally with the sons. Father's share goes to the son who looks after father in his old age. In sharing of property, elder son gets some extra land as *jheastabhagam,* because he is born first. Cattle, goats, etc. are shared equally. Daughters do not have a right to land. But they may be given a goat or buffalo out of affection. On the contrary, some informants mentioned that the share of all the daughters will be equal to that of one son. In the absence of sons, adoption *(dattu)* is resorted to, and adopted son gets a share like a son. If no adoption takes place, daughters/ sons-in-laws share property equally. Sometimes, the son-in-law comes and stays in the dwelling of father-in-law under an arrangement which is locally called as *illitum.* If no children are there, lineage members known as *dayadulu* 'brothers and brothers' children) inherit the property. No outsider gets the property without the approval of *dayadulu.* In the absence of sons, whoever performs the burial/cremation and final rites called as *dinam* will get some part of the property with the approval of *dayadulu.* According to some of the informants, even *illitum* son-in-law does not belong to that surname group. Married sons, though they live separately, have an obligation to assist their parents until all younger brothers and sisters are married. Land will not be partitioned until then and cultivation is done jointly. They draw their shares from common granary. A son, even after separation, is obliged to contribute part of his individual earnings such as from wage labour, towards his share for the parents household consisting of unmarried siblings. Cooperation exists between households of son and father in agricultural activities. Plough, bullocks, fish-trap *(gari),* etc. are shared by them. Mother-in-law and daughter-in-law share kitchen implements such as grinding stone *(vishuru rai),* and pounding stone *(dampudu rolu),* once separation is complete, there will be little cooperation between households. For instance, the head man of the village lamented that his daughter-in-law staying in the next hut, who also happened to be his wife's brother's daughter, does not even give water to his bullocks.

Though a son is supposed to help his father until his sisters are married and younger brothers are settled, non-fulfilment of this obligation does not bar him from getting his share of property. The aged do not resent not being helped by their children. Parents justified their sons by repeatedly saying that "their life is theirs, what they get is not enough for them" *(Valla batuku vallede, vallake chaladu).* Lack of assistance from sons is not a serious offence as grown up children are supposed to look after themselves. Only few individual felt bitter that the children extracted work from them as long as they are fit enough, leaving them to fate after they became weak. Only when the aged parents become sick or invalid, the son gets reminded of his responsibilities by others. Normally the aged are not left for themselves among Chenchus. Villagers say that destitution is alien to Chenchus. People are taken care of, for their assets, for extracting work, or even otherwise also some body will provide a morsel of food *(oka mudda padestaru)* to the old. The old strongly feel that one needs wife/husband for assistance in the old age as friction or incompatibility is expected with daughter-in-law or son-in-law. The following instances reveal the strength of the man-wife bond over that of parent-son or other relations. In one case, a daughter-in-law went away to her natal home along with her five years old son, after her husband joined a residential school for high school studies. The in-laws did not make any attempt to stop her to have their grand-son with them. In another case, pregnant wife of a Chenchu youth went to her natal house for delivery. The youth abandoned his hut temporarily and went to his wife's place, and not to his parents' dwelling.

Land Ownership into a Near Subsistence Economy

Chenchus had a tradition of nuclear families. Vertically extended families occurred rarely. As a custom son establishes a separate dwelling after marriage. Eldest male member had the responsibility of looking after the property and family and had authority over all family affairs. They practice cross-cousin marriages and its implications are seen in the kinship terminology in the use of classificatory term for mothers, brothers, fathers, sisters husband and wife's father. Chenchus had an egalitarian society with little status differentiation. Even the head-man of the village had little authority and mainly functioned as the spokesman (Haimendorf, 1985: 146). Joint families are very rare in hunting and food gathering societies. With a near subsistence economy, traditionally, joint households where parents and married sons live together were rare among Chenchus. The needs of the settled cultivation resulted in the entry of joint household among them. Interaction with parents is more in land owning households when cultivation is done jointly. On the other hand interaction gets reduced over a period of time after partition of land. Economic independence and establishment of separate family relieve the youngsters from their obligations towards aged. In a study conducted in several Chenchu villages Bhowmick (1992: 47) pointed that large sized families which are of recent origin are found only in settled agricultural villages. In the study village, out of 100 total Chenchu households. 71 are nuclear households, 11 are joint households, 5 households having two members each (these include three old couples, one widow and her son, and one mother and her divorced daughter), 3 are single individual households, and the rest being nuclear extended households (both fraternal and paternal). In the past due to the absence of economic surplus, thc obligations and dependency are kept at minimum. After marriage, a separate hut will be erected for the couple and they will be on their own for all practical purposes. The explanation given is in terms of incompatibility between daughters-in-law and parents-in-laws. Bhowmick (1992: 138) lists out lack of privacy, poverty, availability of plenty of land, quarrels, etc. as the reasons for the preference for nuclear households. There are two cases in Garapenta where the sons could not construct their own huts as they could not afford the cost of about Rs. 300. But, they established their separate hearths in the same dwelling. Separation of married sons can also be seen in the light of the fact that the Chenchu huts traditionally are single room huts. Separate living of grown up sons affects the quality of life among the aged Chenchus. Sizes of the granary, cattle shed, and hut give an indication of the economic position of the household in this village. Absence of granary in front of the house generally indicates joint cultivation and shared grain storage. In few cases absence of granary means lack of capacity to store foodgrains due to poverty. No granary is found in front of the houses of seven old individuals in Garapenta. These include the poorest and single individual households. Ownership of land makes a difference in the quality of life of the aged. Even if an elderly person is physically not able to cultivate, and son is not taking interest, the father can give his land on *kowlu* or lease and make a living. Goats, cattle, etc. will be looked after by neighbours, brothers or brothers' children. The position of those who own land in sufficient quantity is better. But, after division, the share of the old father will not be much in most of the cases. Attachment with children is found to be less in cases of divorces and remarriages of the parents which are common in tribal villages. This is one of the reasons for less expectation from children and less attachment between children and parents. In all the eleven joint households, the presence of land ranging from six to fifteen acres is significant. Status differences are visible with some households employing wage labour. Other symbols of status include large semi-permanent houses, lavish celebration of festivals and life cycle ceremonies by inviting Brahmin priest and non-tribals, undertaking pilgrimage, frequent consumption of meat and rice[5] in the household, ownership of jewelry, transistor, gun, etc. Family economic activities are being replaced by individual earnings through wage labour giving the younger generations the freedom to ignore their obligations towards elderly. Apart from wage labour, works like making and sale of wooden furnitures provide opportunities for individual earnings. Fire wood selling is an important source of individual income. Market for firewood is readily available at Pullalachervu, a large non-tribal village located at a distance of 10 kms. Illicit distillation and sale of arrack is another earning option for the individuals.

Widows and Single Individuals

An aged Chenchu staying alone results due to lack children and death of spouse. Single individual household also results with the migration/separation of sons, daughters married-off and death of spouse. The incidence of single member households among aged women is indicative of the distress among women. Women do not have right over property. A widow can stay in the hut of the diseased husband, but she will not have any right to sell anything belonging to her husband. She gets no right to her late husband's land. "What is the use of land to a woman" say the villagers. The Chenchu women who were equal participants in the economic activities of the food gathering economy are relegated to the secondary position with the entry of settled cultivation. Land is owned and inherited by males only. A childless widow or one with younger children is made to depend upon *Dayadulu* for cultivating her husband's land. If there are no children and land, the condition of the individual becomes miserable with advancing age. As long as they are capable, they collect berries, fish, firewood, etc. Old individuals who are staying alone live in pitiable condition. Their earning capacity from forest produce collection, sale of firewood and wage labour comes down steadily with advancing age. For instance, a widow of eighty years of age collects berries, etc. from forest, sends them to nearby village for sale as she cannot walk the distance. Her two grown up living separately are not bothered about as she is able to work. There are three single individual households in the study village (two widows and one widowers). Significantly, the widows have married sons living in the village, but they live separately.

Conclusion

The commonly held view that aged in general enjoy, power, authority and respect in traditional societies is only partially valid in the case of Chenchu. In the traditional setting, the position of the aged needs to be considered in the context of subsistence nature of food gathering economy, the tradition of nuclear families, and less attachment between parents and children due to divorces and remarriages. The entry of settled cultivation into an egalitarian Chenchu society has resulted in economic/status differentiation. With land ownership and the availability of irrigation facilities provided through governmental measures, joint households which are alien to Chenchus are coming into existence. Unlike in the joint households, in poorer households which are by and large nuclear, the obligations towards elderly are neglected. The elderly do not have complete right to their lands, as custom allows sons to demand for their share after marriage. After the death of father, the son is entitled to his share even if he had not looked after him in the old age. The rights of the son take precedence over his obligations. The study points out the need to collect more empirical information on the customary practices and emerging trends in the position of the aged in the tribal and rural areas to overcome the stereotypes coming mainly from the studies on urban middle classes.

NOTES

1. An earlier version of this paper was presented in the anthropology and archaeology section of the Indian Science Congress held at New Delhi (January, 1997).
2. Fieldwork was conducted in this village along with post-graduate students of the Department of Anthropology of University of Hyderabad. I am thankful to my students for the village census data.
3. To facilitate comparability with other studies, all those who are said to be above sixty years of age are considered as aged for the present study.
4. The individual goes into a trance and contacts various gods and spirits through *Pinna Devara* (a Chenchu deity). After contacting the respective deities and spirits, solutions will be offered.
5. Consumption of rice is of recent origin. The staple food of Chenchus consisted of Jowar and Ragi.

REFERENCES

Bhowmick, P.K. 1992. *Chenchus of the Hills and Plateaux a Hunting-gathering Tribe in Transition.* Calcutta: Institute of Social Research and Applied Anthropology.

Fernandes, Walter. 1982. "Aging in South Asia as Marginalization in a Neo-colonial Economy. An Introduction", (pp 1-23) in De Souza Alfred and Walter Fernandes (eds.), *Aging in South Asia.* New Delhi: Indian Social Institute.

Haimendorf, C.V.F. 1943. *The Chenchus: Jungle Folk of the Deccan,* London. Macmillan & Co.

—. 1985. *Tribes of India--Struggle for Survival.* New Delhi: Oxford Publishing House.

Narendra Kumar and Pushpa Saxena. 1987. "Aged among the Tribals of Madhya Pradesh", (pp. 71-76) in R. N. Pati and B. Jena (eds.), *Aged in India.* New Delhi: Ashish Publishing House.

Reddy, G.P. 1979. "Introducing Agriculture in a Tribal Community: The Case of Chenchus", *Man and Life,* 5 (1&2): 81-92.

Sastry, V.N.V.K., 1993. "Chenchu Food Gatherers and Hunters of Nallamala Forest-Problems of Transition", *Man and Life,* 19 (1&2): 83-96

TWENTY

POLITICAL ORGANIZATION AND CUSTOMARY LAWS AMONG THE KAMAR TRIBE

A. K. SINHA and M. DAS

Introduction

Madhya Pradesh is known to be the largest state in the country with a total area of 4,42,841 sq. kms. It has a total population of 6,61,81,170 as per the 1991 census. The total tribal population of Madhya Pradesh as per the same census is 153.99 lakhs, which is the highest in the country as compared to other states. This tribal population comprises 23.27 per cent of the total state's population. The tribal population is found to be scattered in all the 45 districts of the state. Among the 45 districts, Jhabua contains the highest percentage of tribal population (83.5%). There are 46 tribal groups inhabiting Madhya Pradesh which are specified as Scheduled Tribes according to article 342(1) of the Indian Constitution. These 46 tribal groups include 7 primitive tribal groups. Baigas (1,34,357)*, Hill Korwas (27,109), Bharias (2,012), Saharias (4,17,171), and Abujhmarias (17,016), were identified as primitve tribes during the Fifth Five-Year Plan period, while Kamar (13,110) was identified and included in the list during the next Five Year Plan. Further, during the Seventh Five-Year Plan, another tribal group, the Birhors (935) was included in the list of primitive tribes (*Source:* Tribal sub-plan, year plan 1995-96).

General Description of the Kamars

The Kamars inhabit the hills and forests of south-eastern part of Raipur district and have a population of nearly 13,500 as per the 1981 census. In Raipur district the Kamars are found to inhabit two tahsils namely Bindranawagarh and Dhamtari and comes under the Integrated Tribal Development Project (ITDP) Gariaband. This project covers four blocks,

* The figures in the brackets indicate the population of the respective tribes.

namely, Chhura, Gariaband. Mainpur and Nagri. In the Gariaband project area, the Kamars are found in 20 villages. In all, they inhabit 201 villages—134 in Gariaband tehsil and 67 in Dhamtari tehsil.

A systematic literature research reveals that there exists a very limited number of studies on the political organization and customary laws of the tribal communities in general and the Kamar in particular. Most of the existing studies are further fragmentary by nature and thereby fail to provide the readers the required information on this area. Here mention may be made of Dube (1951), Saxena (1974), Russell and Hiralal (1975), Tiwari (1984), Singh (1993), etc. who have done some useful work on the aforesaid area.

The Kamars are descendants of the Dravidian community, having mainly two subdivisions—Bundhrajiya and Makadia. They are generally well-built, having a medium stature and well-proportioned limbs. Their skin colour generally varies from light brown to dark brown and even light black. Their staple food comprises of rice, and now-a-days they even consume wheat, maize, etc. In former days, they used to consume only *madia (Eleusine coracana).* Their food is supplemented by various kinds of fruits, tubers, roots and different kinds of vegetables. The Kamars are very simple in their array. Men generally wear a *langoti* and *patuka* and women commonly wear a *lugda.*

The economy of Kamars is mainly agriculture based. Previously they used to depend upon shifting cultivation, but now-a-days this practice has been stopped. The Kamars cannot be said advanced cultivators. They lack modern implements. Some of the Kamars have adopted fishing. The areas of the Kamar habitat is rich in forest resources. Some of the Kamar families have adopted bamboo work and basket making as their base of economy.

The religion of Kamars is directly linked with their economy. Since their economy was previously based upon hunting, therefore they worship a number of forest deities. Besides these, they also worship deities like *Gaata, Duma, Dharti Mata* (Earth Goddess), *Dulhadeo, Mata Bhai, Devi,* etc.

Speaking about the social organization of the Kamars, they practise clan exogamy. They are divided into mainly six clans or septs namely *Jagat, Netam, Markam, Sori, Marai,* and *Chhedaiha.* Their clans are mainly totemistic ones. Marriage within the sept is forbidden, but is permitted between the children of brothers and children of two sisters. Males generally marry at the age of 18 and females at the age of 15. The five ways of acquiring mates among the Kamars are: *bihav* (regular marriage), marriage by elopement, *paithu* marriage, marriage by service, and widow remarriage. The Kamars are usually monogamous, sometimes polygyny is also found to be practised. Levirate and widow remarriage are also socially sanctioned. Nuclear, patrilineal and patrilocal families are common amongst them, with some exception of matrilineal families.

Political Organization of the Kamars

The modern approach towards state is to study it as a political organization. Today, its study is considered essential and its existence is considered vital for the society. We are governed by state-made laws. But in the primitive societies the rules and regulations are embodied in customs and traditions.

Historical accounts reveal that primitive societies had political organization. But their form of government is different from the government in modern societies. It is particularly to be mentioned that in primitive societies the function of law is discharged by customs.

The traditional political organization among the Kamars is totally based upon the primitive political system which is represented by four basic bodies, viz. the council of elders, village headman, traditional village panchayat and the union of villages or the pargana panchayat. In the case of Kamars, the political system is totally represented by a council of elders.

The representative council of elders of a particular village are responsible for settling minor disputes and trivial matters. This council may or may not be an elected one, they may be selected on the basis of their age, wisdom, experience and power to control the affairs of the tribe and village and even on the basis of heredity.

Following the lines of the foregoing discussion, it can be said that the traditional panchayat of the Kamars is based upon a four-tier hierarchy of a council of elders namely the *raja* or *kurha, dewan* or *sarpanch, chharidar* and *chaprasi.* Sometimes an additional post of a *koshadyaksh* is also included in this hierarchy, but this post is not a common one. It may or may not be present in a traditional panchayat. From among the sample villages of the present study, there was only a *koshadyaksh* in the village Keshodar.

This hierarchy of tribal officials is merely superficial, though, at the very outset, it appears to be quite concrete. This council of tribal authority is based upon the village as a unit. That means, every village or a number of villages or settlements close to one another join together and form a group. A single group is represented and governed by a single council of elders. In fact, there is no common centralized authority for the Kamars as a whole.

The officials of the traditional Kamar panchayat have definite tenures. Their mode of selection is also something different, quite simple and not accompanied by any elaborate procedures. The jurisdiction of these office bearers is also not fixed. It depends upon the area extension and population of the respective villages falling under their jurisdiction. A *raja* has normally 10-12 *palis* (nearly 25 villages) under his jurisdiction. The *dewan* wields power over 20 villages, the *chaprasi* and *chharidar* each have a maximum of five villages under their jurisdiction. The normal tenure of these office bearers extends upto a maximum of five years, which may be extended further if the respective official is found eligible to continue. All these officials are jointly elected by the members of the tribe. The *raja* is considered to be the supreme head of the traditional *panchayat*, whose decision on all matters is sought for and is a compulsion for all the members of the tribe to follow.

The *panchayat* does not meet to settle all disputes or award punishments for every single breach of the tribal laws. In many cases, it has been reported, social disapproval expressed by the elders of the local group is generally enough while others are left for their settlement to the super-natural powers. The *panchayat* assembles and takes into consideration only the comparatively more serious breaches of tribal law and custom. The *panchayats* enjoy wide powers in socio-religious matters. They depend on officials for their work.

For the tribe as a whole there is no central authority. Instead, a group of settlements, adjacent to one another, forms its own *panchayat* which enjoys supreme powers in the socio-religious matters of the members of the tribe living in the constituent settlements. *Panchayats* often depend for their functioning on a hierarchy of officials, such as *kurha* or *raja*, the chief of all the villages; *sarpanch*, the presiding officer of the group panchayat; and *chaprasi*, who runs errands, inform people about the panchayat meetings, their date, place and purpose. None of these officials has a determining voice in the decision of the panchayat. Children, young men and women of all ages are excluded from its membership. The decisions arrived at in the panchayat are either unanimous or by majority. The panchayat hears both the sides along with their witnesses and the persons accused are also given an opportunity to explain their positions. The people assembled can air their views but their opinions are not counted statistically in order to arrive at decisions. There is no superior authority than the panchayat which can itself over-rule decisions of the family elders.

Customary Laws of the Kamar

Tribal customary law has been studied as a part of the study of tribal society. In the process a distinction has been made between sanction in primitive society and the law of the more advanced society; between the uncodified, unwritten customary rules recognized as binding by a tribal community and the larger corpus of the laws enacted and enforced by formal state system. The critical role of tribal customary law in the maintenance of tribal solidarity, and now tribal identity, has generally been overlooked. With the growing understanding of our pluralism there is now an awareness of the need to know more of the tribal customary laws.

Observance of these rules is indispensable for the maintenance of social order and continuity of cultures. As they are inseparable from the content of culture, a brief account of culture is necessary to understand customary laws.

The culture areas of operation of these rules, particularly in the dispensation of civil and criminal justice, also need to be identified. The legal, social and supernatural sanctions which make these rules effective are also to be understood.

A study of the customary laws covers the traditional and normative rules governing and regulating the customs of the tribes.

The Kamar are a very simple, pre-literate tribe of Madhya Pradesh existing on an undeveloped economic and cultural level. Contacts with the British-sponsored judicial system have brought in partial disintegration of the traditional pattern of law and justice and administration. They have to abide by their own customary laws as also by the Indian Penal and Civil Codes. Nonetheless these people have been found to make little use of the Indian courts and larger *panchayats*. This may be due to the stranglehold of traditions over them, and/or their ignorance about the functioning of the courts and larger *panchayats*.

The customary laws of the Kamar deal with various kinds of offences, and the punishments awarded are not similar to those that would be awarded by an Indian court. This difference is explicable with reference to the varying conceptions as to what constitutes crime as between the Indian Penal Code and the traditional law of these people. Thus, homicide is often justified and when it is not, the murderer's crime is pardoned when he gives a penal feast. Stealing grains and forest products from other tribes and government reserves respectively is not regarded as an offence, nor is illicit distillation of liquor. Personal disputes are often traditionally settled through an exchange of blows.

As regards actions which are regarded as crimes against the tribal norms, punishments may be awarded collectively by the *panchayat* or may not be awarded at all in such cases, where supernatural and automatically operative punishment is expected. It is further believed that if the deities do not punish the culprits in this world, they will certainly take them to task in the world to which people go after death. Incest, i.e. sexual intercourse between close relatives, is one such offence, which need not be punished as supernatural wrath is sure to be visited upon the offending pair. However, according to local tradition such a breach of a tribal norm is always socially penalized through ostracizing those guilty of it. They are completely isolated, or even driven out of the village.

Abusing or neglecting to do one's duty is yet another offence which is not punished in the hope that the gods will themselves take revenge.

There are also automatic supernatural punishments for some ordinary breaches of various taboos. Thus, if a menstruating woman violates any of the taboos imposed on her, like entering the shed of the goddess or the kitchen, supernatural punishment is expected not only upon her but her entire family.

An Orderly System

The Kamars maintain the traditionally approved interpersonal relationship and have an orderly system of social relations under the council of elders *(panchayat).* Most of the Kamar villages have a panchayat which functions in accordance with the traditions, customs, ethics and moral values of the society. This village *panchayat* works as watchdog and keeps a strict vigilance on the interpersonal relations of its members. Whenever necessary or when anybody violates any of the customary laws, the Kamar *panchayat* interferes and corrects him by punishing such a person. Here, the *raja* or *kurha* presides over the meeting, the offenders or involved persons are called upon, their grievances are heard patiently in the *panchayat.* In the last phase, the matter is discussed by the members of the *panchayat* where they come to a decision by consulting one another. On certain occasions, when the decision of the Kamar *panchayat* is not acceptable to the offender, the matter is referred to the modern *panchayat.* But this is rarely done so, due to fear of social disapproval from the members of the tribe.

Among the Kamars certain deeds or activities are looked down upon by their customs and traditions. If anybody is involved in such deeds, he is taken to task, sometimes fined, punished, asked to host a communal feast or excommunicated from the society, subject to the sanctioned customary laws of the society.

Kamars' Sense of Superiority

In regional social hierarchy Kamars consider themselves to be superior to *Satnami, Dhobi* and *Nai* castes, but inferior to *Rawat, Teli* and *Gond.* So, usually a person is excommunicated from the society, if he or she is found eating or drinking with or in the hut of an inferior caste or tribe man. Such a person is readmitted to the society only if he or she obliges the villagers with a communal feast.

Customary Laws Regulating Kamar Life

Besides the above mentioned details, Kamars' marriage laws, remarriage laws, laws regulating children of unmarried mothers, rape cases and abortion are very important in regulating their way of life.

Customary Laws Regulating Marriage, Remarriage and Separation

Customary laws of the Kamars have not undergone any major changes. Regarding marriage, the Kamars still follow the usual rule of tribe endogamy, and they also practise clan exogamy and avoid incest. Marriage within the village is permissible and such alliances are not avoided. In fact, village endogamy was a rule in the past, but now-a-days it is not a compulsion. Prescribed and preferential marriage ties are not the rule of the society, while senior levirate and junior sororate are permitted. The Kamars also follow certain rules regarding remarriage and separation. It is seen that women are not easily granted social approval if they go for remarriage and separation. Men can remarry as many times as they wish to but women can only change partners by accepting the *churi* (bangles) offered to them by the concerned persons. Remarriage is also associated with usual rules of marriage, viz. tribe endogamy and clan exogamy. The fines associated with the violation of usual norms are Rs. 500 each for tribe exogamy and clan endogamy. The Kamars also recognize superiority and inferiority in the caste hierarchy. In this connection they follow the practise of hypogamy and hypergamy. They consider the *Rawat, Teli* and *Gond* to be superior to themselves, and if any male or female marries a person belonging to any of these ethnic groups he or she is accepted as a member of the Kamar tribe after expiation of his/her offence by paying the requisite amount of fine and the penal feast. On the other hand, a person marrying any one from the *Satnami, Dhobi* or *Nai* caste is liable of total ex-communication from the tribe. His/her offence is considered to be an extremely serious one, and cannot be expiated by a fine and penal feast. The customary laws of marriage are also associated with certain taboos, and marital relation between the certain persons is regarded as incest, viz. between paternal cousins, between a man and his sister-in-law and between a man and his elder brother's wife. Any person found to be guilty of committing such an offence is liable of punishment, in the form of a fine of Rs. 400. But in exceptional cases, a man is allowed to marry his elder brother's wife, after the death of his brother. In that case, he can expiate his offence by merely arranging for the penal feast, and may be exempted from paying the fine.

On the other hand, the marital relations between a man and his widowed sister-in-law and between maternal cousins are granted social approval. The marriage between maternal cousins takes place in the usual way.

The Kamars also follow certain residential rules regarding marriage. A man is only permitted to adopt his wife's residence, when she has no brothers. He has to some extent claim over his wife's property in that situation. If there are two or more sisters of the wife, then only the husband of the eldest daughter is allowed to adopt his wife's residence.

Customary laws regarding remarriage are not too strict. A man marrying a woman whose husband is still alive has to pay the requisite amount of Rs. 200 to Rs. 1000 to her former husband as *byahtari* (a fine). This is considered as a fine for the man going for remarriage. In some cases, he has also to arrange for a penal feast. A man going for remarriage with a widow may be exempted from punishment and payment of the fine.

The customary laws regarding remarriage impose more strict rules on women than on men. This is seen from the fact that Kamar women are not permitted to keep more than one partner at a time, whereas men are free to stay with more than one wife at a time. But the concerned man cannot keep all his wives under the same roof or in the same village. He is permitted to keep at most two wives in the same village.

The Kamars do not legally sanction anything known as divorce. In fact, divorce can be more precisely referred to as separation. Instances of separation between the husband and wife are common in the Kamar society. Separation is easily followed by remarriages. A man going for remarriage with a separated woman has to pay an amount of fine ranging from Rs. 500 to Rs. 1000 to the former husband of the woman. This fine is known as *chootha daan.* A separated woman can also claim for her share of the husband's property, but only in such cases when she does not go for remarriage with another person. It is normally found that men and women easily go for remarriage after separation, so the question of wife's claim over the husband's property does not arise.

Customary Laws Relating to Property and Inheritance of Property

The customary laws regarding property and inheritance of property are accompanied by slightly complex rules and regulations. Among the Kamars, the rights of property inheritance are usually enjoyed by the sons, and the daughters normally do not have any share in it. Property inheritance mainly refers to inheritance of landed property. The unlanded property is usually not divided or distributed. The eldest son of a family inherits the *jethasi* (an extra share of his father's property). This is done to secure his responsibilities as the eldest child; he is supposed to take up the total responsibility of his father's last rites after death. Property rights and rights of inheritance by widows is also superficial. A widow normally does not stay as a widow for the whole of her lifetime, she usually goes for remarriage by accepting the *churi* from another person. In exceptional cases, when the widow does not go for remarriage, she may be granted 1/4 of the total share of her husband's property, but this is only in such cases where the women stays under the same roof of her deceased husband. Similar are the rules of property inheritance by separated women. Adopted children also have a claim over both their biological father's property and property of their present parents. Ex-communicated persons also retain their usual rights over their share of property, they may claim for it at any time, but only in conditions when they expiate their offence by the fine and penal feast. An illegitimate child has no claim over property from any side.

The Kamars also practise the system of property transfer by barter, by sale, by purchase or by exchange. Though this is a rare occurrence, but is occasionally seen even today among the Kamars. Matters of property transfer are dealt with by the *kotwar, tahsildaar, patel, panch* or *sarpanch.*

Customary Laws Relating to Illegitimate Child

Customary laws regarding the rights of an illegitimate child are also prevalent in the Kamar society. A male person accused of bearing an illegitimate child is pressurized to pay a fine of Rs. 200 to Rs. 300 to the traditional panchayat. An accused female is heavily charged with a fine of Rs. 500 to Rs. 600 and also, sometimes liable of ex-communication if she is not in a position to pay the amount. This order of ex-communication is known as *sobreitnama.*

Customary Laws Relating to Child Adoption

The Kamars also have certain customary laws and provisions regarding child adoption, though rarely child adoption is practised by them. Child adoption is merely a matter of verbal sanction done with the intermediation of the elderly members of the traditional *panchayat.* If in any case it happens that the ex-parents of a child demand for their child's possession from the parents who have adopted the child, then they can do so, but this act of theirs is associated with the paying of a fine known as *nuksani.* The adopted child can claim over his father's property (both ex- and present). The procedure of child adoption is associated with the arrangement of a *panchayati bhoj.*

Customary Laws Relating to Rape and Abortion

Offences such as rape and intentional abortion are of rare occurrence. Still they are regarded as serious and the modes of punishment and judgement are also specified for such types of offences. These are associated with particular amount of fine and penal feasts. Tne cases of rape are handled by the Kamar traditional *panchayat.* The accused male is liable to punishment or even ex-communication. Punishment is offered in the form of a penal feast comprising of 10 bottles of liquor, 1 *katha* rice and the flesh of a goat. The child borne by a victim of rape can claim for property rights from his father, but only on conditions when the "accused" male belongs to the same tribe as that of the victim. In some cases, if the victim (female) marries another person, then she is asked to pay a fine of Rs. 400 to Rs. 500.

Intentional abortion is also taken to be a very sinful act though the Kamars have not devised any definite means of intentional abortion. But intentional abortion, done by any means, is treated as an offence and in such cases the accused male or female (sometimes both) are liable of ex-communication. But the Kamars generally conceive the offence to be committed by the female, hence she is charged a fine of Rs. 100 to Rs. 200.

Customary Law Regulating Beef-eating or Killing of Cow

Beef-eating is also conceived to be an offence on the part of Kamars. The accused Kamar has to expiate his offence by committing to *harin paap* by going to a place of pilgrimage, where he has to arrange for a feast, the cost of which is determined by the priests at the place of pilgrimage. The feast includes usual items like rice and pulses.

Customary Law Relating to Abuse/Personal Assault, Elopement and Incestuous Relations

Matters of abuse and personal assault are often referred to the members of the traditional panchayat. The offender has to pay a fine of Rs. 500 to Rs. 600 to the Panchayat. Now-a-days cases of serious abuse/assault are directly referred to the civil courts.

Elopement is also regarded as an offence among the Kamars. A couple accused of elopement is also liable to punishment. The accused female has to pay a fine of Rs. 150 to Rs. 200 whereas the accused male is subjected to a fine of Rs. 200 to Rs. 300. Otherwise the couple is liable to ex-communication.

Regarding adultery, the Kamars regard certain relations as incest, such as sex relations between paternal cousins, a woman and her husband's elder brother. An accused girl's parents have to pay the *dihar* (a fine of Rs. 500) to the traditional *panchayat.*

Changes in Political Organization and Customary Laws of the Kamars

The changes in political organization of the Kamars can be said to be very limited. The traditional Kamar panchayat was hereditary in nature, but now-a-days, the officials are not merely elected on the basis of heredity, but some other qualities such as age, experience, wisdom, eligibility, power to control and affairs of the village and tribe are also taken into consideration. It was seen that almost 20 to 25 years ago, the Patel system of government was prevalent among the Kamars, and during those days, heredity was the sole factor responsible for the selection of the office bearers.

The traditional Kamar *panchayat* in the former days, used to deal with criminal cases and cases of dispute such as murder, homicide, abuse and assault. Such type of offences could be expiated by only offering a penal feast. The influence of state civil judiciary system has brought about a change in this system in that, such type of criminal cases are now-a-days neither referred to nor dealt with in the traditional *panchayat.*

In former days, the customary laws of the Kamars also had the provision for expiation of such type of offences by merely offering a fine and penal feast. The amount of fine charged for various types of offences was also less, ranging from Rs. 2 to Rs. 4 gradually it amounted to Rs. 50 to Rs. 200, now-a-days, the range varies from Rs. 150 to Rs. 1000. This amount is also likely to increase to a maximum of Rs. 2000.

The items of the Penal feast have also undergone a change in terms of quantity. The flesh of a goat as an item of the penal feast was not a compulsion, but now-a-days items such as rice, pulses, liquor and the flesh of a goat are made compulsorily. In former days, the quantity of rice was a maximum of 4 *katha* (about 7 kg), today it has increased upto a maximum of 9 or 10 *katha*. The quantity of liquor as offered in former days was 1 or 2 bottles, today it has gone upto a maximum of 10 to 12 bottles. The flesh of one goat, as offered in past has also now increased to two.

The imposition of state civil laws on the customary laws of the Kamars is also quite clear. This was evident by some case studies and crime records collected from the survey area. It was found that certain Kamars were arrested under various codes of IPC and Cr.P.C. IPC articles imposed on these Kamars were 325, 307, 381, 302, 381, 451, 376 and 335 (for details see Appendix-I). These accused were charged with different crimes committed by them. A few others were also charged with land disputes under Cr.P.C. code. There were also some cases where a few Kamars were charged with illegal manufacture of liquor, and theft of forest property. Though the number of such cases are less, but still one can clearly view the impact of state civil laws on the customary laws of the Kamars, wherein cases of murder, rape, assault, theft and other associated criminal cases are now-a-days no longer dissolved in the *panchayat.*

Now the question arises, why is law obeyed? A few anthropologists have also presented their views on this question. Example may be cited of Bronislaw Malinowski. It had been said that the primitive obeys laws spontaneously, willingly and slavishly. It was Malinowski who showed that there was no automatic submission to law. What actually made a people obey law was interdependence and mutual obligation. If one does not perform one's duty for others, one cannot expect them to do anything for one's own sake. And no individual nor an individual family is a unit self-sufficient by itself. Malinowski illustrated this mutuality of obligations as it underlies the economic, social and ceremonial ritual life of the Trobriand Islanders. Thus, he showed that unless the beach-dwellers exchange their fish for the garden produce of those living in the interior, and *vice versa,* neither group will be able to survive. Consequently mutual obligations must be fulfilled. These obligations are embodied in tribal laws; and the same are obeyed not slavishly but because of self-interest and its fulfilment. Economic interest is one of the dominant self-interests, which governs the emergence of, and obedience to, laws (quoted by Madan and Majumdar, 1993: 180-181).

Conclusion

Intention and motive are subordinated to the consequences of an act, and punishments are awarded in terms of these consequences. Consequently, no distinction is made between wrongs committed deliberately and those committed unknowingly as a result of chance and accident. Broken-eared people among the Kamar are ostracized. There are prolonged discussions over cases of this type, but majority decisions are always reached and these uphold and conserve the tradition.

A large number of offences can be expiated by giving penal feasts. The items of the feast are dictated by the *panchayat* which may be reduced on the request of the accused. Often the accused takes some time to collect the requirement for the feast. During this time, he has to bear with the punishment awarded to him, e.g. if he has been ostracized, then he shall remain outside the tribe or atleast outside its social life.

Now-a-days cases of such offences as homicide, grievous bodily hurt and thefts of very serious nature are taken to the Indian courts for decision.

Adultery, witchcraft, eating with low-caste people, touching or riding a horse, black magic, killing a cow or a bullock, having vermin in one's wound, being beaten by a low-caste person, after changing four husbands, marrying a fifth one, elopement, and breaking the rule of clan exogamy, are some of the actions which are regarded as breaches of customary law by the Kamar. Offences against person and property are not numerous and are rarely of a serious nature. They are generally treated lightly and are even regarded as justifiable necessities sometimes. Concealment of offences and suppression of evidence is rarely attempted. In fact, rather than being regarded as "crimes", offences are regarded as "sins", which can be expiated in most of the cases by giving a tribal feast and paying a fine. Authority naturally rests with men of age and experience. The elders of the tribe are the guardians of law and order. They are both interpreters of the tribal code and adjudicators of disputes.

Thus, through the simple mechanism described in the foregoing pages the Kamar society controls social relations. Here, whoever violates or goes against the established customary laws is treated as a social offender and the whole Kamar society turns against the offender. So, it is the collective responsibility and the power of the traditional *panchayat* which compels an offender to act according to its verdict.

The impact of the modern forces of change on the customary laws of traditional Kamars has been very little due to Kamars' negligible interactions with the outer world.

APPENDIX-I

DETAILS OF INDIAN PENAL CODE ARTICLES

(1) *Article 302:* Whoever commits murder shall be punished with death or imprisonment for life and shall also be liable to fine.

(2) *Article 307: Attempt to murder:* Whoever does any act with such intention or knowledge, and under such circumstances that, if he by that act caused death, he would be guilty of murder, shall be punished with imprisonment of either description for a term which may extend to ten years, and shall also be liable to fine; and, if hurt is caused to any person by such act, the offender shall be liable either to imprisonment for life, or to such punishment as is herein before mentioned.

Attempts by life-convicts: When any person offending under this section is under sentence of imprisonment for life, he may, if hurt is caused, be punished with death.

(3) *Article 325: Punishment for voluntarily causing grievous hurt:* Whoever, except in the case provided for by Section 335, voluntarily causes grievous hurt, shall be punished with imprisonment of either description for a term which may extend to seven years, and shall also be liable to fine.

(4) *Article 335: Voluntarily causing grievous hurt on provocation:* Whoever voluntarily causes grievous hurt on grave and sudden provocation, if he neither intends nor knows himself to be likely to cause grievous hurt to any person who gave the provocation, shall be punished with imprisonment of either description for a term which may extend to four years, or with fine which may extend to two thousand rupees, or with both.

(5) *Article 376: Punishment for rape:* Whoever commits rape shall be punished with imprisonment for life, or with imprisonment of either description for a term which may extend to ten years, and shall also be liable to fine, unless the woman raped is his own wife and is not under twelve years of age, in which case he shall be punished with imprisonment of either description for a term which may extend to two years or with fine or with both.

(6) *Article 381:* Theft by clerk or servant of property in possession of master—whoever being a clerk or servant, or being employed in the capacity of a clerk or servant, commits theft in respect of any property in the possession of his master or employer, shall be punished with imprisonment of either description for a term which may extend to seven years, and shall also be liable to fine.

(7) *Article 451: House-trespass in order to commit offence punishable with imprisonment:* Whoever commits house trespass in order to committing of any offence punishable with imprisonment, shall be punished with imprisonment of either description for a term which may extend to two

years, and shall also be liable to fine; and if the offence intended to be committed to theft, the term of the imprisonment may be extended to seven years.

REFERENCES

Dubey, S.C. 1951. *The Kamar.* Lucknow: The Universal Publishers Ltd.

Russell, R.V. and R.B. Hiralal. 1975. *The Tribes and Castes of Central Provinces of India.* Vol. 3. Delhi: Cosmo Publications.

Saxena, Usha 1974. *A Text Book of Indian Penal Code* (Hindi). Lucknow: Prakashan Kendra.

Singh, Kumar Suresh. 1993. *Tribal Ethnography, Customary Law and Change.* New Delhi: Concept Publishing Company.

Tewari, D.N. 1984. *Primitive Tribes of Madhya Pradesh.* New Delhi: Ministry of Home Affairs.

NOTES ON CONTRIBUTORS

Babu, B.V. is Senior Research Officer (Social Sciences) at the Regional Medical Research Centre, Indian Council of Medical Research, Bhubaneswar. He was awarded the doctoral degree in Anthropology in 1994 from Andhra University. Dr. Babu has worked as Senior Research Fellow and Research Associate of Council of Scientific and Industrial Research (CSIR) at the Department of Anthropology, Andhra University. He has done extensive fieldwork in tribal areas of the Eastern Ghats of Andhra Pradesh and has published around 40 articles in national and international journals. Presently Dr. Babu is engaged in WHO projects with main emphasis on medical anthropology.

Mailing Address: Senior Research Officer
Regional Medical Research Centre
Indian Council of Medical Research
Chandrasekharpur
Bhubaneswar-751 016
Orissa, India

Behera, Deepak Kumar obtained his Master's degree (Gold Medalist) and Ph.D. from Sambalpur University, where he has been teaching anthropology since 1985. He has more than 50 research publications in reputed journals and edited volumes. Dr. Behera has also published one book and has edited six volumes. Of the six edited volumes, three are jointly with Prof.Georg Pfeffer of Institute of Ethnology of Free University of Berlin (Germany): two on tribal studies *(Contemporary Society: Tribal Studies,* Vol-I & Vol-II, 1997, Concept, New Delhi) and one on childhood matters *(Contemporary Society: Childhood and Complex Order,* 1996, Manak, New Delhi). Another volume edited by Dr. Behera is also on childhood matters *(Children and Childhood in Our Contemporary Societies,* 1998, Kamla-Raj Enterprises, New Delhi). Two other edited volumes on gender issues *(Gender and Society in India,* Vol-I & Vol-II, 1998, Manak, New Delhi) have been recently brought out by Dr. Behera jointly with Prof. R. Indira of Mysore University. He has successfully completed half-a-dozen research projects funded by national bodies like UGC, ICSSR, Ministry of Welfare, National Literacy Mission Authorities, etc. He is a faculty member of the ongoing Shastri Indo-Canadian project entitled "Empowering Women through Forestry: The Role of Indigenous Women...." Dr. Behera has participated in more than a dozen international conferences in Mexico, Germany, Belgium (twice), Sweden, Denmark, and USA, and has lectured at different universities and research institutes there. He was a UGC Visiting Fellow to Israel. Besides conducting research, he delivered a series of lectures in Tel Aviv University, Hebrew University and DCI, during his stay in Israel. Recently he went to South Africa as a Visiting Professor under an Agreement of Co-operation, signed between the Dept. of Anthropology, University of Orange Free State and Dept. of Anthropology, Sambalpur University. The agreement was signed under the initiatives of Dr. Behera, and Prof. Erasmus of the University of Orange Free State. Dr. Behera is the Editor of the international journal—*Journal of Social Sciences.* Recently Dr. Behera has been recently elected as a member of the Executive Board of International Union of Anthropological and Ethnological Sciences (IUAES) for the period 1998-2003. He is the youngest Indian in the long history of IUAES to get elected to the post. He has also been recently elected as Officer-at-Large of the International Sociological Association Research Committee-53—Sociology of Childhood for the session 1998-2002. He is a member of the International Advisory Board of the Journal—*Sociological Analysis* (North Carolina, USA) and also a member of the Editorial Board of Global Gutter Press (Cambridge, UK). Dr. Behera is a member of the core group of IUAES *Commission on Anthropology in Policy and Practice, Commission on Anthropological Dimension of Global Change* and *Commission on Urban Anthropology.* The first two commissions are affiliated to UNESCO through IUAES. Dr. Behera is now taking initiatives to create a new *Commission on Anthropology of Children and Childhood* in IUAES. The said commission is likely to be established by 2000 AD. Recently Dr. Behera chaired two different sessions, namely, *Resource Management through Indigenous Socio-cultural Practices* and *Children without Childhood in our Contemporary Society* at the 14th ICAES, held in Virginia, USA during July-August, 1998. Of the two, one was an officially sponsored session of the International Union of Anthropological and Ethnological Science *Commission on Anthropology in Policy and Practice.* Recently Dr. Behera also organized another session of ISA RC-53 on *Public Images of Childhood* (with Prof. Lucia Rabello de Castro of Brazil as the co-organizer) at the 14th World Sociology Congress, held in Montreal, Canada during July-August 1998. He has successfully guided three Ph.D. and twenty M.Phil scholars. Dr. Behera is the Director of the Institute of Evaluation, Research, Documentation and Training. His current interests in research are tribal studies, childhood matters, inter-ethnic relations and gender issues.

Mailing Address: Dr. Deepak Kumar Behera
Department of Anthropology
Sambalpur University
Jyoti Vihar, Burla
Sambalpur- 768 019
Orissa (India)
Fax: ++91-(0) 663-404000/430158
email: <dkb@cal2.vsnl.net.in> or <dkb@vsnl.com>

Das, Amal Kumar (M.Sc., Ph.D.) retired from the post of Director, Cultural Research Institute, Government of West Bengal in 1992. Since 1993, he has been working as a Member of West-Bengal Backward Classes Commission. He received higher training in Anthropology as a Mellon Fellow from the University of Pittsburgh, U.S.A. Since 1957, he was intimately connected with development administration, research and training in the Research Institute. He has specialized in the study of Scheduled Tribes, Scheduled Castes and other weaker sections of the society. Prior to 1957, he worked in the UNESCO project on "Impact of Industrialization on Productivity", W.H.O., R.C.A. project on "Environmental Sanitation" and AIISW BM Project on "Impact of Industrialization on Factory Labourers". Dr. Das is the author of twenty-seven books and more than two hundred twenty-five research papers dealing with Scheduled Tribes, Castes and other weaker sections. In addition, he is associated with different Universities, learned bodies and organizations, holding important positions. His fields of specialization are advanced social anthropology, applied anthropology and development anthropology.

Mailing Address: 22A, Garcha First Lane
Calcutta - 700 019
West Bengal, India

Das, M. did her Master's and M. Phil degrees in Anthropology at G.G. University, Bilaspur, Madhya Pradesh. She has carried out fieldwork among the primitive tribes of Madhya Pradesh. She has participated in various national seminars. Ms. Das is presently working for her doctoral degree at G.G. University, Bilaspur. Her research interest is primitive tribal communities in India.

Mailing Address: Department of Anthropology and Tribal Development
G.G. University
Koni, Bilaspur
Madhya Pradesh, India.

Das, Rajat Kanti received his Master's and Doctoral degrees from Calcutta University. His first assignment after Master's degree was in the Social Studies Section in the Office of the Superintendent of Census Operations, Shillong, Assam in 1963. He served as Lecturer/Senior Lecturer in Anthropology in D.M. College of Science, Imphal, Manipur during 1964-1987. He joined Vidyasagar University, West Bengal as Reader in Anthropology in the year 1987. Currently he holds the post of Professor of Anthropology in the same University. He has authored two books entitled, *Manipur Tribal Scene: A Study of Society and Change* and *Tribal Social Structure: A Study of the Maring Society of Manipur,* both published by Inter-India publications, New Delhi. He has published a number of research papers on tribal cultures, socio-political movements, social and political change in North-East India with special reference to Manipur and Nagaland. Prof. Das is at present working on a research project entitled, "Problems and Prospects of Development: A Study on Santal, Bhumij and Kharia tribes of Midnapore District, West Bengal," being financed by ICSSR, New Delhi.

Mailing Address: Department of Anthropology
Vidyasagar University
Midnapore
West Bengal, India

Jena, Debendranath got his Master's and Doctoral degrees in Sociology from Utkal University. He joined the teaching profession as Lecturer in Sociology, Ravenshaw College, Cuttack in 1977. In the year 1985 Dr. Jena joined the P.G. Department of Sociology, Utkal University as Lecturer and was elected to the post of Senior Lecturer in 1986. He became a Reader in the same department in 1990 and since then is continuing in the same post. He has published twelve research papers and has authored four books. His research interests are sociology of rural development and social change and mobility.

Mailing Address: Department of Sociology
Utkal University
Vani Vihar
Bhubaneswar
Orissa, India

Krishna Reddy, S. received his Master's and Doctoral degrees in the discipline of Anthropology from Sri Venkateswara University, Tirupati. He has published more than 20 articles in reputed journals and edited volume. He has to his credit a book entitled, *Religious Ecology.* He has presented papers in more than 30 national and international conferences. He is a life member of many professional associations. His main research interest has been in the areas of tribal development, demographic anthropology, urban anthropology, ecological anthropology and folklore.

Mailing Address: Department of Anthropology
S.V. University
Tirupati - 517 502, India

Kusuma, Y.S., is a Research Associate (CSIR) in the Department of Anthropology, Utkal University, Bhubaneswar. Prior to this she was Senior Research Fellow of CSIR in the Department of Anthropology, Andhra University, Waltair. Her doctoral thesis is on epidemiology of blood pressure among cross cultural populations. She has published more than ten research papers in various national and international journals.

Mailing Address: Department of Anthropology
Utkal University
Vani Vihar
Bhubaneswar
Orissa, India

Mandal, Debabrata obtained his Master's and doctoral degrees in Anthropology from Calcutta University. At present he holds the post of Superintending Anthropologist in Anthropological Survey of India, Western Regional Centre, Udaipur, Rajasthan. He is a painstaking fieldworker and has conducted fieldwork in more than ten states covering the Scheduled Caste and Scheduled Tribe populations. So far he has successfully completed seventeen national level projects. He has about fifty research papers to his credit. His book *Social Structure and Cultural Change of the Saharin Tribe* has been recently published and another book *Snake Charmer in India* is in the press. Dr. Mandal's special interest is primitive tribal groups in India.

Mailing Address: Western Regional Centre
Anthropological Survey of India
Udaipur-313 001
Rajasthan, India

Mollick, F. is a lecturer in the Dept. of Anthropology and Tribal Development, G.G University, Bilaspur. He has done intensive fieldwork among the tribes of Madhya Pradesh. He worked on the problem of tribal ethnicity for his Doctoral degree. His areas of research interest are tribal development and inter-ethnic relations.

Mailing Address: Department of Anthropology and Tribal Development
G.G. University
Koni, Bilaspur - 495 009
M.P., India

Mukherjee, B.M. obtained his Master's (Gold Medalist) and doctoral degrees from Ranchi University. He has been in the teaching profession since 1977. At present he is Professor and Head of the department of Anthropology and Dean of the Faculty of Life Sciences, G.G. University, Bilaspur, M.P. Prof. Mukherjee has a good number of research publications including two edited volumes. He has successfully completed five research projects sponsored by U.G.C., Ministry of Welfare, Government of India, CSIR, Museum of Man and C.I.L. Recently he presented a couple of research papers in the 14th ICAES held in Virginia, USA during July-August, 1998. He was also a visiting Professor in an American University for a semester. His research and teaching interests are women studies, medical anthropology and development anthropology.

Mailing Address: Department of Anthropology and Tribal Development
G.G. University
Koni, Bilaspur - 495 009
Madhya Pradesh, India

Naidu, J.M. is Professor of Anthropology and Registrar of Andhra University, Visakhapatnam. He has been teaching anthropology and human genetics in Andhra University since two decades. Prof. Naidu has completed a number of research projects financed by UGC, CSIR, ICSSR, etc. He has done extensive fieldwork among various caste and tribal populations of coastal Andhra Pradesh. Prof. Naidu has more than 80 publications to his credit in different journals.

Mailing Address: Department of Anthropology
Andhra University
Visakhapatnam
Andhra Pradesh, India

Narasimha Raju, M.P. is a Senior Lecturer in the Dept. of Sociology, Sri Venkateswara University, Tirupati. He has published more than twenty articles in various journals and edited books. He is the Principal Investigator of the UGC Major Research Project entitled, "Infant and Child Mortality in a Tribal

Community of Andhra Pradesh." He organised two national level seminars in the department. He has presented papers in a number of national level conferences. His areas of interest in research are infant mortality, tribal studies and development anthropology.

Mailing Address: C/o M. P. Narasimha Raju
Department of Sociology
S.V. University
Tirupati - 517 502,
Andhra Pradesh, India

Nayak, Abhaya Narayana got his Master's (topper) and M.Phil degree in Anthropology from Sambalpur University. As a NET qualified scholar he is presently working on the theme resource management through indigenous socio-cultural practices for his doctoral degree. Mr. Nayak has won a number of medals and prizes both in English and Oriya debates and essay competitions at the state level. His current research interest is developmental anthropology.

Mailing Address: C/o Dr. Deepak Kumar Behera
Department of Anthropology
Sambalpur University
Jyoti Vihar, Burla
Sambalpur - 768 019
Orissa, India

Pfeffer, Georg is Professor of Ethnology at the Freie University of Berlin. He studied Ethnology, Sociology and History of Religions at Frieburg University, Germany where he obtained his doctoral degree in 1990. In 1971 he was appointed Assistant Professor at the South Asia Institute of University of Heidelberg where he was promoted to the position of an Associate Professor in 1979. During his career he has conducted fieldwork for several years in various parts of India and Pakistan and has learnt several Indian languages. Prof. Pfeffer has undertaken ten extended excursions to the tribes of middle India. In addition to his teaching and research obligations in Berlin he is an active member of several national and international academic societies and the co-editor of German Zeitschrift Fur Ethnologie. Prof. Pfeffer has number of research publications in reputed international journals. He has brought out three edited volumes jointly with Dr. D.K. Behera of Sambalpur University, Orissa, India. Of the three, two are on tribal studies and one is on childhood matters. He is a member of the Editorial Board of *Journal of Social Sciences*. Cults and kinship of Scheduled Tribes in Koraput and Phulbani districts of Orissa (India) are Prof. Pfeffer's key areas of interest.

Mailing Address: Institute Fur Ethnologie
Freie Universitat Berlin,
Drosselweg 1-3
14195 Berlin, Germany

Raha, Manis Kumar did his Master's and Doctoral degrees at Calcutta University and completed a course on Management Development Programme for Educational Administrators in the Indian Institute of Management, Calcutta. Dr. Raha retired as Joint Director of the Anthropological Survey of India. He has done empirical studies in different states and union territories of India including Himalayan regions and the Andaman and Nicobar Islands. His Publications include 35 books, more than 80 articles. He has also reviewed 15 books. Dr. Raha has edited the felicitation volumes of Prof. P.K. Bhowmick of Calcutta University, Calcutta. He is the Editor of the Journal–*Journal of Biological and Environmental Sciences.* Dr. Raha is also the Managing Editor of *Man and Life.* He has his expertise in tribal studies, culture change and tribal development.

Mailing Address: 10/3, Jamir Lane
Calcutta-700 019
West Bengal, India

Rathnaiah, K. received his Master's and Doctoral degrees in Sociology from S.V. University. He served as a Lecturer in Sociology during 1980-89 and as a Reader in Home Science (extension) between 1989 and 1993. At present he is a Reader in Sociology, S.V. University. Dr. Rathnaiah has published a number of articles on the socio-economic conditions of Scheduled Castes in Andhra Pradesh in national journals. He has also participated in many national level seminars. Dr. Rathnaiah has successfully organized two national level seminars in S.V. University, Tirupati. Recently he visited Paris for a month under "Indo-French Cultural Exchange Programme", to undertake a study on Indian immigrants. His area of specialization is sociology of minorities.

Mailing Address: Department of Sociology
S.V. University
Tirupati - 517502
Andhra Pradesh, India

Sanyal, Suparna received her Master's degree in Anthropology from Dr. H.S. Gaur University, Sagar, M.P. She had received training in population studies and museum appreciation. Ms. Sanayal is presently working for her Ph.D. on Anglo-Indians in Calcutta. She has to her credit some research publications.

Mailing Address: C/o Debabrata Mandal
Western Regional Centre
Anthropological Survey of India
Udaipur-313 001
Rajasthan, India

Sarkar, R.M. (M.Sc., Ph.D., D.Litt.) is an eminent researcher in the domain of anthropology. Dr. Sarkar's interest in both the principal branches of anthropology has made him conversant in biology and culture of human existence and activities. He has to his credit 80 research papers published in reputed scientific journals. Dr. Sarkar has authored seven books on anthropological science. Through his extensive fieldwork he has been able to make a well-knit study on the theoretical context and empirical findings. Dr. Sarkar has conducted fruitfully a number of research projects sponsored by UGC and ICSSR. He worked as a member of the National Committee for the preparation of Syllabus in Anthropology and Sociology organized by UGC. Dr. Sarkar is a member of the Advisory Committee of Anthropological Survey of India, Government of India. He is intimately associated with the working and the organizational activities of a number of voluntary organizations. For last nine years. Dr. Sarkar has been in intimate association with the renowned anthropological journal, *Man in India,* as its Editor. He is a member of the Advisory Board of *Journal of Social Sciences.* His areas of interest are tribal studies, environmental studies and biosocial studies.

Mailing Address: Mayurakshi
Baghajatin Park
Calcutta-700 094
West Bengal, India

Soheila, Shahshahani got her B.A. (Philosophy) from University of California and Ph.D. in Anthropology from the Graduate faculty of the New School for Social Research in New York. She is now Assistant Professor at Shahid Behesthi University, Tehran. Her research in urban anthropology has concerned the cities of Kashan, Varâmeen and Esfahan. She has also studied the Mamassani, a pastoral nomadic population in Iran, and as rural area is concerned, she has done research in the grotto villages of Meymand in central Iran. Her Publications include three books, namely, *The Four Seasons of the Sun. A Bibliography of Iranian Women in Social Sciences, Humanities and Arts,* and *A Pictorial History of Iranian Headdresses* and many articles in Persian and English.

Mailing Address: B.P. 19585-193
Tehran, IRAN

Sheykhi, Mohammad Taghi got his Master's degree in Sociology (first class first) from Aligarh Muslim University (India) in 1977 and Doctoral degree from Agra University (Agra) in 1980. He worked as a population expert at the Statistical Centre of Iran from 1981-86. At present he is a member of the teaching Staff at Al-Zahra University (Tehran). Dr. Sheykhi is also a member of the Council of Research, Al-Zahra University. He has more than forty research publications both at national and international levels. He has participated in various national and international seminars/conferences. He is a member of the Advisory Board of *Journal of Social Sciences.* Dr. Sheykhi's research interests are population studies, sociology of development, sociology of tribes and nomads and sociology of deviant behaviour.

Mailing Address: Department of Social Sciences
Al-Zahar University
Tehran-19834, Iran.

Sinha, A.K. received both his Master's and Ph.D. degrees from Ranchi University, Ranchi. He started his career as a Research Investigator at the Centre for Advanced Study in Anthropology, Ranchi University, Ranchi. Then he joined as Research Associate in the same department. Presently Dr. Sinha is Reader in Social Anthropology in Punjab University, Chandigarh. Prior to this Dr. Sinha was Senior Lecturer in the Department of Anthropology and Tribal Development, G.G. University, Bilaspur, M.P. He has published around 25 research papers in reputed national journals. Besides, he has also authored three books, namely, *Applied Anthropology, Tribal Development and Primitive Tribes of Madhya Pradesh.* His areas of specialization are social anthropology and tribal studies.

Mailing Address: Department of Anthropology
Punjab University
Chandigarh - 160014, India

Srivastava, A.R.N. got his Master's degree from Wake Forest University and Doctoral degree from Arizona State University, U.S.A. At present he is Professor and Head of the Department of Anthropology, Allahabad University. Earlier he taught at Ranchi University, Ravi Shankar University and Wake Forest University (U.S.A.) Prof. Srivastav has done extensive fieldwork in Chotanagpur and Bastar. Some of his works include *Social Anthropology in India* (1978), *The Development Dimension of Domestic Groups in India* (1979), *Tribal Freedom Fighters in India* (1985) and *Tribal Encounter with Industry* (1990). Besides he has also written three books in Hindi on Cultural Anthropology. His recent publications include *Visual Anthropology* (in press),

What is Anthropology (1992), *Changing Values and Tribal Societies* (1993) and *Anthropology in India* (a collection of original of Indian anthropologists 1955-95).

Mailing Address: 4C/2, Bank Road
University Campus
Allahabad-211002
U.P., India

Suryanarayana, M. did his post-graduation and Ph.D. from Andhra University, Waltair. He worked for his Ph.D. degree on a primitive tribal community (Saoras). He has published six books, besides several contributions in edited volumes and about fifty research papers in reputed national and international journals. In the capacity of a Senior Fellow in Anthropological Survey, he conducted an in-depth study on the Marine Fisherfolk of Andhra Pradesh. He also worked as Research Assistant in Telugu Academy between 1971 and 1972. In July 1972, he joined the Department of Anthropology, Sri Venkateswara University, Tirupati as a Lecturer and presently working as a Professor in the same department. He is a member of the Advisory Board of *Journal of Social Sciences.* His current interest in research is sociology of gerontology.

Mailing Address: Department of Anthropology
S.V. University
Tirupati-517502
A.P., India

Suzuki, Peter T. born in Seattle, Washington, U.S.A., studied anthropology at Columbia University (B.A., M.A.), Yale University (Doctoral studies), and Leiden University, Holland (M.Phil and Ph.D. degrees). His post-doctoral work includes studies at Heidelberg University, Germany and Louvain La Neuve, Belgium. Prof. Suzuki has conducted fieldwork in Turkey, and has done research among Turks in Germany, American Indians in Nebraska, American Blacks in Omaha, and Asian Americans. He is the Frederick W. Kayser Professor at the University of Nebraska at Omaha, Nebraska.

Mailing Address: Department of Public Administration
University of Nebraska at Omaha, Omaha
Nebraska - 68182-0276, USA

Tanner, R.E.S. obtained his B.Sc. in Social Anthropology from Oxford University and Ph.D. in Criminology from Stockholm University. He joined the Tanzanian Administrative Service in 1948 and continued to serve there till 1960. Then he joined the University of East Africa as Lecturer in Adult Education. He was the Chairman of East African Institute of Social Research from 1964 to 1967. He served the University of London as Lecturer in Comparative Religion from 1968 to 1980. He has been actively engaged in research works for the last 17 years. He has authored a number of books like *Homicide in Uganda, Transition in African Belief, An East African Problem, The Social Ecology of Religion* and *The Biology of Religion,* etc. He has contributed a large number of articles on translation problems in religion, religious hysteria, ancestor worship, witchcraft, Tanzanian agriculture, cattle theft, gossip, ecumenism, etc.

Mailing Address: The Footprint
Pudworth Common
Reading
RG 74 QG, United Kingdom

Tripathi, Sabita got her Bachelor's and Master's degrees from Gangadhar Meher College, Sambalpur. She obtained her Ph.D. degree on Sri Aurobindo Literature from Sambalpur University in 1992. After serving as Lecturer in English at Women's College, Jharsuguda, she joined as a faculty member in the Department of English, Sambalpur University in 1993. She has attended a number of national level seminars. Dr. Tripathy's current interests in research are gender issue and translation.

Mailing Address: Department of English
Sambalpur University
Sambalpur - 768 019
Orissa, India

Venkata, Rao, P. obtained his M.A. (1976) and Ph.D. (1983) from Andhra University. Presently he is a Reader in the Department of Anthropology of Hyderabad University. He has one book and thirty research publications to his credit. His areas of research interest include development issues, economic anthropology, complex societies and gerontology.

Mailing Address: Department of Anthropology
University of Hyderabad
Hyderabad - 500 046
Andhra Pradesh, India

INDEX